RUNNING

TO WIN

365 Days of Timeless Wisdom and

Biblical Insight for Growing Christians

RUNNING

TO WIN

ERWIN W. LUTZER

and D. L. MOODY

MOODY PUBLISHERS

CHICAGO

Edited by Avrie Roberts
Interior design: Puckett Smartt
Cover design: Thinkpen Design

ISBN: 978-0-8024-4117-1

Originally delivered by fleets of horse-drawn wagons, the affordable paperbacks from D. L. Moody's publishing house resourced the church and served everyday people. Now, after more than 125 years of publishing and ministry, Moody Publishers' mission remains the same—even if our delivery systems have changed a bit. For more information on other books (and resources) created from a biblical perspective, go to www.moodypublishers.com or write to:

Moody Publishers
820 N. LaSalle Boulevard
Chicago, IL 60610

1 3 5 7 9 10 8 6 4 2

Printed in the United States of America

A NOTE FROM THE PUBLISHER

There are a few ways to use this book. You can simply follow the dates and read one chapter each day for a year. Or you can use the Scripture index in the back to find entries that complement your favorite Bible study or Bible-reading plan. You can also jump straight to subjects that address your current needs and interests. However you read the following pages, we trust you'll benefit from the wisdom of two beloved Bible teachers, separated by a century but united by their passion for the Scriptures and the timeless truths they reveal.

INTRODUCTION

In the race of life, we are not left to run alone. Reflecting on the Scriptures and the wisdom of Dwight Lyman Moody, I am reminded that our journey is not about a creed or a myth but a Person—Jesus Christ. This collection of 365 devotions is designed to draw you closer to Him, equipping you to run with endurance and purpose.

It is my joy to share what the Lord has graciously taught me alongside Moody's timeless wisdom. D. L. Moody's devotional material is taken from *The D. L. Moody Year Book: A Living Daily Message from the Words of D. L. Moody*, compiled by his daughter, Emma Moody Fitt, and originally published in 1900. I've revised and updated some of his text for modern readers but kept as much of Moody's original voice and charm as possible, which includes retaining some British English spelling of words such as Saviour.

Each day, we are encouraged to fix our eyes on Jesus, the author and perfecter of our faith. I'm convinced, more than ever, that only the Word of God has the power to transform us from the inside out.

Let us embark on this year-long journey with humility and gratitude as we look forward to the world to come. As you engage with each devotion, take time to reflect on the Scripture passage, allowing it to speak to your heart. Pray earnestly, seeking God's guidance for your response to His Word. As you learn and grow, share these insights with a friend, inviting them to join you in this spiritual journey. Together, let us bring the gospel of Jesus Christ to a broken world, pointing others to the only One qualified to save us and able to bring us all the way to the finish line.

YOUR ANXIETY FOR HIS PEACE

"Peace I leave with you; my peace I give to you. Not as the world gives do I give to you. Let not your hearts be troubled, neither let them be afraid."
JOHN 14:27

D. L. MOODY

Did you ever think that when Christ was dying on the cross, He made a will? Perhaps you have thought no one ever remembered you in a will. If you are in the kingdom, Christ remembered you in His. He willed His body to Joseph of Arimathea, He willed His mother to John, the son of Zebedee, and He willed His spirit back to His Father. But to His disciples He said, "My peace, I leave that with you; that is my legacy. My joy, I give that to you."

"My joy," think of it! "My peace"—not *our* peace, but *His* peace!

They say a man can't make a will now that lawyers can't break . . . I will challenge them to break Christ's will; let them try it. No judge or jury can set that aside. Christ rose to execute His own will. If He had left us a lot of gold, thieves would have stolen it in the first century; but He left His peace and His joy for every true believer, and no power on earth can take it from him who trusts.

ERWIN LUTZER

The peace of God is better than gold, yet we've all found it difficult to accept this gift when anxiety overtakes us. Anxiety is like a warning light on a car, highlighting that which we have not put under God's complete authority. Or perhaps we haven't yet fully cast our fears upon Him, surrendering every corner of our lives to Him. Christ offers His peace to us *personally*. There is a real sense of well-being and stability from knowing our life is in God's hands.

Jesus gave us the gift of His peace at a time when, in His humanity, He Himself needed peace, for this was the last night before He would be cruelly hung on a cross. Yet even then, He was still the Prince of Peace.

Choose peace this year. Christ's promise of peace belongs to you.

PRAYER

Father, I transfer my anxieties unto your shoulders.
Today, I choose to walk in the peace Jesus promised.

AMEN TO GOD'S PROMISES

For all the promises of God find their Yes in him.
That is why it is through him that we utter our Amen to God for his glory.
2 CORINTHIANS 1:20

D. L. MOODY

Is there any reason why you should not have faith in God? Has God ever broken His Word? I defy any infidel to come forward and put his finger on any promise God has ever made to man that He has not kept.

I can show how, for six thousand years, the devil has lied and how he has broken every promise he has made. What a lie he told Adam and Eve! Yet, I can find a thousand men that will believe the devil's lies sooner than I can find one man that will believe God's truth.

ERWIN LUTZER

Dwight L. Moody approached the promises of the Bible with a simple, unquestioning faith, and was blessed with a ministry that continues to this day, all because he took God at His Word. Scripture gives us many examples of those who believed and were blessed because of their faith. Abraham believed God when the Lord promised that his descendants would be as numerous as the stars in the sky. There are many promises for us in the Scriptures, but the clearest have to do with our eternal salvation. He who believes in Jesus will have "eternal life, and they will never perish, and no one will snatch them out of my hand" (John 10:28). We can always trust God's promises. Our prayers, whether answered or unanswered, are a declaration of our dependence on Him and His promises.

PRAYER

Father, when I feel insecure, may I cleave to Your promises.
When I feel angry, may I submit to Your will.
Thank You for Your sure promises I can rely upon.

A DISCIPLE'S FRAGRANCE

"By this all people will know that you are my disciples, if you have love for one another."
JOHN 13:35

D. L. MOODY

How are you going to tell whether you are a Christian or not? What did Christ say? "By this shall all men know that ye are my disciples, if ye have love one to another."

When I was first converted, I used to wish that every Christian would wear a badge, because I would like to know them; my heart went out toward the household of faith. But I have got over that. Every hypocrite would have a badge inside of thirty days if Christianity should become popular. No badge outside; but God gives us a badge in the heart. The man that hasn't any love in his creed may let it go to the winds; I don't want it. "By this shall all men know that ye are my disciples, if ye have love one to another." Love is the fruit of the Spirit. "If any man have not the Spirit of Christ, he is none of his" (Romans 8:9).

ERWIN LUTZER

I agree with Moody: Wearing a badge would not convince me that someone was a Christian. A better test is love, that fragrance which says to the world, "I may disagree with you, but I love you."

Charles Weigle, best known for writing the hymn, "No One Ever Cared for Me Like Jesus," was preaching at a conference in California. He spent an afternoon visiting some rose gardens in the city. When he went to preach that evening, a number of people asked him how he enjoyed the lovely gardens. He was mystified as to how they knew where he had been until one explained, "You have brought the fragrance of the roses with you."

People will only know we have been in the presence of Jesus when we bring the fragrance of Christ's love along with us. Today, show someone around you Christ's sacrificial love, which is much better than wearing a Christian badge.

PRAYER

Jesus, love through me; care through me; live through me.

YOUR FUTURE HOME

For here we have no lasting city, but we seek the city that is to come.
HEBREWS 13:14

D. L. MOODY

Surely it is not wrong for us to think and talk about heaven. I like to locate it and find out all I can about it. I expect to live there through all eternity. If I were going to dwell in any place in this country, if I were going to make it my home, I would inquire about its climate, about the neighbors I would have, about everything, in fact, that I could learn concerning it. If soon you were going to emigrate, that is the way you would feel. Well, we are all going to emigrate in a very little while. We are going to spend eternity in another world, a grand and glorious world where God reigns. Is it not natural that we should look and listen and try to find out who is already there and what is the route to take?

ERWIN LUTZER

We should take Moody's advice! People who plan a trip to Europe spend hours reading travel books and studying maps about the places they hope to visit. Should we not be even more motivated by the fact that we are traveling to another world? We are leaving the land of the dying for the land of the living.

Death is not the end of the road, it's just a bend in the road. When you go from this life into the next, you are immediately in that realm beyond.

A poor, little boy gazed longingly at toys in the store window. When he was finally gifted a toy for the first time, he exclaimed, "There's no glass between!" In heaven, there will be a whole new reality—a new way of seeing. "For now we see in a mirror dimly, but then face to face" (1 Corinthians 13:12).

You were made for another world. Live today for eternity.

PRAYER

Father, may I live today to give You glory. You are my hope
and eternity is my focus.

NO ONE LIKE HIM

He came to his own, and his own people did not receive him.
But to all who did receive him, who believed in his name,
he gave the right to become children of God.
JOHN 1:11–12

D. L. MOODY

Him—mark you—not a dogma, not a creed, not a myth, but a *Person*!

ERWIN LUTZER

Read Moody's sermons and prayers and you will soon discover there is no fluff, no unnecessary words, just the truth. This devotional has but a single sentence, "Him—mark you—not a dogma, not a creed, not a myth, but a *Person*." Blessed is the preacher who makes little of himself and much about Jesus.

Moody knew, and we all agree, that only the Jesus of the New Testament is able to save us from our sins. He alone has the qualifications to cleanse our hearts, give us the gift of righteousness, and welcome us into our eternal home.

Jesus is qualified because of His divinity. "In the beginning was the Word" (John 1:1). Jesus is the intelligibility, the message, and the communication of God. The Word existed from all eternity. The Word (Jesus Christ) was and is God.

Jesus is also qualified because of His humanity. "The Word became flesh" (John 1:14). This truth shatters the philosophical and religious world. Jesus was a sinless human being, to be sure, but He became one with us. He bridged the gap between God and man. What a beautiful, saving mystery!

What a tragedy to know Isaac Newton, but not as a scientist; to know William Shakespeare, but not as a poet or playwright; and to know Jesus, but not as your Savior. Have you received Him?

PRAYER

Father, help me to see the uniqueness, the credentials, and the beauty of Jesus.
There is no one else like Him.
I don't just admire Him, I receive Him by faith.

AN APPETITE FOR GOD'S WORD

"Heaven and earth will pass away, but my words will not pass away."
MATTHEW 24:35

D. L. MOODY

Notice how that statement has been fulfilled. There was no shorthand reporter following Jesus around taking down His words; there were no papers to print His sermons, and they wouldn't have printed them if there had been any daily papers. The leaders of the people were against Him.

I can see one of your modern freethinkers standing near Christ and hearing Him say: "Heaven and earth shall pass away, but my words shall not pass away." I see the scornful look on his face as he says: "Hear that Jewish peasant talk! Did you ever hear such conceit, such madness? He says heaven and earth shall pass away, but His words will not pass away." My friend, I want to ask you this question—has it passed away? Do you know that the sun has shone on more Bibles today than ever before in the history of the world? They tried in the Dark Ages to burn it, to chain it, and keep it from the nations, but God has preserved it and sent it to the ends of the earth.

ERWIN LUTZER

Moody was right. When you hold the Bible, you hold a book from God. Without it, we wouldn't know how to prepare for the eternity we intuitively know awaits us. We'd have no objective knowledge of right or wrong nor the ability to discover God's purposes. We can be thankful God made Himself known through His Son, Jesus Christ, revealed in the Scriptures. God's Word is dependable, shedding light as we take our next step of obedience and preparing us for our eternal destiny. It is Spirit-given. Its authors wrote under divine supervision and inspiration, showing us God's intention for the redemption of all who believe.

Let us rekindle our hunger for God's Word through meditation, memorizing its promises, and personal worship. Become a lover of God's Book, and you'll be a lover of God.

PRAYER

Father, help me to love the Bible, believe it, memorize it, and be changed by it.

PRAY WITH CONFIDENCE

"Before they call I will answer; while they are yet speaking I will hear."
ISAIAH 65:24

D. L. MOODY

We talk about heaven being so far away. It is within speaking distance to those who belong there.

ERWIN LUTZER

Moody often surprises us with his directness and obvious simplicity. Think of it: Of course, heaven is close to us, as close as God's description given to us in Scripture, and as close as our next breath, which could be our last.

In fact, the Scriptures teach that legally, believers are already in "heavenly places in Christ Jesus" (Ephesians 2:6). Jesus is raised above every principality, power, and name that is named. When we were converted, God legally and judicially put us "in Him" so that we are, even today, with Christ on God's right hand. He loves us, making no distinction between His love for His Son and His love for us. We are invited to draw near to the throne of grace because we belong to Him.

No believer should ever say, "I'm a hopeless case." Instead, we should pray with confidence supported by our Advocate, Jesus. Is it any wonder the apostle Paul prayed that the church might be able to see themselves through God's eyes? (Ephesians 3:14–19).

Jesus is before the throne of God the Father, continuously interceding for us. When we pray, we become a prayer partner with Christ. We join Him before the throne of God on behalf of others. What a privilege to draw near to God in full confidence because of the person and work of Christ.

PRAYER

Father, in my struggles with prayer, may I remember the privilege and priority of coming before You.

SINS BLOTTED OUT

"But Abraham said, 'Child, remember that you in your lifetime received your good things, and Lazarus in like manner bad things; but now he is comforted here, and you are in anguish.'"

LUKE 16:25

D. L. MOODY

I believe that when God touches the secret spring of memory, every one of our sins will come back if they have not been blotted out by the blood of the Lord Jesus Christ, and they will haunt us as eternal ages roll on.

ERWIN LUTZER

Moody's comments are chilling. Imagine existing forever in hell with the memory of your sin upon your conscience. Imagine reliving each lost opportunity, each infraction of the divine law, fully aware of the holiness and justice of God. We must urge people to believe the gospel so that their sins will be blotted out by the blood of Jesus (Acts 3:19).

After writing an essay on the doctrine of hell, I was so burdened that I went to our next-door neighbor who was mowing his lawn and talked to him about his soul. As it turned out, he gave evidence of already being a believer. After he died, I witnessed to his widow, but she was not interested in the gospel and gave no indication that she desired to believe in Christ. She is now deceased and unless she, by God's grace, changed her mind, she and her husband will be separated forever. He in eternal bliss; she in eternal hell, with her sins upon her conscience.

Today, there is someone you know who should hear your testimony and be pointed to Jesus Christ who shields us "from the wrath to come" (1 Thessalonians 1:10).

PRAYER

Father, forgive me for failing to share the gospel with my neighbors, friends, and relatives. Give me wisdom, boldness, and love as I share the good news of Your redemption.

THE BEST OF A BAD DECISION

Then the Lord God said to the woman, "What is this that you have done?" The woman said, "The serpent deceived me, and I ate."

GENESIS 3:13

D. L. MOODY

What had Eve done? She had disobeyed God. She had turned from the fountain of life to the fountain of death, and had drunk from that fountain. She had introduced sin into the world.

God let her live long enough on the face of the earth to see what she had done. The first child that was born after the fall was a murderer (Genesis 4:1–8). She lived nearly a thousand years, if she lived as long as Adam, and had a chance to see something of the untold woe and misery she had introduced into this world.

ERWIN LUTZER

What's the worst decision ever made? Well, as Moody pointed out, it was the sin of Adam and Eve, turning from the fountain of life to the fountain of death. No decision has ever had such far-reaching consequences into eternity.

Like Eve, there are two lies we are tempted to believe. The first lie says, "One sin doesn't matter." The devil's second lie says, "Now that you have fallen, there's no use standing up." But God promised Adam and Eve that redemption would be available. As proof, He gave them garments of skin to cover their shame. Already in the garden, God's plan of redemption began to be realized.

Do you think you have sinned too much for God? You have not. Adam and Eve could not return to their days of innocence; they were kept from returning to Paradise. Not even Satan could keep God from giving fallen humanity forgiveness and redemption.

PRAYER

Father, thank You for Your redemption. Help me to know that there is more grace in Your heart than sin in my past.

DESPERATE BEFORE GOD

If I had cherished iniquity in my heart, the Lord would not have listened.

PSALM 66:18

D. L. MOODY

I sometimes tremble when I hear people quote promises and say that God is bound to fulfill those promises to them when, all the time, there is some sin in their lives they are not willing to give up. It is well for us to search our hearts and find out why it is that our prayers are not answered.

ERWIN LUTZER

To be alone in the presence of God is the only path of self-discovery. Only with total openness in His presence do we know who we are—nothing more, nothing less. Your identity is not who your friends, your family, or even your church thinks you are. Ask yourself, "Who am I in God's presence?"

Moody was right about stressing the need for self-examination. We must pray, "Search me, O God, and know my heart! Try me and know my thoughts! And see if there be any grievous way in me, and lead me in the way everlasting!" (Psalm 139:23–24). We must come to God in desperation, willing to see what He shows us about ourselves. Like Jacob, we often wrestle with God, but just as God crippled Jacob, our weakness will become our strength.

Sin left unconquered saps our joy and steals our fellowship with God.

PRAYER

God, I open my life to You. Search me and show me what You see. Grant me the humility to be able to admit who I am so I can become who You want me to be. I give myself to You unreservedly.

YOUR LIFE AND WITNESS

He answered, "The man called Jesus made mud and anointed my eyes and said to me, 'Go to Siloam and wash.' So I went and washed and received my sight."

JOHN 9:11

D. L. MOODY

He told a straightforward story, just what the Lord had done for him. That is all. That is what a witness ought to do—tell what he knows, not what he does not know. He did not try to make a long speech. It is not the most flippant and fluent witness who has the most influence with a jury.

This man's testimony is what I call "experience." One of the greatest hindrances to the progress of the gospel today is that the narration of the experience of the church is not encouraged. There are a great many men and women who come into the church, and we never hear anything of the Lord's dealings with them. If we did, it would be a great help to others. It would stimulate faith and encourage the more feeble of the flock. The apostle Paul's experience has been recorded three times. I have no doubt that he told it everywhere he went: how God had met him; how God had opened his eyes and his heart; and how God had blessed him.

Depend upon it, experience has its place; the great mistake that is made now is in the other extreme. In some places and at some periods, there has been too much of it—it has been all experience; and now we have let the pendulum swing too far the other way.

ERWIN LUTZER

Have you ever asked, "When it comes to witnessing, what is most important: my life or my lips?" If you share the gospel but don't have the integrity to back it up, people won't listen. They'll say, "Even if it's true, I don't want to hear it from you." Yet, if you're kind but don't tell people about Jesus, they'll simply attribute your niceness to your DNA.

Like wings on a plane, we bear witness with both a spoken and lived testimony.

PRAYER

Father, may I witness to my friends and coworkers
and tell them what Jesus has done for me.

FAITH IN THE FIRE

He answered and said, "But I see four men unbound, walking in the midst of the fire, and they are not hurt; and the appearance of the fourth is like a son of the gods."
DANIEL 3:25

D. L. MOODY

The fourth man was, doubtless, the Son of God. That Great Shepherd of the sheep saw three of His true servants in peril, and He came from His Father's presence and His Father's bosom to be with them in it. He had been watching that terrible attempt to burn the faithful. His tender pitying eye saw they were condemned to death because of their loyalty to Him. With one great leap, He sprang from the Father's presence, from His palace in glory, right down into the fiery furnace, and was by their side before the heat of the fire could come near unto them. Jesus was with His servants as the flames wreathed around them, and not a hair of their heads was singed. They were not scorched; not even the smell of fire was upon them. I can almost fancy I hear them chanting:

"When thou passest through the waters, I will be with thee; and through the rivers, they shall not overflow thee: *when thou walkest through the fire, thou shalt not be burned; neither shall the flame kindle upon thee*" (Isaiah 43:2).

ERWIN LUTZER

These three men were delivered from the fire, but many martyrs have died in the flames for their faith in Jesus Christ. To us, the "Fourth Man" didn't seem to deliver them. We can accept unanswered prayer because we believe God's will is best, and that He is with us even if we're not delivered from fiery trials. Whether we see a miracle or not, let us resolve to trust in God and not swerve in our faith. What God does *in* us is sometimes more important than what God does *for* us.

PRAYER

Father, when I'm angry, disappointed, or bitter because You haven't answered prayer as I expected, speak to me through Your Word by Your Spirit. I believe. Help my unbelief.

RETURN HOME

"For the Son of Man came to seek and to save the lost."

LUKE 19:10

D. L. MOODY

To me, this is one of the sweetest verses in the whole Bible. In this one short sentence we are told what Christ came into this world for. He came for a purpose; He came to do a work. He came not to condemn the world, but that the world through Him might be saved.

ERWIN LUTZER

Yes, we were lost prodigals, but Jesus came to save us. Thanks to Him, our heavenly Father is waiting for us. He says, "I have made provision for you to come back home. I sent my Son, the Lord Jesus Christ, to die on the cross for sinners so that if you receive Him, I will welcome you home."

No matter how lost we are, the Spirit can lead us home.

You may be a backslidden believer, perhaps you have never trusted Christ as Savior, or you may be a wandering prodigal, but God sent Jesus so that, in the words of a hymn, "The vilest offender who truly believes, that moment from Jesus a pardon receives."[1] God redeems our messes; He honors us even as the father honored the wandering prodigal. Don't turn away from the Voice drawing you to Jesus.

PRAYER

Father, who is there except You to reach into my heart
and deal with the anger that keeps prodigals like me away from You?
Today, I'm coming home.

GOD'S EXCLUSIVE TREASURES

And one called to another and said: "Holy, holy, holy is the Lord of hosts; the whole earth is full of his glory!"
ISAIAH 6:3

D. L. MOODY

When we see the holiness of God, we shall adore and magnify Him. Moses learned this lesson. God told him to take his shoes from off his feet for the place where on he stood was holy ground (Exodus 3:5). When we hear men trying to make out that they are holy, and speaking about their holiness, they make light of the holiness of God. It is His holiness that we need to think and speak about; when we do that, we shall be prostrate in the dust.

ERWIN LUTZER

God is holy and altogether separate. Our holiness means we're set apart to God, free of sin's power to be God's exclusive treasure.

Think of what it means to belong to God. Although we are by nature children of wrath (Ephesians 2:3), we have been born again into an entirely different family, reflecting God's nature in purity and love. This requires deep repentance, not just about the sins of the flesh, but also of covetousness or dishonesty. We are also God's treasure. There's no way we could ever accomplish our own redemption. Yet God paid for it with the blood of His beloved Son. How dare we magnify our sins, toying with them, when Jesus paid it all to redeem us from sin!

The call to salvation is a call to holiness. We become saints, God's exclusive treasure, by faith in Christ. Now, it is our responsibility and privilege, by His grace, to pursue holiness in personal experience.

PRAYER

Father, I confess my casual attitude toward my own sin.
Would You give me the grace to do whatever You ask me to do?

HUMBLE REPENTANCE

*"And you, Capernaum, will you be exalted to heaven?
You will be brought down to Hades. For if the mighty works done in you had been done in Sodom, it would have remained until this day."*

MATTHEW 11:23

D. L. MOODY

A man said to me some time ago: "Don't you think David fell as low as Saul?"

Yes, he fell lower because God had lifted him up higher. The difference is that when Saul fell, there was no sign of repentance; but when David fell, a wail went up from his broken heart, there was true repentance.

ERWIN LUTZER

Why did David have to endure twelve years of harassment from Saul, the spear thrower? God wanted to take all of the "Saul" out of David's heart. If God had only exalted David, he would have become another King Saul. Saul was too proud to fall helplessly in God's presence, saying, "Oh God, extinguish this flame of resentment and jealousy. Don't let me go till my heart is pure." He wasn't willing. Yes Saul "repented" five times (1 Samuel 13:11–12; 15:24–25, 30; 24:16–21; 26:21). He would say, "I've played the fool; I have erred exceedingly," but then continued the way he was living. Like an alcoholic or sex addict, his repentance was just another form of manipulation.

While Saul was manipulative, David trusted God. He trusted that Israel was God's kingdom and God could give it to whomsoever He wanted. Rather than throwing the spear back at Saul in vengeance, David didn't, and instead affirmed God would execute vengeance. Even after David's greatest failure, his repentance before God was different. It was a thorough, complete repentance. True repentance is a humble submission to God's will and His way.

PRAYER

Father, I surrender my kingdom, submitting to Your Spirit's mighty work in me.

JANUARY 16

MEDITATION'S GOAL

They read from the book, from the Law of God, clearly, and they gave the sense, so that the people understood the reading.

NEHEMIAH 8:8

D. L. MOODY

We must study the Bible thoroughly and hunt it through, as it were, for some great truth. If a friend were to see me searching about a building and were to come up and say, "Moody, what are you looking for? Have you lost something?" and I answered, "No, I haven't lost anything; I'm not looking for anything in particular," I fancy he would just let me go on by myself and think me very foolish. But if I were to say, "Yes, I have lost a dollar," why, I might expect him to help me to find it.

Read the Bible as if you were seeking for something of value. It is a good deal better to take a single chapter and spend a month on it than to read the Bible at random for a month.

ERWIN LUTZER

There are two ways to read the Bible, just as there are two ways to take a trip. For some, the goal is simple—get to the destination. We set goals to steadily read Scripture, focused on Jesus and the overarching drama of redemption. One danger of an annual Bible reading plan is that if we're busy, we tend to read quickly just to get through the reading for that day. The other way to travel is to enjoy the journey. In Scripture reading, this is meditation. Perhaps choose twelve books of the Bible from different genres—psalms, narratives, or epistles. Then reread, study, and pray through one book each month. Even just a few verses can be food for your soul.

Both styles of travel guide you to encounter God. We should always read to *analyze* by asking thoughtful questions of the text. Then we *personalize*: "How should this text change me?" Finally, we *memorize* specific sections. When we meditate on Scripture daily, we'll be stable in adversity and prosperous in each season of life.

PRAYER

Father, free my restless soul. I rest in You, meditating on Your Word.

UP AGAINST LOVE

Who shall separate us from the love of Christ? Shall tribulation, or distress, or persecution, or famine, or nakedness, or danger, or sword?
ROMANS 8:35

D. L. MOODY

Now, who is going to do it? Devils? Men? Angels? Paul throws down a challenge. He challenges heaven and earth and angels and men and principalities and powers; and not only that, but all things past, present, and to come; all creatures, internal or external; all states, death or life, height or preferment, depth or dungeon, prison or stripes.

Nothing shall separate me from the love of Christ. Let my enemies come collectively or singly, I don't care. Let them come one and all. I have no foes that can overcome me. Why? Because God has justified me. I do not dread death. Why? Because Christ has tasted death for me. I dread no judgment. Why? That is past. I dread no separation, and I anticipate no failure.

ERWIN LUTZER

Where is love when you need it? Our heavenly Father walks with us through our suffering, assuring us that He loves us. His love is continual, personal, and eternal.

Divine love is based on the Lover. There is nothing that can dissuade God from loving those whom He has chosen to redeem. If He stopped loving us and canceled our redemption, He'd have more to lose than we would—we would lose our souls, but He would lose His reputation, breaking His covenant. Faith that He loves us makes us see beyond the visible to the invisible; it sees beyond earth to heaven. Faith in our Father's love makes us realize that what God takes away from us is not as important as what He gives us.

If you are a believer and therefore you belong to Jesus, there is nothing you can ever do to get God to stop loving you.

PRAYER

Father, thank You for all You have done for me in Christ.
Help me to be secure in Your love.

(EXTRA) ORDINARY GLORY

"And those who are wise shall shine like the brightness of the sky above; and those who turn many to righteousness, like the stars forever and ever."
DANIEL 12:3

D. L. MOODY

How empty and short-lived are the glory and the pride of this world! If we are wise, we will live for God and eternity; we will get outside of ourselves and will care nothing for the honor and glory of this world. In Proverbs 11:30 we read: "He that winneth souls is wise." If any man, woman, or child, by a godly life and example, can win one soul to God, their life will not have been a failure. They will have outshone all the mighty men of their day because they will have set a stream in motion that will flow on and on forever and ever.

ERWIN LUTZER

Everything exists for God. Was He egotistical in making everything for His glory? No. If God loves that which is most supreme, He must love Himself. The first commandment applies to God: "You shall have no other gods before me." God enjoys being God, especially through revealing His mercy in the light of the gospel for sinners.

God has chosen to reveal His glory through His imperfect human vessels. "But we have this treasure in jars of clay, to show that the surpassing power belongs to God and not to us" (2 Corinthians 4:7). Human weakness is not a barrier to God's power. God uses ordinary people to glorify Himself. This is why we live to the praise of His glory. Nothing else matters except the glory of God. Only in Him do we find our deepest and greatest purpose and happiness.

PRAYER

Father, be glorified in me, at my expense.

DON'T HIDE

"I the LORD search the heart and test the mind, to give every man according to his ways, according to the fruit of his deeds."

JEREMIAH 17:10

D. L. MOODY

When I was going through the land of Goshen in Egypt a few years ago, as I came near the city of Alexandria, I saw one of the strangest sights I had ever seen. The heavens were lit up with a new kind of light and there seemed to be flash after flash; I couldn't understand it. I found later that the Khedive had died and that a new Khedive was coming into power. England had sent over some war vessels and the moment darkness came on, they had turned their searchlights upon the city. It was almost as light as noonday. Every street was lit up, and I do not suppose that ten men could have met in any part of Alexandria without being discovered by that searchlight.

May God turn His searchlight upon us and see if there be any evil way in us!

ERWIN LUTZER

"The heart is deceitful above all things" (Jeremiah 17:9). The most important part of us is not what others see, but what our God sees—the omniscient, all-knowing One. We all have a public persona useful for our outward appearances, with our secret sins hidden from view. Many people live their lives in two compartments: the outer to impress others, the inner to satisfy our desires. The better we know ourselves, the more clearly we will see that every one of us has the potential for great sin.

When we trust Christ as our Savior, He births within us a new nature, but even then, we still struggle with sin. As our secret sins come under the authority of Jesus, our motives are purified. God is glorified when our inner motives and outer actions are in line with His will.

Have you been misunderstood or lied about? God knows the truth. Are you nurturing sins of the spirit? Do anger or envy fester in your heart? God knows the truth. Ask Him to purify your motives for His glory.

PRAYER

Lord, search me and change me!

A HOLY WALK

Enoch walked with God, and he was not, for God took him.

GENESIS 5:24

By faith Enoch was taken up so that he should not see death,
and he was not found, because God had taken him.
Now before he was taken he was commended as having pleased God.

HEBREWS 11:5

D. L. MOODY

A great deal is being said about holiness. Every true child of God desires to be holy as His Father in heaven is holy. And holiness is walking with God. Enoch had only one object. How simple life becomes when we have only one object to seek, one purpose to fulfill—to walk with God, to please God! It has been said that the utmost many Christians get to is that they are pardoned criminals. How short they fall of the joy and blessedness of walking with God!

ERWIN LUTZER

Moody is credited with saying, "This one thing I do and not these forty things I dabble in." Like Enoch, walking with God should be our highest priority. To walk with God requires agreement. "Do two walk together, unless they have agreed to meet?" the prophet Amos asked (Amos 3:3). Walking with someone means you have common interests and a shared destination. Walking with God also means that we "walk in the light, as he is in the light" (1 John 1:7). Every hidden sin should be confessed and forsaken; our lives must be open to His leading.

You may be thinking, "Can we really know God, so that we might 'walk' with Him?" The answer is *yes*. Through the Scriptures, we are introduced to His mercy, His salvation, and invited to walk each day in dependence and fellowship.

God has not turned His face from us; rather, His arms are outstretched toward us, inviting us to come into His presence through the blood of Christ.

PRAYER

Lord, I want to know You and be holy like You.

JANUARY 21

THE POINT OF NO RETURN

Your evil will chastise you, and your apostasy will reprove you.
Know and see that it is evil and bitter for you to forsake the Lord your God;
the fear of me is not in you, declares the Lord God of hosts.

JEREMIAH 2:19

D. L. MOODY

I have travelled a good deal, but I never found a happy backslider in my life. I never knew a man who was really born of God that ever could find the world satisfy him afterward. Do you think the prodigal son was satisfied in that foreign country? Ask the prodigals today if they are truly happy. You know they are not. "There is no peace, saith my God, to the wicked" (Isaiah 57:21).

ERWIN LUTZER

There's only one way to avoid the point of no return at Niagara Falls: Watch for the currents' warning signs. Just so, we must watch for the warning signs of being swept away by the currents of temptation. We must also be aware of the warning signs of spiritual decline.

First, pay attention for the feeling of self-satisfaction, the feeling you have everything under control. Beware of harboring sin that masters you and causes spiritual blindness. Second, watch for any hidden provisions for defeat; don't put yourself in a place where temptation lurks. The third danger is spiritual coasting. We begin to push God and His Word to the circumference of our lives, and soon, compromises lead us to ultimate disaster. Moody was right in saying that no backslider is a happy person.

I've been on a boat that left the shore so quietly that I scarcely noticed it. That's the way most backsliding happens. Only tragic failure makes us realize how far we have drifted from the shore. Pay careful attention to the warning signs.

PRAYER

Holy Spirit, grant me a sensitivity to sin so that I may grow
in fear and reverence of You.

CHILDREN, COME

"Truly, I say to you, unless you turn and become like children, you will never enter the kingdom of heaven."
MATTHEW 18:3

D. L. MOODY

It is a masterpiece of the devil to make us believe that children cannot understand religion. Would Christ have made children the standard of faith if He had known they were not capable of understanding His words? It is far easier for children to love and trust than for grown-up persons, and so we should set Christ before them as the supreme object of their choice.

ERWIN LUTZER

The Moody Church was founded in 1864 as a Sunday school. D. L. Moody loved children; he began ministry in the worst neighborhood of Chicago—Little Hell. One day someone asked him, "How many people accepted Jesus Christ last night?" He responded, "Two-and-a-half." They said, "Oh, two adults and a child!" Moody said, "Oh no, it was two children and an adult because the adult's life is half over. The children have all their lives to live for God."

A child knows they are dependent, that's why Jesus honored the faith of a child. If you are self-assured, convinced you can manage life on your own, you cannot enter the kingdom of heaven. We enter by faith and humility.

Jesus said, "Welcome children in my name" (see Mark 9:37). God expects us to represent Him to children, whether our own or those of others. They should see God's grace; they should look to us to guide them in the right path. We sing, "Jesus loves the little children." He loves them and so should we.

PRAYER

Father, our greatest honor is that we are Your children.
May we welcome more children into Your kingdom.

TRANSFER OF TRUST

If you confess with your mouth that Jesus is Lord and believe in your heart that God raised him from the dead, you will be saved.

ROMANS 10:9

D. L. MOODY

I do not know of any more important truth to bring before an unconverted person than the answer to the question, "What must I do to be saved?" because that is the beginning of everything with regard to the divine life. A man must know he is saved before there is any peace or joy or comfort. The answer is, "Believe on the Lord Jesus Christ, and thou shalt be saved" (Acts 16:31).

The question that comes right after that from almost everyone is, "What is it to believe?" I believe that Jesus Christ is the Son of God; I believe that He came into the world to save sinners. Well, so do the devils. The devils not only believe, but they tremble (James 2:19). I can believe intellectually that Jesus Christ is able and willing to save and yet be as far from the kingdom of God as any man who never heard about Jesus Christ. To be saved, I must believe in my heart and trust in His atoning work.

ERWIN LUTZER

Moody is correct: Faith in Christ is more than mere mental assent. Some say, "I love and admire Jesus. I attend church. I'm a good person." That's not true faith. Facts alone don't save.

Faith is an attitude of trust, the transferring of trust from ourselves to Christ. Faith presupposes an awareness of our sin, our inability to deal with the guilt, and therefore, our need to call on Jesus to give us both forgiveness and acceptance before God. Right now, you can savingly believe on Jesus through repentance and faith.

PRAYER

Lord, thank You for the great miracle of salvation
that You have done for me and in me.

WANTED: ETERNAL WORSHIPERS

And the ransomed of the LORD shall return and come to Zion with singing; everlasting joy shall be upon their heads; they shall obtain gladness and joy, and sorrow and sighing shall flee away.

ISAIAH 35:10

D. L. MOODY

Joseph Parker of London, a nineteenth-century preacher, uttered something I thought was splendid in regard to the thirty-fifth of Isaiah where it says in verse ten, "Sorrow and sighing shall flee away." Take up an old dictionary, he said, and once in a while, you will come across a word marked "obsolete." The time is coming, he said, when those two words "sorrow" and "sighing" shall be obsolete. Sighing and sorrow shall flee away, to be no more. Thank God for the outlook!

ERWIN LUTZER

Yes, that time is coming! When God restores creation, some things will be no more; indeed, even death will be gone forever. "He will wipe away every tear from their eyes, and death shall be no more" (Revelation 21:4). The hearse will have taken its last journey. There may be some vocations that will continue in heaven, but being an undertaker will not be one of them.

In heaven, we will see things as God sees them, and so our tears will be wiped away. We will say, "Father, on earth there was much we could not understand. Now that we see Your purposes from Your eternal perspective, we praise and bless Your holy name." Weeping is gone forever.

Imagine it! We will be abiding in the glory of God, talking face to face with Him as one speaks with a friend. And we will say, as Philip did, "Show us the Father, and it is enough for us" (John 14:8). And that request will be fully answered. We shall *behold the Father* and be satisfied. A new home! A new city! A new occupation—worshiping the Father and enjoying Him forever.

PRAYER

Father, all that I am, all that I have,
and ever hope to be is Yours forever and ever.

PLEADING FOR JESUS

O Lord, open my lips, and my mouth will declare your praise.
PSALM 51:15

D. L. MOODY

It is a very sad thing that so many of God's children are dumb, yet it is true. The churches are full of them. They can talk about politics, art, and science; they can speak well enough and fast enough about the fashions of the day, but they have no voice for the Son of God.

Dear friend, if Christ is your Saviour, confess Him. Every follower of Jesus should bear testimony for Him. How many opportunities each one has in society and in business to speak a word for Him! How many opportunities occur daily wherein every Christian might be "instant in season and out of season" (2 Timothy 4:2) in pleading for Jesus! In so doing, we receive blessing for ourselves and also become a means of blessing to others.

ERWIN LUTZER

The famous atheist Bertrand Russell was asked, "What if . . . when the time comes, you should meet Him? What will you say?" He said, "God, you gave us insufficient evidence."[2]

Russell was wrong. The Bible teaches that God is not hiding Himself from humanity. We are hiding ourselves from God. Every person is created in God's image and intuitively knows they are sinners and God is holy. In his preaching, Moody appealed to sinners with the confidence that God had already gone ahead of him, preparing hearts to hear the message. Many rejected Moody's message, but tens of thousands responded.

Moody gives us a challenge: Are we pleading with others to accept Jesus? Your friends and relatives might be more open to the gospel than you realize. There is plenty of evidence for the existence of God and the death and resurrection of Jesus. Let's not be ashamed of the one message able to save sinners.

PRAYER

Father, help me to share the gospel with others. Like Moody,
let me plead for people in prayer and witness with confidence.

JANUARY 26

UNITED IN CHRIST, DIVIDED BY SIN

Eager to maintain the unity of the Spirit in the bond of peace.
EPHESIANS 4:3

D. L. MOODY

One of the saddest things in the present day is the division in God's church. You notice that when the power of God came upon the early church, it was when they were "all of one accord" (see Acts 2). I believe the blessing of Pentecost never would have been given but for that spirit of unity. If they had been divided and quarrelling among themselves, do you think the Holy Ghost would have come and those thousands been converted?

I have noticed in our work, that if we have gone to a town where three churches were united in it, we have had greater blessing than if only one church was in sympathy. And if there have been twelve churches united, the blessing has multiplied fourfold; it has always been in proportion to the spirit of unity that has been manifested. Where there are bickerings and divisions, and where the spirit of unity is absent, there is very little blessing and praise.

ERWIN LUTZER

Why was the early church unstoppable? With political authorities and other religions competing for the same minds and the same hearts, Christianity marched along with tremendous strength. Unstoppable! In the book of Acts, it says that "they devoted themselves to the apostles' teaching and the fellowship, to the breaking of bread and the prayers" (Acts 2:42). The Greek word for *fellowship* means they shared something in common. We are united not by common interests but a shared common life—the life of Christ. What unites us is more powerful than what divides us.

Unity—true unity on the part of all who are members of Christ's body—is an unstoppable force.

PRAYER

Father, unite me in love and faith with Your church.

HIDDEN IDOLS

Search me, O God, and know my heart! Try me and know my thoughts!
And see if there be any grievous way in me, and lead me in the way everlasting!
PSALM 139:23–24

D. L. MOODY

If we should all honestly make this prayer once every day, there would be a good deal of change in our lives. "Search *me*"—not my neighbor. It is so easy to pray for other people but so hard to get home to ourselves. I am afraid that we who are busy in the Lord's work are especially in danger of neglecting our own vineyard.

There is a difference between God searching me and my searching myself. I may search my heart and pronounce it all right, but when God searches me as with a lighted candle, a good many things will come to light that perhaps I knew nothing about.

ERWIN LUTZER

I have prayed the above prayer often, and I trust you have too. To what extent are we willing to be obedient to what God asks us to do? God shows us our cherished sins and exposes our idols when we are in His presence. Remember how God tested Abraham to see if Isaac had become an idol in his life? God chooses what is most precious to us to test us.

When David wrote Psalm 139, he began with, "You have searched me and known me" and yet when he came to the end of the psalm, he prayed, "Lord search me." He began by affirming that God had already searched him, and now prays for God to show him what he needs to see. All sins or idols compete with the greatest commandment: "You shall love the Lord your God with all your heart and with all your soul and with all your mind" (Matthew 22:37).

PRAYER

Father, only You can expose the idolatries of my heart.
Search me and lead me to You.

DIRTY, UGLY TREASURE

"For where your treasure is, there your heart will be also."
MATTHEW 6:21

D. L. MOODY

It does not take long to tell where a man's treasure is. In fifteen minutes' conversation with most men, you can tell whether their treasures are on earth or in heaven. Talk to a patriot about his country, and you will see his eye light up; you will find he has his heart there. Talk to businessmen and tell them where they can make a thousand dollars, and see their interest; their hearts are there. Talk to people who are living just for fashion, of its affairs, and you will see their eyes kindle, they are interested at once, their hearts are there. Talk to a politician about politics, and you see how suddenly he becomes interested. And talk to a child of God, who is really laying up treasures in heaven, about heaven and about his future home, and he responds at once, there are chords in his heart that vibrate at the thought of heaven and home.

ERWIN LUTZER

The temptations of this world are unrelenting, and we know this world is a rather dirty place—moral and spiritual pollution is everywhere. All that incites us to sin would be quite manageable if only there wasn't something within us that desires to sin. Sometimes we follow distantly behind Christ. That's why, as Moody said, we sometimes find it easier to talk about matters of earth rather than matters of heaven.

The first step in cleaning up our mouths is to clean up our hearts. If you believe what the Bible teaches and yet you are not walking in obedience, how can you expect to speak of Christ? As Jesus put it, "Out of the abundance of the heart the mouth speaks" (Matthew 12:34).

Who is your master? Are you dirty in the world or clean in Christ? Repent of all that makes you more conversant about the things of earth than the things of heaven.

PRAYER

Father, forgive me for serving the world.
May my treasure be found in You.
And may I joyfully speak of heavenly things to others.

THE WORLD IS NOT ENOUGH

Godliness with contentment is great gain.
1 TIMOTHY 6:6

D. L. MOODY

Would to God we might all be able to say with Paul—"I have coveted no man's silver, or gold, or apparel" (Acts 20:33). The Lord had made him partaker of His grace, and he was soon to be a partaker of His glory, and earthly things looked very small. "Godliness with contentment is great gain," he wrote to Timothy; "having food and raiment let us be therewith content" (1 Timothy 6:6, 8). Observe that he puts godliness first. No worldly gain can satisfy the human heart. Roll the whole world in and still there would be room.

ERWIN LUTZER

Godliness with contentment. We have all met many people who are discontent—perhaps even most of them are. And no doubt, we ourselves are guilty of the same sin. Someone has described contentment as accepting what God gives and does not crave more.

Of course, God may sometimes take us from a high place and bring us low, or He may ask us to change vocations. When Peter decided to follow Jesus, he had to leave the fishing business. Undoubtedly he thought, "Without the fishing business to depend upon for an income, will I be able to depend on Christ to meet my needs?" He would have to learn to submit to a new Master and abide by a new lifestyle—and to be content. How do we learn contentment? The first and most important step is to give God praise right where we are, even in the midst of discouragement, reversals, and discontentment. When we thank God for what He has brought into our lives, we begin to learn how to be content no matter where we find ourselves.

PRAYER

Father, You never abandon us. Strengthen me today so I might believe You are working in my circumstances and that I will be content.

LIE TO ME

And he said, "I heard the sound of you in the garden,
and I was afraid, because I was naked, and I hid myself."
GENESIS 3:10

D. L. MOODY

Most of us live away from home. We are hiding as Adam did in the bushes of Eden. There was a time when God's voice thrilled Adam's soul with joy and gladness, and he thrilled God's heart with joy. They lived in sweet fellowship with each other. God had lifted Adam to the very gates of heaven and had made him lord over all creation. I haven't a doubt that He had plans to raise Adam still higher—higher than the angels, higher than seraphim and cherubim, higher than Gabriel, who stands in the presence of Jehovah, and Michael, the archangel. But the man turned and became a traitor to Him who wanted to bless him.

ERWIN LUTZER

Adam and Eve lived in a perfect environment. They were created in an enchanting orchard where they could eat from a variety of trees. Just one was forbidden. Satan, of course, focused in on that one tree, that one negative. He does the same today. Satan tells us that if God were good, we would be able to eat of any tree, even the tempting trees of the world. He wants to blind us to all the promises and blessings we have in Christ. Eve was deceived—it was genuine deception. She was deceived by thinking the words of the serpent were more reliable than those of God.

Adam was not deceived (1 Timothy 2:14); he knew it was wrong, but he ate anyway. He was willingly deceived.

Standing next to the forbidden tree, the terrible consequences of their sin was hidden from them. The same is true today: We do not see the terrible consequences even one sin can bring about. Let us not fall into the deceptions of the world.

PRAYER

Father, I'm prone to deception and I desire to do my own thing.
Would You come to me in power? Show me Your grace and Your glory.

FREE TO SAY NO

To all who did receive him, who believed in his name,
he gave the right to become children of God.
JOHN 1:12

D. L. MOODY

Yes, sons of God! Power to overcome the world, the flesh, and the devil; power to crucify every besetting sin, passion, lust; power to shout in triumph over every trouble and temptation of life, "I can do all things through Christ which strengtheneth me!" (Philippians 4:13).

ERWIN LUTZER

Power to overcome sin! That is power at its best. Slaves don't tell their master what to do; they do the master's bidding. To be a slave of sin means to be overpowered by it, driven by it, controlled by the lusts burning within the soul. Most people think they can control sin, but they can't. For that, divine power is needed.

Jesus said it clearly, "Everyone who practices sin is a slave to sin" (John 8:34). Sin gives the orders, you obey. Though this is especially seen in the lives of addicts, it can be true of our lives too; if we do not master sin, sin will master us.

Jesus said of the Pharisees, "You are of your father the devil, and your will is to do your father's desires" (John 8:44). Contrast this with our heavenly Father who liberates us from sin and gives us the desire and the strength to master what enslaves us.

Moody was not exaggerating when he said we had power in Christ to crucify every besetting sin, passion, lust, and sinful power. This power is found in Christ. In fact, all the necessary legal work for such power has already been accomplished by Christ. In Him, our sinful nature has been crucified, dead, and buried.

PRAYER

Father, help me to see Your power overcome sin in my personal life.

THE LIGHT OF OUR SAVIOR

Even though I walk through the valley of the shadow of death, I will fear no evil, for you are with me; your rod and your staff, they comfort me.
PSALM 23:4

D. L. MOODY

Must not there be light where there is shadow? Can you get a shadow without light? If you doubt it, go down into the cellar tonight without a light and find your shadow if you can. All that death can do to a true believer is to throw a shadow across his path. Shadows never hurt anyone. You can walk right through them as you can through fog. There is nothing to fear.

I pity down deep in my heart any man or woman that lives under the bondage of death! If you are under it, may God bring you out today! May you come right out into the liberty of the blessed gospel of the Son of God!

ERWIN LUTZER

In the Bible, the word *light* is frequently used to convey the idea of truth and reality. To the scientist, light means *energy*. To the person who is walking in moral cleanness, light means *purity*. To the philosopher, light means *knowledge* and *understanding*. Jesus is all these things and more as the "Light of the world." Scripture says, "The light shineth in darkness; and the darkness comprehended it not" (John 1:5 KJV).

Today, there are people who fight against the light; they prefer the darkness that hides their deeds. They try to extinguish the light. Those who walked in darkness crucified Jesus to extinguish the light. Although they crucified Him, they could not destroy Him; His light still shines. We are invited to "walk in the light, as he is in the light" (1 John 1:7). Christ is the light that guides us all the days of our lives until we cross through death and into glory. We find our hope and comfort in Him.

PRAYER

Father, I thank You for the coming of Jesus.
I thank You that the light has come; help me to walk in that light today.

THE NEW MIRROR

Therefore, if anyone is in Christ, he is a new creation.
The old has passed away; behold, the new has come.
2 CORINTHIANS 5:17

D. L. MOODY

"That which is born of the flesh is flesh; and that which is born of the Spirit is spirit" (John 3:6), and a man can soon tell whether he is born of the Spirit by the change in his life. The Spirit of Christ is a Spirit of love, joy, peace, humility, and meekness, and we can soon find out whether we have been born of that Spirit or not; we are not to be left in uncertainty.

ERWIN LUTZER

Moses was with God for forty days and forty nights. When he came down, his face was glowing. Don't you think he was changed after being on the mountain in the presence of God? Did he come down from that mountain still loving sin? It's hard to be in the presence of God and to remain unchanged, and certainly Moses spoke to God face to face. He was permanently changed by the encounter. Wouldn't it be wonderful if you were Moses, to go into God's presence and be transformed?

As Moody said, when we are in Christ, we are a new creation; we love what we once hated and hate what we once loved. The privilege that God gave Moses is open to everybody for the same transformation and for perhaps even a deeper one. We all have the opportunity to see God. Jesus said, "Whoever has seen me has seen the Father" (John 14:9). We behold Him, and then we reflect Him. The bottom line is this: What we gaze at is what we become.

PRAYER

Father, let me gaze upon and reflect Your Son,
and rejoice that the "new" has come!

MINISTERING TO PRODIGALS

"For the promise is for you and for your children and for all who are far off, everyone whom the Lord our God calls to himself."
ACTS 2:39

D. L. MOODY

It is not only our privilege to have our names written in heaven, but also those of the children whom God has given us; and our hearts ought to go right out for them. Many a father's and many a mother's heart is burdened with anxiety for the salvation of their children. If your own name is there, let your next aim in life be to get your children's there also.

ERWIN LUTZER

In Matthew 15:22–23, we meet a praying mother, "And behold, a Canaanite woman from that region came out and was crying, 'Have mercy on me, O Lord, Son of David; my daughter is severely oppressed by a demon.' But he [Jesus] did not answer her a word." But a few verses later, we read, "Then Jesus answered her, 'O woman, great is your faith! Let it be done for you as you desire.' And her daughter was healed instantly" (v. 28).

For those of you who are praying for your children, are you put off by the apparent silence of God? Initially, Jesus didn't answer this woman, and He appeared indifferent. But let us always remember that the silence of God is never a sign of the indifference of God. We see that, in the end, Jesus was plotting mercy toward this woman and her child.

God can do what we can't, so we must be willing to pray, "Lord, they are yours," and "Lord, change their heart." That is the power of a praying parent! God is waiting for our faith to put a stake in the ground, saying, "Satan, you will not have my child." We must pray with that confidence.

PRAYER

Father, may I get alone with You and spill out my heart before You for my family, for the church, and for all of us.

KNOWN AND LOVED

"For from within, out of the heart of man, come evil thoughts, sexual immorality, theft, murder, adultery, coveting, wickedness, deceit, sensuality, envy, slander, pride, foolishness."

MARK 7:21–22

D. L. MOODY

If a man should advertise that he could take a correct photograph of people's hearts, do you believe he would find any customers? There is not a man among us whom you could hire to have his photograph taken if you could photograph the real man. We got to have our faces taken, with our carefully arranged clothes and hair, and if the artist flatters us, we say, "Oh, yes, that's a first-rate likeness," and we pass it around among our friends. But let the real man be brought out, the photograph of the heart, and see if we will pass that around among our neighbors! Why, we would not want our own wives to see it! We would be frightened even to look at it ourselves.

ERWIN LUTZER

The grace of God extends to those who are in need, those who are willing to face their sin honestly. You show me someone who is wretched and broken down, I will show you someone to whom the grace, mercy, attention, and the love of Christ is extended. Jesus is our High Priest in heaven and He intercedes for us, He reminds God the Father that we have been purchased at high cost. We have been bought. We have been redeemed. We are special and we belong to Him, and He knows everything about us.

Moody was right: Within us are the seeds of every kind of evil. I want to invite you today to come to Jesus, who can forgive even those sins we attempt to hide. He takes our life with its failures, and says in effect, "If you come to me, I will forgive your sin and use your past to show my grace. Come to me, you've been away from home too long."

PRAYER

Father, let me be honest about my deep need of Your constant grace.
Forgive and restore me as only You can.

THE SATISFIED LIFE

He asked life of you; you gave it to him, length of days forever and ever.
PSALM 21:4

D. L. MOODY (Born February 5, 1837)

I was down in Texas and happened to pick up a newspaper, and there they called me "Old Moody." Honestly, I never got such a shock from any paper in my life before! I never had been called old before; I cannot conceive of getting old. I have a life that is never going to end. Death may change my position but not my condition, not my standing with Jesus Christ. Death is not going to separate us.

Old! I wish you all felt as young as I do here tonight. Why, I am only sixty-two years old! If you meet me ten million years hence, then I will be young. Read Psalm 91, "With long life will I satisfy him." That doesn't mean seventy years. Would that satisfy you? Did you ever see a man or woman of seventy satisfied? Don't they want to live longer? You know that seventy wouldn't satisfy you. Would eighty? Would ninety? Would one hundred? If Adam had lived to be a million years old, and then had to die, he wouldn't be satisfied. "With long life I will satisfy him"—life without end! Don't call me old. I am only sixty-two. I have only begun to live.

ERWIN LUTZER

Moody thought he wasn't old at sixty-two; as I write this, I am twenty years older than he was when he wrote that. We spend so much of our time thinking about today that the reality of the life to come is only a distant anticipation. So, let's take a moment and reflect on eternity, specifically, the New Jerusalem. Who dwells there? God and His people: "Behold, the dwelling place of God is with man. He will dwell with them, and they will be his people, and God himself will be with them as their God" (Revelation 21:3).

If your name is written in the Book of Life, there is nothing permanent that can happen to you on earth because you have a place reserved in heaven. There's a crown only you can wear. There's a room only you can enter. There's an assignment only you can perform. You will be there reigning with Christ forever and ever.

PRAYER

Father, may I always live with eternal values in a transitory world.

FEBRUARY 6

PRIDE VERSUS GOD

"Now I, Nebuchadnezzar, praise and extol and honor the King of heaven, for all his works are right and his ways are just; and those who walk in pride he is able to humble."

DANIEL 4:37

D. L. MOODY

When you find that a man has got to praising God, it is a good sign. Nebuchadnezzar's earlier edict said much about other people's duty toward the God of the Hebrews, but nothing about what the king himself should do. Oh, let us get to personal love, personal praise! That is what is wanted in the church in the present day.

We may surely hope that his was a "repentance to salvation not to be repented of." If so, we may well believe that today Nebuchadnezzar the king and Daniel the captive are walking the crystal pavement of heaven arm-in-arm together.

ERWIN LUTZER

I expect to see Nebuchadnezzar in heaven! The king who opposed Daniel went insane, eating grass like an animal. After God intervened, the king extolled the Most High. I agree with Moody, the king's speech appears to show a "repentance to salvation."

Contrast the humility of Nebuchadnezzar with the pride of Belshazzar. "King Belshazzar made a great feast . . . [and] commanded that the vessels of gold and of silver that Nebuchadnezzar his father had taken out of the temple in Jerusalem be brought" (Daniel 5:1–2). They used the vessels to drink to their pagan gods. Belshazzar blasphemed God, shaking his fist at the God of Abraham, Isaac, and Jacob.

Nebuchadnezzar died humbly bowing to God; Belshazzar died at a drunken orgy. One died in humility in the presence of God; the other died pridefully, thinking he was in charge of his own fate. Humility made the difference. "Whoever exalts himself will be humbled, and whoever humbles himself will be exalted" (Matthew 23:12).

PRAYER

Father, teach me to humble myself so that I might serve You with humility. May You shape me for Your use.

FOR ALL TO READ

You yourselves are our letter of recommendation,
written on our hearts, to be known and read by all.
2 CORINTHIANS 3:2

D. L. MOODY

I remember reading of a blind man who was found sitting at the corner of a street in a great city with a lantern beside him. Someone went up to him and asked what he had the lantern there for, seeing that he was blind and the light was the same to him as the darkness. The blind man replied: "I have it so that no one may stumble over me."

Where one man reads the Bible, a hundred read you and me. That is what Paul meant when he said we were to be living epistles of Christ, known and read of all men. I would not give much for all that can be done by sermons if we do not preach Christ by our lives. If we do not commend the gospel to people by our holy walk and conversation, we shall not win them to Christ.

ERWIN LUTZER

Many unbelievers stumble over the gospel because our witness is not a shining light showing the way to God. We must point the way through the Word of God that transforms us; then we can tell others what God has done for us. When we are satisfied with God, saying no to temptation is easy, and all the circumstances swirling around us don't matter because we accept whatever God brings our way.

When our lamp grows dim, as Moody pointed out, the people around us stumble; they don't know there's a way out of the darkness. We can only keep our lamp lit by meditating on God's Word. Ask the text some questions. Analyze the text and ask yourself, "What does this text tell me about God?" Don't ever close the Bible until you've found some food for your soul. Then we can point the way out of the darkness. "Thy word is a lamp unto my feet, and a light unto my path" (Psalm 119:105 KJV).

PRAYER

Father, may no one stumble over me because my lamp is not lit.
Today, help me to point the way for some person walking in darkness.

PURE LOVE

If I speak in the tongues of men and of angels, but have not love, I am a noisy gong or a clanging cymbal. And if I have prophetic powers, and understand all mysteries and all knowledge, and if I have all faith, so as to remove mountains, but have not love, I am nothing.

1 CORINTHIANS 13:1–2

D. L. MOODY

A man may have wonderful knowledge, may be able to unravel the mysteries of the Bible, and yet be as cold as an icicle. He may glisten like the snow in the sun. Sometimes you have wondered why it was that certain ministers who have had such wonderful magnetism, who have such a marvelous command of language, and who preach with such mental strength, haven't had more conversions. I believe, if the truth was known, you would find no divine love back of their words, no pure love in their sermons.

ERWIN LUTZER

Yes, without love we will be empty and repel people from the gospel rather than attract them. But we must distinguish human love from divine love. Human love is good, but it seldom is able to survive a storm. It says in effect, "As long as you are doing something for me, I can love you." Only divine love endures by saying, "I love you no matter what." Human love says, "I can only take so much." It is only divine love that lasts.

God loved us when we were unlovable, unresponsive, and in rebellion (Romans 5:8). Our love can endure because love comes from God. Christian love, the kind in 1 Corinthians 13, is a supernatural gift from God. The world can out-entertain us, the world can out-finance us, the world can outnumber us, but let it never be said that the world can out-love us.

PRAYER

Father, as I mediate on 1 Corinthians 13, may Your love flow through me to others, even to those who regard me as their enemy.

PERFECT PEACE

"You keep him in perfect peace whose mind is stayed on you, because he trusts in you. Trust in the Lord forever, for the Lord God is an everlasting rock."

ISAIAH 26:3–4

D. L. MOODY

As long as our mind is stayed on our dear selves, we will never have peace. Some people think more of themselves than of all the rest of the world. It is self in the morning, self at noon, and self at night. It is self when they wake up and self when they go to bed. They are all the time looking at themselves and thinking about themselves instead of "looking unto Jesus" (Hebrews 12:2). Faith is an outward look. Faith does not look within; it looks without. It is not what I think or what I feel or what I have done, but it is what Jesus Christ is and has done that is the important thing for us to dwell upon.

ERWIN LUTZER

Peace is what we all long for. I've often thought about those who take a long vacation to a beautiful place in the world and yet they take their own fears and insecurities with them. Peace comes, not by a change of location, but a change of focus. Faith in itself does not have the power to transform something hurtful into something helpful. The old idea that says, "It doesn't matter what you believe as long as you are sincere," is nonsense. The reason that those whose mind is focused on God have peace is because God gives them peace; He is the source of peace. "Therefore, since we have been justified by faith, we have peace with God through our Lord Jesus Christ" (Romans 5:1). And peace with God often leads to peace with others.

Do you need peace? Seek Christ; focus on Him and let the Word of God bring you to a point of surrender. Give what troubles you into God's loving hand.

PRAYER

Father, show me how I can focus on You; may I be willing to penetrate the darkness and experience the "peace that passes understanding" (Philippians 4:7).

FEBRUARY 10

NO MORE THIEVES

The Lord spoke to Moses, saying, "Speak to Aaron and his sons, saying, Thus you shall bless the people of Israel: you shall say to them, The Lord bless you and keep you; the Lord make his face to shine upon you and be gracious to you; the Lord lift up his countenance upon you and give you peace."

NUMBERS 6:22–26

D. L. MOODY

I think these are about as sweet verses as we find in the Old Testament. I marked them years ago in my Bible, and many times I have turned to this chapter and read them. They remind us of the loving words of Jesus to His troubled disciples, "It is I; be not afraid" (John 6:20). The Jewish salutation used to be, as a man went into a house, "Peace be upon this house," and as he left the house the host would say, "Go in peace."

ERWIN LUTZER

We return to the topic of peace because everyone seeks for peace. The Sunday school teacher wants peace, the drug dealer wants peace, and the alcoholic wants peace. We all seek for peace. The question is, "Where can it be found?"

There are certain thieves that steal our peace. One is an inner thief, such as a sense of guilt or regret; then there's another thief, the outer circumstances of our lives. In talking about peace, I'm talking about a sense of stability, a sense of being guided by God. It is very close in meaning to the word "hope."

Regardless of your past, you can be brought into God's presence to experience the joy of reconciliation. That's what Jesus does for people. The world gives a peace that is based on circumstances. Jesus Christ promised, "My peace I give to you" (John 14:27). He gives us peace even if circumstances do not change. He gives peace no matter what the future holds.

PRAYER

Father, when I lack peace, remind me of Christ's promises and favor.

OUR ETERNAL COMPANION

"The secret things belong to the Lord our God, but the things that are revealed belong to us and to our children forever, that we may do all the words of this law."
DEUTERONOMY 29:29

D. L. MOODY

There are many things which were dark and mysterious to me five years ago, on which I have since had a flood of light; and I expect to be finding out something fresh about God throughout eternity.

I make a point of not discussing disputed passages of Scripture. An old divine has said that some people, if they want to eat fish, commence by picking the bones. I leave such things till I have light on them. I am not bound to explain what I do not comprehend. "The secret things belong unto the Lord our God: but those things which are revealed belong unto us and to our children forever"; and these I take and eat and feed upon in order to get spiritual strength.

ERWIN LUTZER

I've walked with God for many years and there are still so many mysteries about Him that I don't understand. The challenge for us is to live up to what we do understand. The disciples were beginning to feel abandoned when Jesus kept telling them, "I'm going to go away, I'm going to leave you." So, Jesus had to give them some reassurance. He said, "I will ask the Father, and He will give you another Helper" (John 14:16). He is referring to the coming of the Holy Spirit. It is the responsibility of the Holy Spirit to substitute for the physical presence of Jesus in our lives.

Faced with the mysteries of God, we turn to Christ and know that the Holy Spirit is our Helper, our companion, and teacher. He illuminates God's Word for us. We are given enough truth to bring transformation. We read that we received the Spirit, "that we might understand the things freely given us by God" (1 Corinthians 2:12). We do not know God fully, but we do know Him truly.

PRAYER

Father, let me respond to all the truth You show me; let the mysteries of Your character lead me to worship and trust in Your promises.

FEBURARY 12

THE GREAT REVERSAL

About midnight Paul and Silas were praying and singing hymns to God, and the prisoners were listening to them.

ACTS 16:25

D. L. MOODY

An old gentleman got up once in a meeting and said he had lived nearly all his life on Grumble Street, but not long ago, he had moved over on Thanksgiving Street. His face showed it. Paul and Silas in jail at Philippi, when they had received stripes on the back and had their feet in the stocks, still sang praises to God. If some of us were in jail with our feet in the stocks, I don't think we would sing much. We want a cheerful Christianity.

ERWIN LUTZER

Can we give thanks to God for an evil act when God uses it for good? In Los Angeles, a baby was born to a teenage girl who was raped. The baby girl grew up and became a soloist and blessed the hearts of millions of people. She was Ethel Waters, who sang the beloved gospel song at the Billy Graham crusades, "His Eye Is on the Sparrow."

This is an example of how we can give thanks to God for how He sometimes uses evil to bring about good. We don't give thanks for the evil, but we do give thanks for the good He brings forth from it. Do not ever underestimate God's ability to take a sorrow and to turn it into a joy. He does that today, even for you and for me.

As we discover in Acts 16, Paul and Silas could sing hymns to God while unjustly prisoned. They saw God above the pain and unjust events of life. If you are going through a trial today, give thanks to God for it. You will bring glory to His name and help you look at it from a divine perspective. God, in His grace, may bring something beautiful from what you are going through. Give thanks right now; God is able and the war has been won.

PRAYER

Father, You can take the deepest of sorrows and bring hope. Help me to thank You in all things. Let me sing praises to You despite unanswered questions.

UNBOUND SIN

"Let all the house of Israel therefore know for certain that God has made him both Lord and Christ, this Jesus whom you crucified." Now when they heard this they were cut to the heart, and said to Peter and the rest of the apostles, "Brothers, what shall we do?" And Peter said to them, "Repent and be baptized every one of you in the name of Jesus Christ for the forgiveness of your sins, and you will receive the gift of the Holy Spirit."

ACTS 2:36–38

D. L. MOODY

One thing I have noticed is that some conversions don't amount to anything; that if a man professes to be converted without conviction of sin, he is one of those stony-ground hearers who don't bring forth much fruit. The first little wave of persecution, the first breath of opposition, and the man is back in the world again. Let us pray that God may carry on a deep and thorough work, that men may be convicted of sin so they cannot rest in unbelief. Pray this conviction and confession may begin in our own church. I would a great deal rather see a hundred men thoroughly converted, truly born of God, than to see a thousand professed conversions where the Spirit of God has not convicted of sin.

ERWIN LUTZER

It has been my belief that the reason we have so many who turn away from the faith after professing to be converted is because they got saved when they didn't even know they were lost. And so like Judas, they professed faith in Christ and appeared to fit in with the church but were never really converted. Judas represented humanity, showing the deception of the human heart without restraints, without the intervention of God's grace, and without repentance—human nature in all its contradictions. Judas reminds us that the gate to hell is right next to the gate to heaven. For three years, he was able to be with Jesus, to learn from Him, to become a part of the family of His disciples. Yet, for all that, his heart was unchanged. He walked past the gate of heaven and yet ended in hell.

PRAYER

Father, grant me a genuine faith; a faith that knows my great need and comes to Christ in repentance to have that need met.

FEBRUARY 14

JESUS PAID OUR BILL

For you know the grace of our Lord Jesus Christ, that though he was rich, yet for your sake he became poor, so that you by his poverty might become rich.
2 CORINTHIANS 8:9

D. L. MOODY

Men talk about grace but, as a rule, they know very little about it. Let a businessman go to a banker's to borrow a few hundred dollars for sixty or ninety days. The banks give what they call "three days' grace" after the sixty or ninety days, but they will make the borrower pay interest on the money during these three days, and if he does not return principal and interest at the appointed time, they will sell his goods; they will perhaps turn him out of his house and take the last piece of furniture in his possession.

That is not grace at all, but that fairly illustrates man's idea of it. Grace not only frees from payment of the interest, but of the principal also. The grace of God frees us from the penalty of our sin without any payment on our part. Christ has paid the debt and all we have to do is to believe on Him for our salvation.

ERWIN LUTZER

"Jesus paid it all; all to him I owe. Sin had left a crimson stain; He washed it white as snow."[3] Paul says in Romans 3 that we are all sinners before God. There is nothing we can do about it, and our very attempt to do something only makes it worse. We are alive physically but spiritually, apart from Christ, we are dead. "But God, being rich in mercy, because of the great love with which He loved us, even when we were dead in our trespasses, made us alive together with Christ—by grace you have been saved" (Ephesians 2:4–5).

When we come to Christ, we bring nothing except our sin. We don't come to Christ saying, "If I got serious about this, I could take care of it. But I need Your assistance." No. You come blind and helpless. Have you invited Christ to cleanse your heart and open your spiritual eyes?

PRAYER

Father, let me praise You for the gift of salvation and paying our debt.
Help me to constantly rejoice in Your grace toward me.

THE POWER OF THE NEW BIRTH

For you did not receive the spirit of slavery to fall back into fear, but you have received the Spirit of adoption as sons, by whom we cry, "Abba! Father!"
ROMANS 8:15

D. L. MOODY

I want to say very emphatically that I have no sympathy with the doctrine of universal brotherhood and universal fatherhood; I don't believe one word of it. If a man lives in the flesh and serves the flesh, he is a child of the devil. That is pretty strong language, but it is what Christ said. It brought down a hornet's nest on His head, and helped to hasten Him to the cross, but nevertheless it is true. Show me a man that will lie and steal and get drunk and ruin a woman—do you tell me he is my brother? Not a bit of it. He must be born into the household of faith before he becomes my brother in Christ. He is an alien, he is a stranger to the grace of God, he is an enemy to God, he is not a friend. Before a man can cry, "Abba, Father," he must be born from above, born of the Spirit.

ERWIN LUTZER

God loves to remake spoiled vessels. His grace outweighs our sins, and He loves to remake people as it pleases Him. In Christ, "the old has passed away; behold, the new has come" (2 Corinthians 5:17). Remaking us isn't easy; the transformation comes only when our love for Christ is greater than our love of sin. God is the divine Potter: He puts the vessels into a kiln and turns up the heat. There are some sins and past values we won't give up except by the conviction of the Holy Spirit and seeing the consequences of our actions.

No matter where you find yourself, submit to the Potter; do not resist the divine hand upon your life; He is in the process of remaking us for His honor and glory and our good. God, our loving Father, is shaping us. As Moody said, we cannot cry, "Abba, Father" unless we have been born from above.

PRAYER

Father, thank You for working in my life to make me look more like Jesus. Thank You for difficult circumstances which remake me toward Your eternal purpose for me. Cause me, Father, to submit gladly to You.

TRAGEDY AND GLORY

Jesus said to her, "I am the resurrection and the life. Whoever believes in me, though he die, yet shall he live."
JOHN 11:25

D. L. MOODY

When a young man, I was called upon suddenly, in Chicago, to preach a funeral sermon. A good many Chicago businessmen were to be there, and I said to myself, "Now, it will be a good chance for me to preach the gospel to those men, and I will get one of Christ's funeral sermons."

I hunted all through the four gospels trying to find one of Christ's funeral sermons, but I couldn't find any. I found He broke up every funeral He ever attended! He never preached a funeral sermon in the world. Death couldn't exist where He was. When the dead heard His voice they sprang to life.

ERWIN LUTZER

Yes, Christ gives life to all who believe on Him; but physically, we must die. We do everything we possibly can to avoid death, to eke out one last week of existence. Yet the Bible presents a very different story. Death is the chariot; it's the limousine God sends to bring us to Him. When we arrive, we meet the Doorman—the One we have come to trust in this life. He is there to meet us on the other side. For the Christian, death is a gift. Paul says, "All things are yours, whether . . . life or death" (1 Corinthians 3:21–22). He also writes about our suffering using the imagery of a scale: If one side held all of your trials and sorrows, this does not compare to the counterweight, "the eternal weight of glory" that will be revealed in us (2 Corinthians 4:17). God's glory is so much heavier and so much greater than any tragedy we encounter en route to the heavenly city.

When it is time for someone to preach our funeral sermon, may our loved ones and friends experience sorrow mingled with joy. The one who redeemed us will be with us forever.

PRAYER

Father, encourage me and Your people to look at the events of life from a standpoint of the eternal glory in Your presence.

WHEN GOOD ENOUGH IS NOT GOOD ENOUGH

The heart is deceitful above all things, and desperately sick; who can understand it?
JEREMIAH 17:9

D. L. MOODY

Nobody knows what is in the human heart but Christ. We do not know our own hearts; none of us have any idea how bad they are. Some bitter things have been written against me, but I know a good many more things about myself that are badder than any other man. There is nothing good in the old Adam nature. We have got a heart in rebellion against God by nature, and we do not even love God unless we are born of the Spirit.

This is a truth that men do not at all like, but I have noticed that the medicine we do not like is often the medicine that will do us good. If we do not think we are as bad as the description, we must just take a closer look at ourselves.

ERWIN LUTZER

The moral gap between us and God is infinite. I believe God never shows us the seeds of wickedness and deceit that exist in every man and woman; if He did, we might not be able to endure it. Many of us think we are good people or good enough to enter heaven, but we don't take into account the fact that God's hatred of sin is beyond our comprehension. And thankfully, Jesus Christ supplies all that God demands. He is our perfection and based on Him our entrance into heaven is assured.

Don't let your heart deceive you! By nature, we run from God; we come to Him only because He searches for us! We are sinners, helpless and needy in the presence of a God whose holiness burns brighter than the sun. Were it not for His grace in Christ, we would be damned forever. Even our good works are tainted with sin. Perhaps He would even call them "works of lawlessness." Thank God for the perfection of Christ.

PRAYER

Father, You have searched me; show me what You see so I may deeply repent. Please open my heart to show me my need for You.

AN EVERLASTING HARVEST

Since you have been born again, not of perishable seed but of imperishable, through the living and abiding word of God.

1 PETER 1:23

D. L. MOODY

We hear nowadays so much about "culture." Culture's all right when you have something to cultivate. If I should plant a watch, I shouldn't get any little watches, would I? Why? Because the seed of life is not there. But let me plant some peas or potatoes and I will get a crop.

Don't let any man or woman rest short of being born of the Spirit of God. Don't cultivate a dead and corrupt thing, first make sure that you have that divine nature, then cultivate it.

ERWIN LUTZER

Jesus taught that the true seed is the Word of God (Luke 8:11). The gospel of the kingdom Jesus proclaimed was breaking into Satan's kingdom and rescuing people from his grip. Jesus told a parable where sometimes the seed of the Word fell on hard soil and took no root; at other times the seed was choked by the cares of this world. But then there was the good soil that brought forth fruit. In each case, the same seed was planted, but the condition of the soil determined whether it bore fruit. And when the seeds bear fruit, they reproduce themselves. Why? It's because within them is life, and within God's Word there is life, and you and I can share that seed with others.

We sow by our witness, and when we sow the gospel in the lives of other people, we are trusting and believing that God will breathe life into those who hear it. If we are believers, the gospel has been sown in our own hearts that we might bear fruit, and in turn, we sow the imperishable seed in the lives of others.

PRAYER

Father, I thank You for the gospel.
Grant me opportunities to sow Your seed on fruitful ground.

THE CHOICE: TO FOLLOW OR NOT TO FOLLOW CHRIST

"See, I am setting before you today a blessing and a curse: the blessing, if you obey the commandments of the LORD your God, which I command you today, and the curse, if you do not obey the commandments of the LORD your God, but turn aside from the way that I am commanding you today, to go after other gods that you have not known."

DEUTERONOMY 11:26–28

D. L. MOODY

Take the two Sauls: The first Saul got a kingdom and a crown; he had a lovely family (no father ever had a better son than Saul had in Jonathan); he had the friendship of Samuel, the best prophet there was on the face of the earth; and yet he lost the friendship of Samuel, lost his crown, his kingdom and his life, all through an act of disobedience.

Now take the Saul of the New Testament. When God called him, he was obedient to the heavenly vision, and he was given a heavenly kingdom.

The act of obedience gained all, and the act of disobedience lost everything. I believe the wretchedness and misery and woe in this country today comes from disobedience to God. If they won't obey God as a nation, let us begin individually. Let us make up our minds that we will do it, cost us what it will, and we will have peace and joy.

ERWIN LUTZER

God has been unofficially banned in America from the public square, from education and science, and He's being banned from the workplace. People say God must stay on the other side of that thick, high wall called "the separation of church and state."

When most Americans say, "God bless America," they mean, "Oh God, keep us from terrorist attacks, keep my children healthy, and don't let the stock market crash." But it should mean: "God bless America with a spirit of repentance and revival." We need to ask ourselves if we are on God's side, not the other way around. God is faithful to all those who seek Him (Hebrews 11:6).

PRAYER

Father, build my faith and help me to be a good witness wherever You plant me.

PRAY LIKE BREATHING

If one turns away his ear from hearing the law,
even his prayer is an abomination.
PROVERBS 28:9

D. L. MOODY

Think of that! It may shock some of us to think that our prayers are an abomination to God, yet if any are living in known sin, this is what God's Word says about them. If we are not willing to turn from sin and obey God's law, we have no right to expect He will answer our prayers. The prayer of the humble and the contrite heart is a delight to God. There is no sound that goes up from this sin-cursed earth so sweet to His ear as the prayer of the man who is walking uprightly.

ERWIN LUTZER

Some look at prayer like an oxygen mask—it comes in handy when a crisis arises. For believers, prayer is oxygen itself. We pray when we have needs, but we need fellowship with God more than we need our prayers answered.

Prayer yields us to the will of God. Jesus taught us to pray, "Your kingdom come, your will be done, on earth as it is in heaven" (Matthew 6:10). Prayer is submission to God's will. Jesus in Gethsemane said, "My Father, if it be possible, let this cup pass from me; nevertheless, not as I will, but as you will" (Matthew 26:39). If your prayer does not lead to submission before God, you haven't really prayed.

Come to God with an honest and cleansed heart. Tell Him why you love Him. Quote verses of Scripture that remind you of His promises and His love for you. Enjoy fellowship with God. You are His child, and God loves it when you show up—especially if it's just the two of you.

PRAYER

Father, forgive me for concentrating on all other things,
and forgetting to seek You first.

FEBRUARY 21

OVERFLOWING WELLS

On the last day of the feast, the great day, Jesus stood up and cried out, "If anyone thirsts, let him come to me and drink. Whoever believes in me, as the Scripture has said, 'Out of his heart will flow rivers of living water.'"

JOHN 7:37–38

D. L. MOODY

When a boy upon a farm in New England, we had a well, and I used to have to pump the water from that well on wash-day, and to water the cattle; and many a time I had to pump until my arm got tired. But they have a better way now. They dig down until they strike what they call a lower stream, and then it becomes an artesian well, which needs no labor as the water rises spontaneously from the depths beneath.

I think God wants each of His children to be a sort of artesian well; not to keep pumping, but to flow right out. Why, haven't you seen ministers in the pulpit just pumping, pumping, pumping? I have, many a time, and I have had to do it too. I know how it is. They stand in the pulpit and talk and talk and talk, and the people go to sleep, they can't arouse them. What is the trouble? Why, the living water is not there; they are just pumping when there is no water in the well.

ERWIN LUTZER

When Jesus promised that those who believed in Him would find within themselves "rivers of living water," He was referring to the blessed Holy Spirit. John adds that the Holy Spirit had not yet been given "because Jesus was not yet glorified" (John 7:37–39).

But now, all believers are indwelt by the Spirit, though many don't know the Spirit's power. How do you experience the filling of the Spirit? Think of it this way: How did you become a Christian? You put faith in the crucified Christ. How do we become filled with the Holy Spirit? You put faith in the ascended Christ! Make sure that the Spirit is not just resident, but president.

PRAYER

Father, thank You for Jesus' ascension, pouring forth the gift of the Holy Spirit so I can walk in His power today.

FAITHFUL DOUBTING

Now Thomas, one of the twelve, called the Twin, was not with them when Jesus came. So the other disciples told him, "We have seen the Lord." But he said to them, "Unless I see in his hands the mark of the nails, and place my finger into the mark of the nails, and place my hand into his side, I will never believe."

JOHN 20:24–25

D. L. MOODY

I often think that Thomas was the most unhappy man in Jerusalem during the week that followed. It would have been far more reasonable for him to have believed those who saw Jesus, rather than to have doubted their word. But unbelief is the most unreasonable thing in the world.

ERWIN LUTZER

Many people doubt God's promises, and some doubt their salvation. As they think about their future, they have a very vague hope that all will be well and say, "I just hope that God will be gracious." God can handle your doubts. It is okay to doubt because as it has been said, "He who has never really doubted has never really believed."

Some people should doubt their salvation because they are not saved. Saving faith is the deep settled conviction that what Jesus Christ did on the cross for us is sufficient for us to be welcomed by God. If you have doubts, bring them to Jesus. As the song "Just as I Am" reads, "Just as I am, though tossed about with many a conflict, many a doubt, fightings and fears within, without, O Lamb of God, I come."[4]

PRAYER

Father, help me to believe that trust in Jesus is enough.

CRADLED IN LOVE

For I am sure that neither death nor life, nor angels nor rulers, nor things present nor things to come, nor powers, nor height nor depth, nor anything else in all creation, will be able to separate us from the love of God in Christ Jesus our Lord.

ROMANS 8:38–39

D. L. MOODY

There can be no true peace, there can be no true hope, there can be no true comfort, where there is uncertainty. I am not fit for God's service, I cannot go out and work for God if I am in doubt about my own salvation.

ERWIN LUTZER

There are some people who say you can lose your salvation. You can come to saving faith in Christ, you can be sealed with the Holy Spirit of God, and then, because of backsliding and rebellion, you lose your status with God—and if you died, you'd be lost. Can you imagine if we lost our salvation every time we sinned?

What kind of a shepherd loses sheep? Jesus says, "My sheep hear my voice, and I know them, and they follow me. I give them eternal life, and they will never perish, and no one will snatch them out of my hand" (John 10:27–28).

Somebody says, "Oh yes, but we can snatch ourselves out of His hand." But we are not only in His hand, we are a part of His hand, members of His body. And we have this assurance, "My Father, who has given them to me, is greater than all, and no one is able to snatch them out of the Father's hand" (John 10:29). The hands of the Son and the hands of the Father are in harmony with each other.

PRAYER

Father, thank You that I am held in hands that are much stronger than I am.

THE DANGER OF LIVING IN SODOM

They also took Lot, the son of Abram's brother, who was dwelling in Sodom, and his possessions, and went their way.
GENESIS 14:12

D. L. MOODY

For awhile, Lot made money very fast in Sodom and became a very successful man. If you had gone into Sodom a little while before destruction came, you would have found that Lot owned some of the best corner lots in town, and that Mrs. Lot moved in what they called the *bonton* society or upper ten; and you would have found she was at the theatre two or three nights in the week. If they had progressive euchre, she could play as well as anybody; and her daughters could dance as well as any other Sodomites. We find Lot sitting in the gates, he is getting on amazingly well. He may have been one of the principal men in the city; Judge Lot, or the Honorable Mr. Lot of Sodom. They might have elected him Mayor of Sodom. He was getting on amazingly well; wonderfully prosperous.

But by and by there comes a war. If you go into Sodom, you must take Sodom's judgment when it comes; and it is bound to come. The battle turned against those five cities of the plain, and they took Lot and his wife and all that they had.

ERWIN LUTZER

Remember how Lot chose the best pastureland? Abraham gave him the option, and he selfishly chose the best for himself. He pitched his tent toward Sodom, eventually moving within its walls. He and Mrs. Lot had a house, land, and their wealth was there. Sodom was good to Lot; he didn't want to let go of it. Yet, God rescued him.

How does Lot end? He and his two daughters go to a cave after the destruction of Sodom. The daughters get him drunk and have relations with him. Each bears him a child born of incest. The descendants of both children became thorns in the flesh for Abraham's descendants. How costly is sin? Remember Galatians 6:7, "Do not be deceived: God is not mocked, for whatever one sows, that will he also reap."

PRAYER

Father, turn my heart away from the world so that I may rest in You.

OUR RIGHTEOUSNESS IS FILTHY RAGS

"A certain moneylender had two debtors. One owed five hundred denarii, and the other fifty. When they could not pay, he cancelled the debt of both."

LUKE 7:41–42

D. L. MOODY

Very few people think they are lost. You seldom meet a bankrupt sinner. Most of them think they can pay about seventy-five cents on the dollar; some 99 percent—they just come short a little, and they think the Almighty will make it up somehow.

Don't let Satan make you think you are so good that you don't need the grace of God. We are a bad lot, all of us, with nothing to pay.

ERWIN LUTZER

At an evangelical conference, a man interviewed several participants. His question: "Is it necessary to be perfect to enter into heaven?" And this interviewer couldn't find anybody who would say yes. That's astounding. These Christians, who should have known better, said, in effect, "Well no, of course not."

Here is God who is holy and without stain, and He's going to let imperfect people into heaven? It's unthinkable. It shows you the extent of our theological naïveté. If you are not as holy as God, don't even think about being admitted into heaven. Don't even let the thought cross your mind.

Our problem is so massive that there is nothing we can do to solve it. But in Christ, God solved the problem for us. We give to Christ our sin and He gives to us what we do not have, namely, God's righteousness. We are declared perfectly holy because of Christ's gift to us.

PRAYER

Father, I thank You that I am credited with the righteousness of a perfect Savior. Thank You for Jesus' sacrifice on our behalf.

BUILD UP THE CHURCH

"Remember the words of the Lord Jesus, how he himself said, 'It is more blessed to give than to receive.'"
ACTS 20:35

D. L. MOODY

What makes the Dead Sea dead? Because it is all the time receiving, but never giving out anything. Why is it that many Christians are cold? Because they are all the time receiving, never giving out.

ERWIN LUTZER

God has ordained that, in one way or another, we should serve others. If any one of us is not doing his or her part, the work of God suffers. God has given us gifts, the purpose of which is so that nobody would ever have to do the job alone, but work together as the body of Christ to do what God expects.

I can't remember a Christmas at the Lutzer family where there was a gift under the tree that was left unopened. It is a tragedy that God has given us gifts, but often they lie dormant, unopened because of fear or a variety of other excuses. I have often noted how Christians complain if they are not edified by the church, but they themselves neglect the opportunity to edify others. This is what I promise: If we take the time to invest in others, we ourselves will be blessed in return. As Moody said, let's not be like the Dead Sea that stagnates, but may our lives be a stream of blessing for others.

PRAYER

Father, I want to thank You that Jesus Christ ordained that we all be
a part of something greater than any one of us.
May I be committed to blessing others even as You have greatly blessed me.
Grant me opportunities to serve the body of Christ with the gifts You gave me.

FEBRUARY 27

DON'T BE EASILY SATISFIED

My speech and my message were not in plausible words of wisdom, but in demonstration of the Spirit and of power.

1 CORINTHIANS 2:4

D. L. MOODY

What the church of God needs today is the old power that the apostles had: If we have that in our churches, there will be new life. Then we will have new ministers—the same old ministers renewed with power, filled with the Spirit.

I remember when, in Chicago, many were toiling in the work and it seemed as though the car of salvation didn't move on, a minister began to cry out from the very depths of his heart, "Oh, God, put new ministers in every pulpit." The next Monday, I heard two or three men say, "We had a new minister last Sunday—the same old minister, but he had got new power." I firmly believe that is what we want today all over the land. We want new ministers in the pulpit and new people in the pews. We want people quickened by the Spirit of God.

ERWIN LUTZER

Believers need a "quickening," a constant filling of the Spirit every day. We need Christians whose hearts match their lifestyle. Jesus told the Sardian church, "Wake up" (Revelation 3:1–3). Though outwardly appearing alive, God said, "You are spiritually dead." They had prosperity and health, but they lacked spiritual vitality. Physically active; spiritually dead.

Jesus rebuked the Pharisees and in effect said, "You sing the right songs, you hear the right words, you honor me with your lips, but your heart is far from me" (see Matthew 15:1–9). That can apply to anyone of us. If it does, we are quenching the Holy Spirit. We can grieve the blessed Holy Spirit through our indifference, hypocrisy, and failure to deal with known sin (see Ephesians 4:25–30). My plea to all of us is to be renewed through repentance and submission to receive what Moody called "the quickening of the Spirit of God."

PRAYER

Father, may I wake up to the reality of my condition and repent of my sin.

THE INFINITE LADDER

"Strive to enter through the narrow door.
For many, I tell you, will seek to enter and will not be able."
LUKE 13:24

D. L. MOODY

Who are we to strive with? Not with the gatekeeper. The gatekeeper stands with the gate wide open, and he says, "Come in, come in!" All the striving is with the flesh; it is with this old carnal nature of ours.

ERWIN LUTZER

Some think to themselves that the way to heaven is really a tall ladder and God gives us grace to climb it rung by rung. And when God sees how sincere we are, He comes and His grace picks us up and takes us all the way to the top. This kind of thinking is sometimes summarized as "God helps those who help themselves."

This actually is the broad way that leads to destruction (Matthew 7:13). This view overestimates the goodness of man and it underestimates the glory, holiness, and perfection of God. It assumes that somehow we can cooperate with God in the process of salvation. Trying to climb that ladder only means that it is done with my power and my energy—energy that may be given to me of God, but energy that is mine nonetheless.

But salvation is not a cooperative process. God has to come down, scoop us up and carry us all the way to the top. This is done for all who repent and believe in the free gift of eternal life.

PRAYER

Father, let me not trust in my own power but instead
find my hope in Christ alone.

ENDURE TO DEATH

"God raised him up, loosing the pangs of death, because it was not possible for him to be held by it."
ACTS 2:24

D. L. MOODY

I can imagine when they laid our Lord in Joseph's tomb, one might have seen Death sitting over that sepulchre, saying, "I have Him; He is my victim. He said He was the Resurrection and the Life. Now I hold Him in my cold embrace. They thought He was never going to die; but see Him now. He has had to pay tribute to me."

Never! The glorious morning comes, the Son of Man bursts asunder the hands of death, and rises, a conqueror, from the grave. "Because I live," He shouts, "ye shall live also."

Yes, *we shall live also*—is it not good news?

ERWIN LUTZER

For the Christian, death is simply following Jesus to the grave and entering heaven where He is today. Jesus will never ask us to endure something that He Himself has not already endured. Thankfully, our body will be raised and, "Because He lives, we too shall live" (John 14:19). We will be shepherded through the door of death by the One who was dead and is alive forever more. He will take us all the way home to the Father.

Is it any wonder Jesus invites us to follow Him into suffering? "Blessed are you when others revile you and persecute you and utter all kinds of evil against you falsely on my account…for so they persecuted the prophets who were before you" (Matthew 5:11–12). Someday the suffering will end, conflicts with the world will vanish, and we will be free forever, knowing that it was worth it all. The resurrected Christ will make us alive, and Paul says our bodies will be transformed to be like His glorious body.

Let us live in light of eternity for we have trusted a living Savior who has promised to share His resurrection life and eternity with us.

PRAYER

Father, help me to live for Christ in all things without fearing death, knowing that Christ will meet me on the other side.

FOUR FACTS ABOUT FAITH

"If this be so, our God whom we serve is able to deliver us from the burning fiery furnace, and he will deliver us out of your hand, O king. But if not, be it known to you, O king, that we will not serve your gods or worship the golden image that you have set up."

DANIEL 3:17–18

D. L. MOODY

Shadrach, Meshach, and Abednego spoke respectfully, but firmly. And mark, they did not absolutely say that God would deliver them from the burning, fiery furnace; but they declared that He was able to deliver them. "But *if* not,"—if in His inscrutable purposes He allows us to suffer—"still our resolve is the same: We will not worship the golden image which thou hast set up." They were not afraid to pass from the presence of the king of Babylon to the presence of the King of kings.

ERWIN LUTZER

How do we keep believing when God doesn't deliver us like we expect? Scripture reveals four facts regarding faith. First, sometimes faith changes our circumstances. Hebrews 11 lists many victories because of faith—military conquests, healings, and divine miracles. Second, sometimes faith does not change our circumstances. My wife and I have been to Rome and have stood where many believers did not receive deliverance and were thrown to the lions. Third, faith does not judge God by circumstances. We believe God loves the world, not because the world appears to be a loving place, but because His Word tells us He sent His Son to redeem us. And finally, faith always leads to ultimate victory for Christians; live or die, we are the Lord's. Let's not judge God's care for us by what we see but by the promises of the world to come.

PRAYER

Father, may the gold of my faith be refined even as
You walk with me through the fire.

AN INDESCRIBABLE INHERITANCE

"The one who conquers will have this heritage,
and I will be his God and he will be my son."
REVELATION 21:7

D. L. MOODY

I used to have my Sabbath-school children sing, "I want to be an angel;" but I have not done so for years. We shall be above angels: We shall be sons of God. Just see what a kingdom we shall come into. We shall inherit all things! Do you ask me how much I am worth? I don't know. The Rothschilds cannot compute their wealth. They don't know how many millions they own. That is my condition—I haven't the slightest idea how much I am worth. God has no poor children. If we overcome, we shall inherit all things.

ERWIN LUTZER

God welcomes us into His family as a son or daughter with all the associated rights and the privileges. Though we can begin to enjoy our inheritance right away on earth, the eventual, ultimate enjoyment will be heaven. Whether you have been saved for forty years or are a brand-new Christian, our status as a son or daughter before God is the same. Your spiritual condition might be that of a baby, but your position is that of an adopted son or daughter of God.

When it comes to the matter of adoption and becoming a child of God, the entire Trinity is involved. We are welcomed by our Father, assured of our security by the Spirit, and given an inheritance shared with us by the Son (Ephesians 1:3–14). There is nothing that belongs to Jesus which He does not share with us as joint heirs (Romans 8:17). We will be trophies of God's grace forever. And yes, we shall inherit all things!

PRAYER

Lord, thank You for Your indescribable grace
in declaring me to be a child of the Most High.

THE FRUIT OF FAITH

What good is it, my brothers, if someone says he has faith but does not have works? Can that faith save him?

JAMES 2:14

D. L. MOODY

I believe in a faith that you can see; a living, working faith that prompts to action. Faith without works is like a man putting all his money into the foundation of a house; and works without faith is like building a house on sand without any foundation.

You often hear people say: "The root of the matter is in him." What would you say if I had a garden and nothing but roots in it?

ERWIN LUTZER

Moody put it well. Our faith must indeed be grounded in God's Word and there should be a direct connection between the Word of God and our lifestyle. In fact, people who are in the Word consistently are most often committed to the church in their service and generosity. That's why James commands us to look intently and persevere in the Word, so we may be changed.

The Word of God, says James, is like a mirror. We must respond to what we see. When we persevere in the "law of liberty," we will be blessed in our deeds (James 1:25). A prime example is controlling our tongue. It doesn't matter how many sermons we've heard or songs we've sung, if you cannot control your tongue your religion is "vain" (James 3:1–12).

Let's not deceive ourselves. We can say, "Look, I've heard the Word; I've memorized the Scripture." But hearing the Word doesn't mean it's gone deep into our heart. Our faith becomes practical and real when we respond and obey. Let's not just invest in the foundation but build upon what we learn.

PRAYER

Father, grant me the grace to bear the fruit of a living faith.

MARCH 5

THE CHRISTIAN'S BEST FRIEND

"When the Spirit of truth comes, he will guide you into all the truth, for he will not speak on his own authority, but whatever he hears he will speak, and he will declare to you the things that are to come."

JOHN 16:13

D. L. MOODY

There is not a truth that we ought to know but the Spirit of God will guide us into it if we will let Him. If we will yield ourselves up to be directed by Him and let Him lead us, He will guide us into all truth. It would have saved us from a great many dark hours if we had only been willing to let the Spirit of God be our counselor and guide.

Lot never would have gone to Sodom if he had been guided by the Spirit of God. David never would have fallen into sin and had all that trouble with his family if he had been guided by the Spirit of God.

There are many Lots and Davids nowadays. The churches are full of them. Men and women are in total darkness because they have not been willing to be guided by the Spirit. "He shall guide you into all truth."

ERWIN LUTZER

When the Spirit has His way, any real transformation is an inner transformation. This is not behavior modification; the Spirit of God changes our desires. When we trust Christ as our Savior, one of the first desires He changes is that we begin to love God. The Spirit transforms us, yes, but we must also seek the Spirit of God. Are you willing to be open to the Spirit to let Him have His way? There's a cost involved. Oh, receiving the Spirit is a gift that is free but there's a cost to walk in the Spirit, and that is to get serious. The Spirit does not enter closed doors.

PRAYER

Father, may Your Holy Spirit have His way in my life and lead me into truth regardless of the cost.

NO AFFLICTION, NO GROWTH

It is good for me that I was afflicted, that I might learn your statutes.
PSALM 119:71

D. L. MOODY

Could a life of ease ruin a man? Yes. If he had nothing but prosperity, he would be ruined. A man can stand adversity better than prosperity. I know a great many who have become very prosperous, but I know few such that haven't lost all their piety, that haven't lost sight of that city eternal in the heavens, whose builder and maker is God. Earthly things have drawn their heart's affections away from eternal things.

ERWIN LUTZER

Every adversity or famine we encounter is a test of our trust in God. In Genesis 12, God told Abraham to leave all he knew and to go into the land He would show him. Abraham obeyed but discovered the land was already inhabited. Abraham built an altar of worship, confirming God had chosen the land of Canaan for him. Yet in that very land, a severe famine came and Abraham began to panic. He fled to Egypt, and there he sinned. To save his life, he lied to Pharaoh about his wife, saying she was his sister. When the truth was revealed, Abraham was forced to leave in disgrace and return to the land God had given him. Once again, the altar appeared, and Abraham was back in fellowship with God (Genesis 13:3–4). Simply put: Because of fear, he had failed the test God had given him. What we do when the wells of our life are dry is a test of our character.

But in the end, Abraham died a pilgrim, looking forward to a city and a hope beyond this present world (Hebrews 11:10). God says, in effect, "I will sustain you in the midst of the famine. It may be difficult, but don't give up hope." And the reason we should not give up hope is because God doesn't leave us—even when we leave Him.

PRAYER

Father, grow my faith in You all the more in times of difficulty.
Let me believe in You even when I see no way out of my predicament.

ROTTEN TO THE CORE

"Your evil will chastise you, and your apostasy will reprove you. Know and see that it is evil and bitter for you to forsake the LORD your God; the fear of me is not in you, declares the Lord GOD of hosts."

JEREMIAH 2:19

D. L. MOODY

I do not exaggerate when I say that I have seen hundreds of backsliders come back, and I have asked them if they had not found it an evil and a bitter thing to leave the Lord. You cannot find a real backslider who has known the Lord, but will admit that it is an evil and a bitter thing to turn away from Him; and I do not know of any one verse more used to bring back wanderers than this very one.

Look at Lot. Did not he find it an evil and a bitter thing? He was twenty years in Sodom and never made a convert. Men would have told you that he was one of the most influential and worthy men in all Sodom. But alas! alas! he ruined his family. And it is a pitiful sight to see that old backslider going through the streets of Sodom at midnight, after he has warned his children, and they have turned a deaf ear to him.

ERWIN LUTZER

Our propensity to turn from the Lord reveals the human heart for what it is. We deny our sin, and when we are found out, we minimize it. Left to ourselves, without the intervention of God's grace, without the intrusion of His light, we are lovers of darkness. The reason we love the darkness is that the darkness is more consistent with our desires. We do what we want to do, and darkness enables us to do that. How much will it cost you to come to the light and repent?

PRAYER

Father, help me to walk in Your Word and not forsake You.

MEETING CHRIST AT THE GATE

"Rejoice that your names are written in heaven."
LUKE 10:20

D. L. MOODY

A soldier, wounded during our Civil War, lay dying on his cot. Suddenly the death-like stillness of the room was broken by the cry, "Here! Here!" which burst from the lips of the dying man. Friends rushed to the spot and asked what he wanted.

"Hark" he said, "they are calling the roll of heaven, and I am answering to my name."

In a few moments he whispered, "Here!" once more and passed into the presence of the King.

ERWIN LUTZER

All of us want to live as long as possible, but when your number strikes on God's clock of your life, if you are a believer in Christ and have embraced His promises, He will be there to meet you. People bury our body, but they do not bury us. Our souls go into the heavenly kingdom.

Is everybody going to be in heaven? No! Jesus said, "The way to heaven is narrow" (see Matthew 7:13–20). Why? It's because we must admit our helplessness, our sinfulness, and cleave to Christ. For those of us who have trusted Christ alone as our Savior, heaven will be our destination one minute after we die. There we'll see angels, loved ones and, best of all, Christ Himself. I'm sure you join me in looking forward to that day when we answer the roll call!

PRAYER

Father, though the curtain separating me from
eternity seems thick and veiled, You have, in Your grace,
given me a glimpse of the other side through Your Word.
Thank You, Father, for those who are even now in Your presence.
May I live today in light of the coming eternity.

PRAYER THAT MAKES A DIFFERENCE

You also must help us by prayer, so that many will give thanks on our behalf for the blessing granted us through the prayers of many.
2 CORINTHIANS 1:11

D. L. MOODY

You have heard the story of the child who was rescued from the fire that was raging in a house away up in the fourth story. The child came to the window and, as the flames were shooting up higher and higher, cried out for help. A fireman started up the ladder. The wind swept the flames near him, and it was getting so hot that he wavered. Thousands looked on, and their hearts quaked at the thought of the child having to perish. Someone in the crowd cried: "Give him a cheer!" Cheer after cheer went up and, as the man heard, he gathered fresh courage. Up he went into the midst of the smoke and the fire, and brought down the child in safety.

If you cannot go and rescue the perishing yourself, you can at least pray for those who do, and cheer them on. If you do, the Lord will bless the effort. Do not grumble and criticize; it takes neither heart nor brains to do that.

ERWIN LUTZER

When you look at Paul's prayers, every one of them are focused on people's relationships with God, and almost nothing was said about their physical needs or conflicts. Paul was convinced that people who are rightly related to God and better understand their life in Christ can endure whatever they are going through.

PRAYER

Lord, teach me to pray—to pray Your thoughts back to You
and to pray Your agenda and not mine.
I also pray for those on the front lines who are "rescuing the perishing."

A DEAD SINNER OR A LIVING CHRISTIAN

So he said to them again, "I am going away, and you will seek me, and you will die in your sin. Where I am going, you cannot come."
JOHN 8:21

D. L. MOODY

One sentence from the lips of the Son of God in regard to the future state of unbelievers has forever settled it in my mind. And you "shall die in your sins; whither I go, ye cannot come." If a man has not given up his drunkenness, his profanity, his licentiousness, his covetousness, heaven would be hell to him. Heaven is a prepared place for prepared people. What would a man do in heaven who cannot bear to be in the society of the pure and holy down here?

ERWIN LUTZER

Perhaps you have noticed the word *sin* has basically dropped from our culture's vocabulary. But if you have a wrong view of sin, you will be wrong about everything in the world that really matters. Your understanding of sin determines who you are as a person and your understanding of God's grace. Without understanding "the sinfulness of sin" we will trivialize our sin.

When sin is exposed, our first tendency as humans is to deny it, then we minimize it, and finally, we compare our sin to someone else who we think is worse than we are. So we go our way through life managing our sin, doing the best we can. We who love evil cannot begin to love good. We need God's intervention. Through Christ's work on the cross, God opens our hearts to believe in Him and then we begin to hate sin. Apart from God, we remain dead in our sins and eternally separated from Him.

PRAYER

Lord, show me the enormity of my sin so that I might rejoice in the enormity of Your grace.

MARCH 11

A GODLY PORTFOLIO

"Moreover, look for able men from all the people, men who fear God, who are trustworthy and hate a bribe, and place such men over the people as chiefs of thousands, of hundreds, of fifties, and of tens."

EXODUS 18:21

D. L. MOODY

Isn't it extraordinary that Jethro, the man of the desert, should have given this advice to Moses? How did he learn to beware of covetousness? We honor men today if they are wealthy and covetous. We elect them to office in church and state. We often say they will make better treasurers because we know them to be covetous. But in God's sight, a covetous man is as vile and black as any thief or drunkard. David said: "The wicked boasteth of his heart's desire, and blesseth the covetous, whom the LORD abhorreth" (Psalm 10:3). I am afraid that many who profess to have put away wickedness also speak well of the covetous.

ERWIN LUTZER

Our wealth is God's, and we are managers. God cares about what you do with what He owns. As for covetousness, the Lord does abhor it. Money should be transmuted into profitable and safe eternal investments.

Our temptation is to think we can have two masters: God and money. But let us listen carefully to Jesus, "One who is faithful in a very little is also faithful in much, and one who is dishonest in a very little is also dishonest in much. . . . You cannot serve God and money" (Luke 16:10–13). Picture the California Gold Rush. People sacrificed their families and their children. They took incredible risks with their lives—all to get the gold. Yet we read this about the promises of God, "More to be desired are they than gold, even much fine gold" (Psalm 19:10). Without God's perspective on money, we will switch the price tags; we will put great value on cheap goods and neglect that which is eternal.

PRAYER

Father, help me to invest in Your eternal rewards
and not the things of this world.

BORN INTO GOD'S FAMILY

Beloved, we are God's children now, and what we will be has not yet appeared; but we know that when he appears we shall be like him, because we shall see him as he is.

1 JOHN 3:2

D. L. MOODY

The reason why there are so many in the churches who will not go out and help others is that they are not sure they have been saved themselves. If I thought I was dying myself, I would be in a poor condition to save anyone else. Before I can pull anyone else out of the water, I must have a firm footing on shore myself.

We can have this complete assurance if we will. It does not do to *feel* we are all right, we must *know* it. The apostle John says, "Beloved, *now* are we the sons of God." He does not say we are going to be.

ERWIN LUTZER

One of the greatest errors we can make is to view our relationship with God as a religion rather than a relationship. Nobody illustrates this like Nicodemus, a high-ranking official of the Jews. Jesus told Nicodemus, who came secretly by night, that we must be born again to "enter the kingdom of God" (see John 3:5–7).

The new birth brings us back in contact with God. Nicodemus would have understood rebirth from Ezekiel, "I will cleanse you. And I will give you a new heart" (Ezek. 36:25–27). The life of God is created within us, making "all things new" (Revelation 21:5). As this new life grows, we experience radical change. We are born into God's family, enjoying all of our privileges as sons and daughters.

PRAYER

Father, grant me assurance of the truth that I am Yours.

THE PASSAGEWAY TO ETERNITY

"Truly, truly, I say to you, whoever hears my word and believes him who sent me has eternal life. He does not come into judgment, but has passed from death to life."
JOHN 5:24

D. L. MOODY

In my native village in New England, it used to be customary as a funeral procession left the church, for the bell to toll as many times as the deceased was years old. How anxiously I would count those strokes of the bell to see how long I might reckon on living! Sometimes there would be seventy or eighty tolls, and I would give a sigh of relief to think I had so many years to live. But at other times, there would be only a few years tolled, and then a horror would seize me as I thought that I too might soon be claimed as a victim by that dread monster, Death. Death and judgment were a constant source of fear to me till I realized the fact that neither shall ever have any hold on a child of God.

ERWIN LUTZER

Death for a believer means we will finally be exempt from the pressures, the pulls, the heartaches, and the pains of this world. Death becomes the passageway into everlasting bliss. It is part of God's total package of redemption for humanity.

Death for an unbeliever—one who has never personally put faith in Jesus Christ and transferred their trust to Him alone—will ultimately be judged in hell. That truth comes from the Son of God, who says, "I have the keys of Death and Hades" (Revelation 1:18). Only He is qualified to tell us what lies on the other side.

PRAYER

Father, I pray for my family and friends who do not know You.
Open their hearts to receive Your gospel.

THE CURSE OF IDOLATRY

"For their rock is not as our Rock; our enemies are by themselves."
DEUTERONOMY 32:31

D. L. MOODY

Has the human heart ever been satisfied with false gods? Can pleasure or riches fill the soul that is empty of God? How about the atheist, the deist, the pantheist? What do they look forward to? Nothing! Man's life is full of trouble; but when the billows of affliction and disappointment are rising and rolling over them, they have no God to call upon. They shall "cry unto the gods unto whom they offer incense: but they shall not save them at all in the time of their trouble" (Jeremiah 11:12). Therefore, I contend "their rock is not as our Rock."

ERWIN LUTZER

Idols not only can't save us, they distract us from knowing the true and living God. Jesus told this story in Luke 12:16–21:

> "The land of a rich man produced plentifully, and he thought to himself, 'What shall I do, for I have nowhere to store my crops?' And he said, 'I will do this: I will tear down my barns and build larger ones, and there I will store all my grain and my goods. And I will say to my soul, "Soul, you have ample goods laid up for many years; relax, eat, drink, be merry."' But God said to him, 'Fool! This night your soul is required of you, and the things you have prepared, whose will they be?'"

Then Jesus adds, "So is the one who lays up treasure for himself and is not rich toward God."

This man's idol was riches. But false gods always disappoint their worshipers. This man discovered that his riches could not give him what he needed most: the forgiveness of God. The world feeds the monster of materialism and possessions but, in the end, like all idols, they will prove inadequate. Christ is the only treasure worth having and the only Master worth following.

PRAYER

Father, show me my hidden idols so I can destroy them in Your name.

LOVED BEFORE TIME

"And as Moses lifted up the serpent in the wilderness, so must the Son of Man be lifted up, that whoever believes in him may have eternal life."

JOHN 3:14–15

D. L. MOODY

I heard of a woman who thought there was no promise in the Bible for her; she thought the promises were for others, not for her. There are many of these people in the world. They think it is too good to be true that they can be saved for nothing. This woman one day got a letter, and when she opened it, she found it was not for her at all; it was meant for another woman who had the same name; and she had her eyes opened to the fact that if she should find some promise in the Bible directed to her name, she would not know whether it meant her or someone else that bore her name. But you know the word *whosoever* includes each and every one in the wide world!

ERWIN LUTZER

Yes, the promises of God are for all who will believe them. In fact, God even gives us the ability to believe His promises, for we cannot believe them without His intervention and help. To be clear: All the promises of God are yes in Christ (2 Corinthians 1:20). And again, we read, "He has granted to us his precious and very great promises, so that through them you may become partakers of the divine nature, having escaped from the corruption that is in the world because of sinful desire" (2 Peter 1:4).

As you read God's promises for believers, insert your own name into them; they are intended for you and me. God is always personal. Jesus calls His own sheep by name (John 10:3). Your friends might forget your name; indeed, there are people who struggle with memory loss and your own mother or father might forget your name, but God does not.

PRAYER

Father, thank You for choosing me, and may I claim Your promises for myself.

MARCH 16

UNITED IN CHRIST

For the mind that is set on the flesh is hostile to God, for it does not submit to God's law; indeed, it cannot.

ROMANS 8:7

D. L. MOODY

Jesus Christ, the purest being who ever came to this earth to save mankind, was crucified. I believe if Gabriel should come down from heaven with all the glory of that upper world and try to save men, they would try to blacken his character inside of a week. The ungodly do not like the godly. The impure do not like the pure. There is enmity still. Men may make petty objections, and discuss as much as they like, but there is the fact. God's prediction is fulfilled. The serpent shall have its head bruised, and every one of us should do all he can to bruise it. Our worst enemy is sin.

ERWIN LUTZER

Satan does not have a divided kingdom. Could you imagine if Satan began to cast out his own demons? Obviously, his kingdom would be weakened, and his kingdom would fall. You just don't have that kind of division in the evil world.

When Jesus died, He disarmed all principalities and powers and made a show of them openly triumphing over them (Colossians 2:15). Jesus took away Satan's armor. How did Jesus do that? He invaded the kingdom of darkness in a rescue mission saying, "I'm going to turn these captives under condemnation to restoration." Because of Jesus, we are not condemned but restored—reconciled to God.

A divided kingdom can't stand, at least not very long. This is also true of our churches. Our fellow believers in the pews are not our enemy. We are fighting a spiritual battle with unseen weapons. The devil and his own are united, so also the church must be united against a common enemy.

PRAYER

Father, in our spiritual battle, unite Your church for Your glory.

BELIEVE, THEN GROW

For good news came to us just as to them, but the message they heard did not benefit them, because they were not united by faith with those who listened.

HEBREWS 4:2

D. L. MOODY

Faith is very important. It is the link that binds us to every promise of God—it brings us every blessing. I do not mean a dead faith, but a *living* faith. There is a great difference between the two. A man may tell me that ten thousand dollars are deposited in a certain bank in my name. I may believe it, but if I don't act upon it and get the money, it does me no good. Unbelief bars the door and keeps back the blessing.

Someone has said there are three elements in faith—knowledge, assent, laying hold. Knowledge! A man may have a good deal of knowledge about Christ, but that does not save him. Our knowledge about Christ does not help us if we do not act upon it. But knowledge is very important. Many also assent and say, "I believe"; but that does not save them. Knowledge, assent, then laying hold: It is that last element that saves, that brings the soul and Christ together.

ERWIN LUTZER

The object of faith is much more important than the amount of faith. A small amount of faith in the true Jesus is much better than absolute confidence in the wrong Jesus. Those who believe in the wrong "Jesus" will be barred from heaven even if they outwardly appear to have a faith that saves (Matthew 7:21–23). Faith is not merely information, but an attitude of trust; and that trust must be in the Jesus of the New Testament as He's revealed Himself.

PRAYER

Father, grow my faith in You. In my lack of faith, grow me.

THE ULTIMATE WEDDING

"And if I go and prepare a place for you, I will come again and will take you to myself, that where I am you may be also."
JOHN 14:3

D. L. MOODY

If my wife were in a foreign country, and I had a beautiful mansion all ready for her, she would a good deal rather I should come myself and bring her to it than have me send someone else to bring her to it. Christ has prepared a mansion for His bride, the church, and He promises for our joy and comfort that He will come Himself and bring us to the place He has been preparing.

ERWIN LUTZER

Think of the most joyous wedding you've ever attended. Now consider the ultimate marriage in heaven—a wedding ceremony—one that is distinctly out of this world. The heavenly wedding has no such vows saying, "Until death do us part," because there is no death that will ever part us. It is the marriage between Jesus Christ and His church. Wedded to Him forever!

Believers in Christ are engaged to the bridegroom. Our dowry was paid with the blood of Jesus. While we wait for Him, He is preparing our new homes and the wedding feast. And when He returns for us, we will be revealed with Him in glory.

Why is our welcome in glory called the "marriage supper of the Lamb?" I believe the reason is because we fell in love with the Lamb, and it is the Lamb who gave Himself for us (see Revelation 19:7–10). Jesus is the only groom who laid down His life for His bride and rose again to redeem her, cleanse her, and marry her.

PRAYER

Father, today and throughout all of eternity, let me repeatedly sing with the saints, "Worthy is the Lamb who was slain" (Revelation 5:12).

MARCH 19

GOD SPEAKS IN THE PAGES OF SCRIPTURE

Open my eyes, that I may behold wondrous things out of your law.
PSALM 119:18

D. L. MOODY

We have a great many prayer meetings, but there is something just as important as prayer, and that is that we read our Bibles, that we have Bible study and Bible lectures and Bible classes so that we may get hold of the Word of God. When I pray, I talk to God, but when I read the Bible, God is talking to me; and it is really more important that God should speak to me than that I should speak to Him. I believe we should know better how to pray if we knew our Bibles better.

ERWIN LUTZER

Christianity claims to be a revealed religion. And there are other religions claiming to be revealed. Joseph Smith claims he had a revelation from an angel. Of course, Muhammad claims to have had a revelation. But when you talk about revelations, you must test them for authenticity and consistency. Do they make sense? You also must test them for their truth value. Do they really explain reality? There is much about the Bible that commends it as the very Word of God.

Christianity is totally unique and different. Instead of one author, there are least forty distinct authors of the book that we call the Bible, and they were all addressing the same issues—God, man, sin, and redemption. And Scripture points to one Redeemer: the Word made flesh. As Moody said, when we read the Bible, God is talking to us.

Let us read the Scripture and let us pray the Scripture. Then we shall have rest for our souls.

PRAYER

Father, guide me to love Your Word and to live by Your will.

MARCH 20

GARDENS OF DESIRE

Do not be deceived: God is not mocked, for whatever one sows, that will he also reap.
GALATIANS 6:7

D. L. MOODY

This law is just as true in God's kingdom as in man's kingdom; just as true in the spiritual world as in the natural world. If I sow tares, I am going to reap tares; if I sow a lie, I am going to reap lies; if I sow adultery, I am going to reap adulterers; if I sow whisky, I am going to reap drunkards. You cannot blot this law out, it is in force. No other truth in the Bible is more solemn.

ERWIN LUTZER

God enables us to grow like fruit, but we have a responsibility of sowing rightly in the Spirit. The desire you give in to the most often is the desire that will become the strongest. If you sow to the flesh, your fleshly desires will grow stronger and stronger and stronger. But if you sow to the Spirit, the flesh will become weaker, and the work of the Spirit will grow stronger. When we are out of agreement with the Holy Spirit, we are vulnerable to sow to the flesh and will reap accordingly.

As fallen human beings, we often succumb to the flesh despite the power of the Holy Spirit who is available to strengthen us. Our great desire should always be that we walk in the Spirit not the flesh. At a time of temptation, let us remember that "he who is in you is greater than he who is in the world" (1 John 4:4). Let us walk in that truth today!

PRAYER

Lord, today I choose to walk in the Spirit,
and I choose to sow to the Spirit not the flesh.

MARCH 21

EVEN THE WORST

"Come to me, all who labor and are heavy laden, and I will give you rest."
MATTHEW 11:28

D. L. MOODY

I like to have a text like this because it takes us all in. "Come unto me, all ye that labour." That doesn't mean a select few—refined ladies and cultured men. It doesn't mean good people only. It applies to saint and sinner. Do you think that Christ would shut the door in any one's face, and say, "I did not mean all; I only meant certain ones"? If you cannot come as a saint, come as a sinner. Only come!

A lady told me once that she was so hard-hearted she couldn't come. "Well," I said, "my good woman, it doesn't say all ye soft-hearted people come. Black hearts, vile hearts, hard hearts, soft hearts, all hearts come. Who can soften your hard heart but Himself?"

ERWIN LUTZER

Yes, Jesus invites all sinners to Himself, even the hardest of hearts. Can you see Jesus dying on that cross between two thieves? One reviled him, "If you are the Son of God, do something," while the other says, "Jesus, remember me." To the second thief Jesus responds, "Truly, I say to you, today you will be with me in paradise" (Luke 23:43).

I marvel at the faith of this man who put so much confidence in someone in a position as bad as his own. Jesus didn't appear any better than the other two dying men. Yet the thief says, "Though He's dying, I'm going to believe in Him anyway." And Jesus assured the man of eternal rest.

I love the hymn with this line, "The vilest of offender who truly believes, that moment from Jesus a pardon receives."[5]

PRAYER

Father, thank You for the invitation that all who trust in Your Son are saved.

DIVINE METAMORPHOSIS

When he calls to me, I will answer him; I will be with him in trouble; I will rescue him and honor him.

PSALM 91:15

D. L. MOODY

If we call on God for deliverance and for victory over sin and every evil, God will not turn a deaf ear to our call. I don't care what the past record has been, I don't care how disobedient or how one may have backslidden and wandered, if one really wants to come back, God accepts the willing mind, God will hear prayer, and answer.

Some people say they can't call. Perhaps you cannot make an eloquent prayer—I hope you can't—I have heard about all the eloquent prayers I want to. But you can say, "God be merciful to me a sinner" (Luke 18:13). I have been forty years in Christian work, and I have never known God to disappoint any man or woman who was in earnest about their soul's salvation or were seeking a more consecrated life. I know lots of people who pretend to be in earnest, but their prayers are never answered.

ERWIN LUTZER

Can humans really change? Society says only behaviorism brings change, that we are the product of our environment. But Adam and Eve had a perfect environment, yet they blew it. Society also says education can change the individual; people only do bad things because they don't know better. This assumes people would do good if they knew what good was, but we all have not lived up to what we know to be what God expects. Only Jesus can transform us into who we should be. All of us have defenses and denial mechanisms making it impossible to see ourselves in the light of His presence. Just as vacillating Simon was transformed into Peter, Jesus can change you (Matthew 16:18). If you admit your sins to Him and ask for His help, He will begin the transformation process. Jesus knows who we are; He also knows who we can become. Figuratively speaking, He changes our name, and yes, as the Good Shepherd, He knows our names.

PRAYER

Father, change me into the image of Your Son, Jesus.

MARCH 23

INTO THE CLOUDS

Go on up to a high mountain, O Zion, herald of good news.
ISAIAH 40:9

D. L. MOODY

A traveler once made arrangements with a guide to take him to the top of a high mountain to see the sunrise. They had not journeyed long when there arose a terrible thunderstorm. "It's no use to go on," the gentlemen said. "We cannot see the sunrise in the midst of this fearful storm." "O, sir," said the guide, "we shall soon get above the storm." They could see the lightning playing about them, and the grand old mountain shook with the thunder, and it was very dark; but when they passed up above the clouds, all was light and clear. So, if it is dark here, rise higher; it is light enough up around the throne. If I may rise up to the light, I have no business to be in darkness. Rise higher, higher, higher. It is the privilege of the child of God to walk on unclouded.

ERWIN LUTZER

What if God wanted to take us where we have never been before—a whole new level of devastation and suffering most of us have never experienced? As Moody said, when we are in darkness, we must rise to the light. The goal of life is not to try to figure out how to live an extra day. The goal of life is to glorify Jesus no matter what situation we are in or what is happening around us. That's why we must ascend to the throne, As Paul said, "For me to live is Christ, and to die is gain" (Philippians 1:21), and so the big C in our lives is not calamity or cancer; the big C in our lives is Christ. He is the good news.

PRAYER

Father, when I am scared and don't know what to do,
grant me the strength to persevere in You.

MARCH 24

GLORY IS COMING

And suddenly, looking around, they no longer saw anyone with them but Jesus only.
MARK 9:8

D. L. MOODY

What a dark night it would have been if our Lord and Master had been caught up with Moses and Elijah, and no Christ had died for our sins. Oh, how Jesus Christ has lit up this world! But suppose He had gone up to heaven on the other side of Calvary and had never finished His work. Suppose that God, in His love for His Son, had said: "I can't let those men spit upon you and smite you; I will take you back to my bosom." What darkness would have settled down on this world! But Moses disappeared, and Elijah disappeared, and Christ only was left, for Christ is all. The law and the prophets were honored and fulfilled in Him.

ERWIN LUTZER

When Jesus left heaven for earth, He set His glory aside. But at the Mount of Transfiguration, His inner nature broke forth. Jesus revealed to His followers a sliver of His radiant glory. Jesus had already told His disciples He was going to die, but they vehemently protested. Even at Moses' and Elijah's appearing, they began discussing Jesus' "departure" (Luke 9:30–36).

For Jesus, pleasing the Father with the redemption of sinners, was worth the "joy set before Him" (Hebrews 12:2). First comes the cross then comes the crown. First comes agony, then comes glory. That's why Jesus brought His disciples up the mountain—to encourage them to know that although He would die, they should remember the glory that awaits them.

In John 17:22, Jesus prayed to the Father for us that "the glory that you have given me I have given to them." The glory the disciples saw on the mountain, will some day be ours too!

PRAYER

Father, thank You that every believer will enjoy and participate
in the glory of Christ. I look forward to the day when I will be like Him,
when I shall see Him as He is (1 John 3:2).

MARCH 25

CLEAN HEARTS, CLEAN FEET

I acknowledged my sin to you, and I did not cover my iniquity; I said, "I will confess my transgressions to the LORD," and you forgave the iniquity of my sin.

PSALM 32:5

D. L. MOODY

We are good at confessing other people's sins, but if it is true repentance, we shall have as much as we can do to look after our own. When a man or woman gets a good look into God's looking glass, they are not finding fault with other people: such are fully occupied with their own sins.

ERWIN LUTZER

Take a deep look into your heart. What do you really see? No doubt you see some good, but you'll also see, if you're honest, a lot of ugly things. As sinners, when we learn more about God's holiness, we become more overwhelmed with even the "small" sins in our life. When Adam and Eve sinned, the smudge of sin settled on every human heart. That sense of guilt we've all experienced is the conviction that we are alienated from God (Ephesians 4:18).

He who washed the disciples' feet is the One who can also wash our hearts. Who needs to be cleansed? The answer, of course, is everyone. In John 13:10, when Jesus washed the disciples' feet, He said, "The one who has bathed does not need to wash, except for his feet." He was talking about two different kinds of baths. There is the bath of regeneration when you become a Christian. That is the bath that all of us need in order to get into heaven. The other bath, the "washing of feet," is confession. When you sin, that sin has to be confessed so that you can stay reconciled to your heavenly Father.

PRAYER

Father, overcome my love of sin by granting me a greater love for You.

REDEEMING SUFFERING

"He will glorify me, for he will take what is mine and declare it to you."
JOHN 16:14

D. L. MOODY

The world can get on very well without you and me, but the world cannot get on without Christ and therefore, we must testify of Him.

The world today is just hungering and thirsting for this divine, satisfying portion. Thousands and thousands are sitting in darkness, knowing not of this great Light; but when we begin to preach Christ honestly, faithfully, sincerely, and truthfully, holding Him up, not ourselves; exalting Christ, and not our theories; presenting Christ, and not our opinions; advocating Christ, and not some false doctrine; then the Holy Ghost will come and bear witness. He will testify that what we say is true.

ERWIN LUTZER

Christianity is the only religion whose God has wounds. Isaiah spoke of One who was wounded and punished by God, yet he also said of this Suffering Servant, "With his wounds we are healed" (Isaiah 53:5). What kind of healing should we experience?

Jesus died to redeem us—body, soul, and spirit. We were purchased by God, every part of us—not just our souls, not just our spirits, but our bodies were purchased. We were bought by Christ in total, in completeness. When Jesus died on the cross, He purchased all that we will ever need to take us into the presence of God.

But, and this is critical, we do not experience complete healing in this life. When we die, our bodies go to the grave while our spirits go to Christ. The full healing of the body will take place on the day of resurrection.

This good news motivated Moody to preach the gospel to tens of thousands. He shared the good news that Christ is a Savior, a Light to the world. To all who come unto God by Jesus, He saves them completely.

PRAYER

Father, thank You for Jesus, who endured what I shall never have to endure, paving the way to bring me all the way home.

LOVE THE BRIDE

Beloved, let us love one another, for love is from God, and whoever loves has been born of God and knows God.

1 JOHN 4:7

D. L. MOODY

The first impulse of a young convert is to love. Do you remember the day you were converted? Was not your heart full of sweet peace and love?

I remember the morning I came out of my room after I had first trusted Christ. I thought the old sun shone a good deal brighter than it ever had before. I thought that the sun was just smiling upon me. I walked out upon Boston Common and heard the birds in the trees and I thought that they were all singing a song for me. Do you know I fell in love with the birds? I never cared for them before, but now it seemed to me that I was in love with all creation. I had not a bitter feeling against any man, and I was ready to take all men to my heart. If a man has not the love of God shed abroad in his heart, he has never been regenerated.

ERWIN LUTZER

I remember praying with a woman who fell into the sin of alcoholism. The first words out of her mouth were, "Father, you know that I love you!" To me, that was proof she was regenerated even though she was struggling with sin. The regenerated heart not only loves God but the "household of God" as well (Ephesians 2:19). The Holy Spirit connects us, but we also must connect with one another. "All the members of the body, though many, are one body, so it is with Christ. For in one Spirit we were all baptized into one body" (1 Corinthians 12:12–13). The church's strength lies in our unity, loyalty, and love. We love Him because He first loved us.

PRAYER

Father, grow my love for others—especially the household of faith.

THE PENALTY BOX

"And take in your hand this staff, with which you shall do the signs."
EXODUS 4:17

D. L. MOODY

When God Almighty linked Himself to that rod, it was worth more than all the armies the world had ever seen. Look and see how that rod did this work. It brought up the plagues of flies and the thunderstorm and turned the water into blood. It was not Moses, however, nor Moses' rod that did the work, but it was the God of the rod, the God of Moses. As long as God was with him, he could not fail.

ERWIN LUTZER

Where did Moses get the rod? He picked up the rod while in the "penalty box," that is the desert where he herded sheep, suffering his fate because of manslaughter. There in the desert, he found a limb from a tree, perhaps six feet long, and used it to herd his flock. But God had greater plans for this shepherd. After the fire burned and Moses reluctantly said yes to God, that rod had divine significance.

As Moody said, wherever Moses went, he took that rod with him. He used it to part the sea, and later, God instructed Moses to hit the rock and water gushed out. The rod of Moses then became the rod of God.

Let me ask: What did you pick up in your desert that God is using today? The desert tests our loyalty and depth of commitment. In the desert, God helps us see who we are and who He is. There we learn lessons that living in a palace could not teach us. It is in the desert we learn servanthood, obedience, and faith. It's there where we receive insight and help that enables us to move to the next level of our ministry and impact.

PRAYER

Father, use everything, including my desert,
to equip me to serve You effectively.

RUIN AND RESTORATION

"They shall keep my laws and my statutes in all my appointed feasts, and they shall keep my Sabbaths holy."

EZEKIEL 44:24

D. L. MOODY

No nation has ever prospered that has trampled the Sabbath in the dust. Show me a nation that has done this and I will show you a nation that has got in it the seeds of ruin and decay. I believe that Sabbath desecration will carry a nation down quicker than anything else. Adam brought marriage and Sabbath with him out of Eden, and neither can be disregarded without suffering.

ERWIN LUTZER

Why is it that the law was given? There are three reasons. The first is to reveal the holiness of God. The word *holy* means separate and pure. God is entirely beyond us and unlike us. Holiness is the only attribute in the entire Bible that is elevated to a third degree, "Holy, holy, holy!"

The second reason for the law is to reveal humanity's sinfulness. Once we get a glimpse of God's holiness, nothing is in more stark contrast than our sinfulness.

The third purpose of the law is to reveal our need for grace because a great chasm exists between God and humanity. Our ability to approach God is based squarely on His grace, not on our ability to keep the law. In God's white light of holiness, He cannot accept any of our good works, polluted and tainted as they are.

Under the new covenant of grace, we stand where the fire of God's judgment has already fallen. We must flee to Jesus Christ, who alone can restore us to a holy God. The full counsel of God keeps us from losing sight of God's holiness, our sinfulness, and our need for His grace.

PRAYER

Father, show me my need for Your grace through Christ.

MARCH 30

TWO MOUNTAINS

"For what does it profit a man to gain the whole world and forfeit his soul?"
MARK 8:36

D. L. MOODY

O that we would wake up to the thought of what it is to be lost! The world has been rocked to sleep by Satan who is going up and down telling people it doesn't mean anything. I believe in the old-fashioned heaven and hell. Christ came down to save us from a terrible hell, and any man who is cast down to hell from here must go in the full blaze of the gospel and over the mangled body of the Son of God.

We hear of a man who has lost his health, and we sympathize with him, and we say it is very sad. Our hearts are drawn out to sympathy. Here is another man who has lost his wealth, and we say, "That is very sad." Here is another man who has lost his reputation, his standing among men. "That is sadder still," we say. We know what it is to lose health and wealth and reputation, but what is the loss of all these things compared with the loss of the soul?

ERWIN LUTZER

All forms of contemporary spirituality say humanity is essentially good. Many believe they are the judge of their own soul. But we are lawbreakers. In Exodus 19, God told the people to consecrate themselves at Mount Sinai where God revealed Himself. But they couldn't even touch the edge of the mountain without perishing. In other words, God was emphasizing His holiness against humanity's sinfulness.

Thank God for Christ who mediates between us and God; He stands in for us, having been made sin on our behalf. Within us is nothing good. Our faith must be in Jesus, and were it not for His grace, we would be banished from His presence forever. Unless we see ourselves as lawbreakers, we will never rely on the One who kept the law perfectly. We cannot understand Calvary until we understand Mount Sinai. Sinai shows us the great sinners we are, and Calvary shows us God's great grace. And as Moody said, what a tragedy for a soul to be lost.

PRAYER

Father, I am a needy sinner, please draw my soul to You.

BELIEVE THE MISSION

"But you will receive power when the Holy Spirit has come upon you, and you will be my witnesses in Jerusalem and in all Judea and Samaria, and to the end of the earth."

ACTS 1:8

D. L. MOODY

I have little sympathy with the idea that Christian men and women have to live for years before they can have the privilege of leading anyone out of the darkness of this world into the kingdom of God. I do not believe, either, that all God's work is going to be done by ministers and other officers in the churches. This lost world will never be reached and brought back to loyalty to God until the children of God wake up to the fact that they have a mission in the world. If we are true Christians, we shall all be missionaries. Christ came down from heaven on a mission, and if we have His Spirit in us, we will be missionaries too. If we have no desire to see the world discipled, to see men brought back to God, there is something very far wrong in our religion.

ERWIN LUTZER

What was it about the early Christians that helped them transform their world and culture? It was faith—faith that the gospel could spread no matter the opposition. They believed that no heart was too hard. No situation was too difficult. They did not look at the laws of the land as being a hindrance to their proclamation of the gospel. They did not allow the situation, the persecution, or the beatings to hinder them. They just kept on going because they believed that God was in everything, even the opposition against them.

PRAYER

Father, may I be willing to follow You, and lovingly share my faith with others.

A MOST ATTRACTIVE SNARE

But those who desire to be rich fall into temptation, into a snare, into many senseless and harmful desires that plunge people into ruin and destruction.

1 TIMOTHY 6:9

D. L. MOODY

Think of Balaam. He is generally regarded as a false prophet, but I do not find that any of his prophecies that are recorded are not true; they have been literally fulfilled. He stepped over a heavenly crown for the riches and honors that Balak promised him. He went to perdition backward. His face was set toward God, but he backed into hell. He wanted to die the death of the righteous, but he did not live the life of the righteous. It is sad to see so many who know God miss everything for riches.

ERWIN LUTZER

We are raising a generation that feeds on greed; a generation driven by consumerism. Greed is a feeling of possessiveness, a feeling of entitlement that says, "This life is the only one that matters; I will put money above worship, and possessions above heavenly rewards." Jesus said, "No servant can serve two masters, for either he will hate the one and love the other, or he will be devoted to the one and despise the other. You cannot serve God and money" (Luke 16:13).

Money makes the same promises as God: "I will be with you in good times and bad; in sickness and in health; when the economy is strong and when it tanks." This deception is the reason why the New Testament warns against riches because with wealth comes temptation. We tell ourselves that we really don't love money; we just think about it continuously and do all we can to get more of it. As Moody reminds us, Balaam was willing to sacrifice his eternal future for temporal wealth.

Let us be warned: The pursuit of money can easily dwarf our worship of God. It may make the same promises as God, but it cannot keep those promises.

PRAYER

Father, show me what I cannot see on my own;
help me to repent of substituting the love of money with love for You.

LET US RID OURSELVES OF SIN'S LINGERING ODOR

If we confess our sins, he is faithful and just to forgive us our sins and to cleanse us from all unrighteousness.

1 JOHN 1:9

D. L. MOODY

There may be some confessions we need to make to be brought into close fellowship with God. We must cooperate with God. If there is any sin in my heart that I am not willing to confess and to give up, I need not expect a blessing. The men who have had power with God in prayer have always begun by confessing their sins. Take the prayers of men like Jeremiah and Daniel. We find Daniel confessing his sin when there isn't a single sin recorded against him.

ERWIN LUTZER

There was a time when I had two briefcases: one for travel and one for daily use. Once, after a trip, a flight attendant handed me a ham sandwich carefully wrapped in cellophane. I put it in my travel briefcase and forgot about it. A few days later, there was a musty smell in my study. A month later, when I had to travel, I found the rotten sandwich, all mushy and green. Just so, we carefully wrap our sin, and set it aside, but there is always a musty odor; try as we might, we cannot keep it hidden, it is there to trouble us and to ruin our otherwise normal life.

John is writing to believers. "If we confess our sins, he is faithful and just to forgive us our sins and to cleanse us from all unrighteousness" (1 John 1:9). When we trust in Christ as Savior, we begin to walk with God, but the sin we tolerate ruins our fellowship, it creates a barrier between us and God. We might try to put it out of our mind, but like the ham sandwich, we are reminded it is there and will steal our joy. John tells us we can "walk in the light, as [God] is in the light" (1 John 1:7), but we can only do that if we are repentant and confess our sins. In fact, if we walk in the light as God is in the light, we have fellowship with God—and God has fellowship with us!

PRAYER

Lord, give me honesty to confess my sins so I might walk in the light and stand before You as forgiven, and we can have fellowship together.

WORSHIP IS THE KEY

"You shall not make for yourself a carved image, or any likeness of anything that is in heaven above, or that is in the earth beneath, or that is in the water under the earth."

EXODUS 20:4

D. L. MOODY

I would a great deal sooner have five minutes' communion with Christ than spend years bowing before pictures and images of Him. Whatever comes between my soul and my Maker is not a help to me, but a hindrance. God has given different means of grace by which we can approach Him. Let us use these, and not seek for other things that He has distinctly forbidden.

ERWIN LUTZER

I agree with Moody. Images often become idols, but the good news is that we can come directly to God through the "one mediator between God and men" (1 Timothy 2:5).

Moses saw a glimpse of God's glory in the rock, but God has revealed His glory to all of us through Jesus. We cannot know the glory of God except through Jesus. John 1:14 says, "The Word became flesh and dwelt among us, and we have seen his glory, glory as of the only Son from the Father, full of grace and truth." Jesus is the one who came to restore the glory. It is through Him that we worship and glorify God. The only intermediary we need is Christ.

We all should strive to live for the glory of God. We do not need images, crucifixes, or altars. Through Christ, we can directly and boldly "draw near to the throne of grace, that we may receive mercy and find grace to help in time of need" (Hebrews 4:16). When we put God's glory first and worship Him, we grow in our relationship with Him.

PRAYER

Father, draw me close to Your heart. Deliver me from all other concerns and those idols I put in the place of Your glory and Your holiness.

A CONFLICT OF CONSCIENCE

Then these men said, "We shall not find any ground for complaint against this Daniel unless we find it in connection with the law of his God."
DANIEL 6:5

D. L. MOODY

What a testimony from his bitterest enemies! Would that it could be said of all of us! He had never taken a bribe, he had never been connected with a "ring." Ah, how his name shines! He had commenced to shine in his early manhood, and he shone right along. Now he is an old man, an old statesman, and yet this is their testimony. Character is worth more than money.

Character is worth more than anything else in the wide world. I would rather, in my old age, have such a character as that which Daniel's enemies gave him; that would be much better than to have raised over my dead body a monument of gold reaching from earth to sky.

ERWIN LUTZER

How do you handle a conflict of conscience? Difficult choices either prove or disprove our love for Christ. A young pastor asked me, "What advice do you have for young pastors?" I said, "Guard your character; once your reputation is called into question, your ability to minister will end."

There comes a time when we draw a line in the sand, refusing to bow down to sin's temptations for the sake of God and His gospel. Jesus was honored because He loved righteousness and hated iniquity (Hebrews 1:9). He died forsaken by others, but no one could honestly accuse Him of sin.

Often, people will not make up their minds about God until they have made up their minds about us. If we say we are believers but our character betrays us, they will use us as a reason to reject the gospel. Daniel maintained his character while in a hostile culture. What guardrails do you have in place to maintain an upright character?

PRAYER

Father, I ask in Jesus' name that, in a confused culture, those of us who are redeemed might actually look and act redeemed.

APRIL 5

THE SEED OF STRENGTH

But he said to me, "My grace is sufficient for you, for my power is made perfect in weakness." Therefore I will boast all the more gladly of my weaknesses, so that the power of Christ may rest upon me.

2 CORINTHIANS 12:9

D. L. MOODY

When we are weak, then we are strong. People often think they have not strength enough; the fact is, we have too much strength. It is when we feel that we have no strength of our own that we are willing that God should use us and work through us. If we are leaning on God's strength, we have more than all the strength of the world.

ERWIN LUTZER

Sometimes we think to ourselves, "Jesus can't be my example because, after all, He was God. He had a divine nature, so He really doesn't understand me and my weakness." Yet, Jesus did not depend on His divine nature when He lived as man. That's why He prayed; that's why He was thirsty; that's why He was weary on His journey and sat on a well. Jesus was not afraid to show His weakness. See Him there in Gethsemane as He invites three of His disciples to pray with Him that He might endure His agony. He was committed to do the will of the Father, and His own apprehension and weakness did not stand in the way. We need to pray even when God does not answer as we might wish.

Removed from pride, in our weakness, we can turn to God and say, "Not my will, but yours, be done" (Luke 22:42).

Weakness is not a barrier, it is used to display God's strength.

PRAYER

Father, in my weakness lead me to You. Your will be done.

PEACE PURCHASED BY THE CROSS

Making peace by the blood of his cross.
COLOSSIANS 1:20

D. L. MOODY

A great many people are trying to make their peace with God, but that has already been done. God has not left it for us to do; all that we have to do is to enter into it, to accept it. It is a condition, and instead of our trying to make peace and to work for peace, we should cease all that and simply enter into peace that has been purchased for us.

ERWIN LUTZER

Sin makes us enemies of God, and because we're born sinners, we are, by nature, enemies of God. We are not only separated from God, we're even separated from ourselves. Jesus has made peace for us by the blood of His cross. And as Paul explains, now that we are justified by faith, "we have peace with God through our Lord Jesus Christ. Through him we have also obtained access by faith into this grace in which we stand" (Romans 5:1–2). Only Jesus can make peace between us and a holy God. And once we have peace with God, we can have peace with others and peace with ourselves. Peace is not always dry-eyed. It's sometimes mingled with tears when we experience the tragedies of life. It's not a state of tranquility where we deny everything going on around us and just pretend all is well. It is a peace that is compatible with a funeral. It's a peace that's compatible with the tears and heartache of a broken marriage. It is a peace that trusts and knows God will work out all things for the good of those who love Him.

PRAYER

Father, may I see You as the God of peace and share that peace with others through faith in Jesus.

APRIL 7

INFECTIOUS COMFORT

I will be with him in trouble.

PSALM 91:15

D. L. MOODY

It is a great thing to have a place of resort in the time of trouble. How people get on without the God of the Bible is a mystery to me. If I didn't have such a refuge, a place to go and pour out my heart to God in such times, I don't know what I would do. It seems as if I would go out of my mind. But to think, when the heart is burdened, we can go and pour those burdens into His ear, and then have the answer come back, "I will be with you," there is comfort in that!

I thank God for the old Book. I thank God for this old promise. It is as sweet and fresh today as it has ever been. Thank God, none of those promises are out of date or grown stale. They are as fresh and vigorous and young and sweet as ever.

ERWIN LUTZER

No matter what our trial, we need two friends: a friend that "sticks closer than a brother" (Proverbs 18:24), namely Jesus Christ, and at least one friend in the body of Christ. When I think of God's comfort, I am reminded of the upper room where Jesus promised to send the Holy Spirit. The Greek word for Holy Spirit is *paraklétos*. It means to "call along, beside of." Jesus sent us the Comforter "who will abide with us forever. He will guide you into all truth" (see John 14:16–17; 16:13 KJV). God has ordained that He would be our friend who walks with us, be with us forever, and then give us others within the body of Christ who will walk with us through our trials.

PRAYER

Father, let me be comforted so that I may, in turn, be a comfort to others.

APRIL 8

DEATH: THE OTHER SIDE OF THE CURTAIN

"In my Father's house are many rooms. If it were not so, would I have told you that I go to prepare a place for you?"

JOHN 14:2

D. L. MOODY

What has been, and is now, one of the strongest feelings in the human heart? Is it not to find some better place, some lovelier spot, than we now have? It is for a place of rest that men everywhere are seeking, and they can have it if they will; but instead of looking down, they must look up to find it. As men grow in knowledge, they vie with each other more and more in making their homes attractive, but the brightest home on earth is but an empty barn compared with the mansions Jesus has gone to prepare.

ERWIN LUTZER

Although Jesus conquered death, it is still our enemy. It ruptures relationships. It brings tears. It brings loneliness. It brings heartache. This side of the curtain—mystery? Yes! Fear? Yes! If we are unsure what lies on the other side, we know it could be worse than what we're experiencing right now.

But the good news is that the Bible sheds some light as to what we can expect when we die. Jesus has the "keys of Death and Hades" (Revelation 1:18) and stands ready to welcome those who belong to Him into their heavenly home. Jesus has gone to heaven to prepare a place for us, and He promised to return to receive us to Himself (John 14:2–3).

Paul, facing the prospect of death, longed to "depart and be with Christ, for that is far better" (Philippians 1:23). When Stephen was being stoned, he saw Jesus in heaven, standing, ready to welcome him (Acts 7:55).

As for those who do not trust Christ, the prospect of death is terrifying. On the other side is outer darkness, weeping and wailing. A terrifying eternal existence. Knowing Christ makes the difference.

PRAYER

Father, thank You that Jesus has opened heaven's door for me.
Help me to live in light of eternity.

FIGHTING FOR THE SOUL

I will arise and go to my father, and I will say to him, "Father, I have sinned against heaven and before you."
LUKE 15:18

D. L. MOODY

One of the greatest battles ever fought was being fought in the heart of the prodigal. Everything holy and heavenly was beckoning him home. The powers of darkness were trying to keep him from returning.

"You go back and they'll all laugh at you. What'll they say?" said the devil.

No doubt there was an angel hovering over him, watching for the decision, and when he said, "I will arise," the angel bore it on high.

"Make another crown. Get another robe ready. There's another sinner coming!"

That "I will" echoed and reechoed, and there was joy in the presence of the angels. He is saved. His heart has got home already. The battle with pride and sin is over.

ERWIN LUTZER

Prodigals stay in the far country for many reasons. Perhaps it's the shame of going back empty-handed, a desire to avoid the rules of the farm, or even an aversion to an older brother's self-righteousness. The reluctance and stubbornness is on our part, not God's. He is gracious and merciful, waiting for sinners just like us to come home. So we must hurry to the Father. "But while he was still a long way off, his father saw him and felt compassion, and ran and embraced him and kissed him" (Luke 15:20).

Our heavenly Father is waiting. God says, "I have made provision for you to come back home. I sent my Son, the Lord Jesus Christ, to die on the cross for sinners. Receive me and I will accept you." How much does God love us? Jesus stretched out His hands on the cross and said, "This much!" That's how great the love of God is.

PRAYER

Father, I throw myself helplessly before You in Your presence.
Here I am, receive me back home.

APRIL 10

THE KING'S RETURN

"For I tell you, you will not see me again, until you say, 'Blessed is he who comes in the name of the Lord.'"
MATTHEW 23:39

D. L. MOODY

When Christ returns, He will not be treated as He was before. There will be room for Him at Bethlehem. He will be welcome in Jerusalem. He will reveal Himself as Joseph revealed himself to his brethren. He will say to the Jews, "I am Jesus," and they will reply, "Blessed is He that cometh in the name of the Lord." And the Jews will then be that nation that shall be born in a day.

ERWIN LUTZER

Christ's return will happen in God's time and in God's way. There are several reasons for the glorious return of Christ. First, Jesus will come to judge the world because of its evil (Matthew 25:31–32). Second, He will come to establish His kingdom on earth (Isaiah 11). Finally, His return to Jerusalem will fulfill all the promises God made to His people throughout the Old Testament about a coming golden age (Daniel 9:24–27).

Jesus will say to those who believe in Him, "Come, you who are blessed by my Father, inherit the kingdom prepared for you from the foundation of the world" (Matthew 25:34). We are going to be ruling with Jesus Christ over certain territories and have responsibilities in the millennial kingdom, rejoicing that God's promises are then fulfilled (Revelation 20:4–6). After a time, the devil will be released, and he will deceive many from all over the world (Revelation 20:7–8). Then Satan will be cast into the eternal lake of fire, and all who are not in Christ will join him. Then Jesus will reign for all eternity, and we shall reign with him. "Blessed is he who comes in the name of the Lord."

PRAYER

Father, one day every tongue will confess Christ is Lord; that is, even now, my confession as I anticipate that great day!

APRIL 11

WATERED BY THE WORD

"You will seek me and find me, when you seek me with all your heart."
JEREMIAH 29:13

D. L. MOODY

These are the men who find Christ—those who seek for Him *with all their heart.* I am tired and sick of half-heartedness. You don't like a half-hearted man; you don't care for anyone to love you with a half-heart, and the Lord won't have it. If we are going to seek for Him and find Him, we must do it with all our heart.

I believe the reason why so few people find Christ is because they are not *terribly* in earnest about their soul's salvation. God is in earnest; everything He has done proves that He is in earnest about the salvation of men's souls. What is Calvary but a proof of that? And the Lord wants us to be in earnest when it comes to this great question of the soul's salvation. I never saw men seeking Him with all their hearts and not finding Him.

ERWIN LUTZER

The psalmist speaks of two men, two paths, and two very different destinies (Psalm 1). God blesses those whose hearts are perfect toward Him (2 Chronicles 16:9), who meditate in the law of the Lord. God knows the way of the transgressor; they are like chaff that the wind blows away. If we meditate day and night, we will be like a tree planted by the rivers of water (Psalm 1:2).

We don't become spiritual by osmosis. It takes discipline! We must be committed to giving God and His Word our time, energy, and focus. The Word of God has such transforming power that when we are exposed to it in a meaningful way, it will guide and direct us even during our darkest hours. Even those of us who already know Christ should continue to seek Him!

PRAYER

Lord, open my heart to behold wondrous things out of Thy law.
I seek You with all my heart.

RELINQUISHED REGRET

"Watch and pray that you may not enter into temptation. The spirit indeed is willing, but the flesh is weak."
MATTHEW 26:41

D. L. MOODY

The flesh is weak. Is there anyone on earth that dares to dispute that statement? Is there anything weaker under the sun than the human flesh? The spirit is willing. Most men would rather do the right thing, and even think they will do it. Tell them that they will do evil things inside of twelve months, and they would say, as the king did, "Is thy servant a dog, that he should do this great thing?" No, never (2 Kings 8:7–15). But they will do it just the same. "The spirit is willing, but the flesh is weak."

ERWIN LUTZER

What hope is there when we blow it? What if we deny that which we know to be true and live contrary to what we believe? What happens when we don't live up to our expectations and ideals? On the night Jesus Christ was betrayed, Peter boasted too much, prayed too little, acted too soon, followed too far, and thought too late. When Peter began to realize he had betrayed Jesus, he wept bitterly (Mark 14:72). The regret washed over his spirit. But after the resurrection, Jesus restored him (John 21:15). His blessed voice says to all of us, "I want to restore you fully to your relationship with me."

Have you fallen? Have you betrayed the One you love? You can move from regret to restoration because Jesus has His arms outstretched saying, "Come home. You've been away far too long."

PRAYER

Lord Jesus, restore me. I have good intentions, but the flesh overwhelms me. Grant me the grace of obedience.

IRONCLAD PROMISES

"The Lord bless you and keep you."
NUMBERS 6:24

D. L. MOODY

God can do what He has done before. He kept Joseph in Egypt, Moses before Pharaoh, Daniel in Babylon, and enabled Elijah to stand before Ahab in that dark day. And I am so thankful that these I have mentioned were men of like passions with ourselves.

ERWIN LUTZER

Yes, as Moody said, God can keep us. But sometimes our faith wavers.

God said to Abraham, "All the land that you see I will give to you and to your offspring forever" (Genesis 13:15). But soon Abraham had doubts. In fact, when there was a famine in the land of promise, Abraham and his family went down to Egypt. There he sinned by trying to deceive Pharaoh. Abraham shamefully betrayed his wife by lying, saying she was not his wife. He had to leave Egypt in disgrace. On another occasion he said in effect, "God you must understand I am old, and Sarah is old. We can't bear children anymore. What about Eliezer of Damascus? He is my trusted servant. Could he be my heir?" But God says, "Abraham, the answer is 'No.' The one who comes from you, your very own son is going to be the heir of the promise" (see Genesis 15:1–6).

My point: We can't stand against the pressure trials bring unless we are "standing on the promises," as the song reminds us. We must believe God despite evidence to the contrary. So when God said to Abraham, "Look toward heaven, and number the stars, if you are able to number them. . . . So shall your offspring be" (Genesis 15:5), that was not just a reminder of God's power, but also a promise that was fulfilled. The Lord did for Abraham and Sarah just as He had promised. And He will do so for us.

Only those who kneel before God's promises will stand when the trials come.

PRAYER

Father, no matter how hard the winds blow, help me
to keep standing on Your promises.

ETERNAL LIFE IS NOW!

"Whoever hears my word and believes him who sent me has eternal life."
JOHN 5:24

D. L. MOODY

A man once prayed for me that I might obtain eternal life *at last*. I could not have said "Amen" to that. I obtained eternal life over forty years ago when I was converted. What is the "gift of God," if it is not eternal life? And what makes the gospel such good news? Is it not that it offers eternal life to every poor sinner who will take it?

ERWIN LUTZER

Eternal life starts the moment we believe and continues into eternity. Eternal life is to know God and His Son, Jesus Christ (John 17:3). God invites us into His fellowship as members of His eternal family. So let us draw near, taking advantage of the welcome the Father gives to His children. I have a friend who prays for me regularly, and he always signs his texts, "Christ is life!"

After Jesus cried, "It is finished" (John 19:30), the veil of the temple was torn in two from top to bottom by an invisible hand (Matthew 27:51). We have confidence to enter into the most holy place by the blood of Jesus (Hebrews 9–10). It is Jesus who gives us that right and that authority to come directly to the Father. That is our privilege as those who have inherited eternal life and already enjoy its benefits.

It's as if Jesus delivered us to the Father and says, "These are the redeemed; they belong to us both—now and forever." All of life, until we see Him face to face, can be lived in the here and now in the very presence of God. As my praying friend reminds me, even now, "Christ is life."

PRAYER

Father, I stand amazed at the gift of eternal life. And because of that, we can boldly enter into Your presence by the blood of Christ.

JESUS WALKS WITH US THROUGH THE FIRE

"But I see four men unbound, walking in the midst of the fire."
DANIEL 3:25

D. L. MOODY

It does my heart good to think that the worst the devil can do is to burn off the bonds of God's children. If Christ be with us, the worst afflictions can only loosen our earthly bonds and set us free to soar higher.

ERWIN LUTZER

Nebuchadnezzar promoted Shadrach, Meshach, and Abednego to high positions in his land. But due to an ego problem, he set up an image of himself (Daniel 3:5). When these three men wouldn't bow to the image, the king had them thrown bound into a burning, fiery furnace. How did these men have the courage to stand there and say, "Throw us into the fire, but whether we are delivered or not, we'll not deny God"?

They were willing to trust God's unknown providence. They did not have absolute assurance of being delivered; but they said to the king, "*But if not . . .*" In other words: We won't bow before the image. God doesn't deliver everyone; many Christians have died as martyrs for their faith. Daniel was delivered from the lions, but many Christians were thrown to lions. We cannot discern God's hidden purposes, but we must continue to believe even when we do not understand.

We should not judge God by our immediate circumstances. We should go on believing Him even without a miracle of deliverance because we have come to know and trust the living and the true God. Sometimes He delivers us; sometimes He comforts us; we know God is with us.

He never abandons His children in the flames; He is there.

PRAYER

Father, let me remember the promise that You will never leave me nor forsake me (Hebrews 13:5). Through fire, famine, or plenty, You walk with me all the way home.

A BEAUTIFUL FUTURE

Prepared as a bride adorned for her husband.
REVELATION 21:2

D. L. MOODY

There are constant sounds around us we cannot hear, and the sky is studded with bright worlds our eyes have never seen. Little as we know about this bright and radiant land, there are glimpses of its beauty that come to us now and then.

Perhaps nothing but the shortness of our range of sight keeps us from seeing the celestial gates all open to us, and nothing but the deafness of our ears prevents our hearing the joyful ringing of the bells of heaven.

ERWIN LUTZER

The eternal bride of Christ will radiate beauty and glory, adorned for her husband, Christ Himself. We will be in that New Jerusalem that is coming down out of heaven as a bride.

Just as the Most Holy Place (Holy of Holies) of the Old Testament tabernacle was a cube, so will be the New Jerusalem. And we will dwell in the Most Holy Place throughout all eternity! With no fear of being contaminated by sin, we will be holy and totally free of all sin. Imagine the presence of God directly without sin coming in between.

In the New Jerusalem there is no temple, "for its temple is the Lord God the Almighty and the Lamb. And the city has no need of sun or moon to shine on it, for the glory of God gives it light, and its lamp is the Lamb" (Revelation 21:22–23). This will be our first experience with uncreated light. We will have direct immediate access to God with no need for a mediator. God and His people will dwell together in the New Jerusalem—forever.

PRAYER

Father, why do You so honor us? Help me to marvel at Your great love that would redeem me and bring me into Your presence forever.

THE GREATEST EVENT

"Whoever hears my word and believes him who sent me . . .
He does not come into judgment."
JOHN 5:24

D. L. MOODY

In a prairie fire, when the wind is strong, the wall of flame often rolls along twenty feet high, destroying man and beast in its onward rush. The frontiersmen know they cannot run as fast as that fire. Not the fleetest horse can escape it. But they just take a match and light the grass before them. These flames sweep a space, and men follow and take their stand in the burned district, and are safe. Over the place where they stand, the fire has already passed and there is nothing left to burn. So, there is one spot on earth that the judgment of God has swept over. Centuries ago the storm burst on Calvary and the Son of God endured it; and now, if we take our stand by the cross, we are safe for time and for eternity.

ERWIN LUTZER

Jesus came to earth to protect us "from the wrath to come" (see 1 Thessalonians 1:10). The crucifixion represents God's farthest reach. God came our way. The chasm that exists between us and God, our inability to live up to His standard of holiness—all of that was bridged by God Himself. In effect, God says, "I am not just descending to humanity with a ladder, asking them to crawl on the ladder toward me. No, they are dead in trespasses and sins. I'm going to scoop them up and bring them to myself." To do that, Jesus had to bear the wrath of God on our behalf.

PRAYER

Father, I love You because You first loved me.
I wish I loved You more, and I thank You that I stand under
the shelter of Christ's great work on the cross.

THE CUP OF JOY

So [Zacchaeus] hurried and came down and received [Jesus] joyfully.
LUKE 19:6

D. L. MOODY

Did you ever hear of anyone receiving Christ in any other way? Zacchaeus received Him *joyfully*. Christ brings joy with Him. Sin, gloom, and darkness flee away; light, peace, and joy burst into the soul.

ERWIN LUTZER

Christ does bring joy, but sin causes the cup of joy to spring a leak. If we are troubled by our consciences, if we find ourselves in conflict with the world, our joy can turn into guilt or grief.

As believers, we find ourselves beset with many different kinds of trials and miseries. We can't live with our troubled past and fear of an unknown future. Zacchaeus, as Moody pointed out, received Christ with joy, but then he had to deal with the reality of his past deceptions as a tax collector. He pledged to give back four times the amount to those whom he had cheated. No doubt his obedience, which had to be difficult, restored his joy.

When Jesus spoke to His disciples, He promised He would give them a joy no one could take from them (John 16:22). Our feelings and regrets of our past oftentimes distract us. But our true self-worth is really based on who we are in Jesus Christ. That's why we receive Jesus joyfully—no matter the cost to us. Our self-worth is based on the costliest work of all that Christ has done, and on that basis, He calls us to be a son or a daughter of the Most High. God wants us to be free to love and serve Him with joy. As David put it, "My cup overflows" (Psalm 23:5).

PRAYER

Father, even when trials come, increase my joy! Give me joy in spite of my tears, joy in spite of regrets, joy in knowing Christ.

FORGIVEN AT CALVARY

And he said to them, "Go into all the world and proclaim the gospel to the whole creation."
MARK 16:15

D. L. MOODY

I can imagine Jesus saying: "Go search out the man who put that crown of thorns on my brow; tell him I will have a crown for him in my kingdom if he will accept salvation; and there shall not be a thorn in it. Find out that man who took the reed from my hand and smote my head, driving the thorns deeper into my brow. Tell him I want to give him a scepter. Go, seek out that poor soldier who drove the spear into my side; tell him that there is a nearer way to my heart than that. Tell him I want to make him a soldier of the cross and that my banner over him shall be love."

ERWIN LUTZER

Please reread the words of Moody printed above! His preaching was vivid, immediate, and filled with colorful insights. Little wonder he connected with the common people; like Jesus, he was understood by those who knew they were sinners and humble enough to accept the hope of the gospel.

"Father, forgive them, for they know not what they do" (Luke 23:34). Those are the words of the One who chose to become a victim of history's greatest crime. Jesus prayed out of love for His enemies. When was this prayer prayed? It was prayed at the very time His nerves were not yet dulled, when the pain was the freshest, when the jolt of anguish that went through His body was the sharpest. These were His first words while on the cross.

Jesus commanded us to take this message of hope to a broken world. Yes, even those who crucified Him could receive His forgiveness. Let us find the greatest of sinners and tell them that they too have a place in heaven if they will repent and believe the gospel.

PRAYER

Father, grant me the ability to forgive others even as You have forgiven me. Let me remind people that great sin is not a barrier to great grace.

ALL I NEED IS CHRIST

I can do all things through him who strengthens me.
PHILIPPIANS 4:13

D. L. MOODY

Take Christ for your strength, dear soul. He'll give you power. Power to overcome the world, the flesh, and the devil; power to crucify every besetting sin, passion, lust; power to shout in triumph over every trouble and temptation of your life, "I can do all things through Christ which strengtheneth me."

ERWIN LUTZER

Christ's strength is sufficient; we can move forward in the worst of circumstances; Paul lived a life deprived of the comforts he was used to, but he was content. As Christ strengthens us, we can endure a ruptured relationship; we can live through disappointment with an inner sense of peace. The presence of God through the Holy Spirit dwells within us by our faith in Jesus Christ.

Today's verse does not mean we can do anything we want; it means we have the strength to do what God calls us to do. God works in and through our disappointments, our fears, and our weaknesses. Think of the dilemma Moses was in, yet God's promise was one of victory. "I am the LORD, and I will bring you out from under the burdens of the Egyptians, and I will deliver you from slavery to them, and I will redeem you with an outstretched arm" (Exodus 6:6).

We can overcome the obstacles in our path through Christ. To repeat: We can do only that which God has called us to do. Nothing more; nothing less.

PRAYER

Father, give me strength to do Your will,
to walk in obedience in the power of Christ.

MORE THAN CONQUERORS

"One man of you puts to flight a thousand."
JOSHUA 23:10

D. L. MOODY

When in Glasgow, a friend was telling me about a man who was preaching one Sabbath morning on Shamgar. He said: "I can imagine that when he was ploughing in the field, a man came running over the hill all out of breath and shouted: 'Shamgar! Shamgar! Shamgar! There are six hundred Philistines coming toward you.' Shamgar quietly said: 'You pass on; I can take care of them, they are four hundred short.' So he took an ox goad and slew the whole of them. He routed them hip and thigh." "One shall chase a thousand." Nowadays it takes about a thousand to chase one, because we do not realize that we are weak in ourselves and that our strength is in God.

ERWIN LUTZER

Scripture reveals only this much of Shamgar, "After him was Shamgar the son of Anath, who killed 600 of the Philistines with an oxgoad, and he also saved Israel" (Judges 3:31). In the time of the Judges, God gave His rebellious people Spirit-filled leadership to lead them out of their woes. All the odds were against Shamgar, but his strength was in God.

Sometimes faith changes our circumstances. God can intervene to deliver us as Shamgar experienced. But sometimes faith doesn't change our circumstances. As Hebrews 11:37–38 says of the some of the heroes of the faith, "[Some were] destitute, afflicted, mistreated—of whom the world was not worthy." God, in His good purposes, doesn't deliver everyone from their enemies. But both groups—those who are delivered and those who die as martyrs—are all heroes of faith.

Faith is the ability to accept whatever God gives us. In fact, faith always leads to ultimate victory. We must keep believing, trusting, and accepting, whatever the outcome will be.

PRAYER

Father, help me to remember that my faith is perfected in weakness.
Let me never judge You by the size of my circumstance, but to judge my circumstance against Your vast power.

APRIL 22

AN ETERNAL PROMISE

Precious and very great promises.
2 PETER 1:4

D. L. MOODY

Let men feed for a month on the promises of God and they will not be talking of their "leanness." It is not leanness, it is laziness. There is an abundant supply for us if we will only rouse ourselves to take it.

ERWIN LUTZER

Everything that God promises, He has the ability and the resources to accomplish. Ahaziah, like the rest of us, often wondered whether God's promise would be fulfilled. When King Ahaziah fell ill, he sought the false god, Baal, for answers (2 Kings 1). Elijah confronted him three times, asking, "Is there no God in Israel to care for you?" Now, we're always going to turn for help to others. The real question is whether we turn to God and His promises first.

Moody was right to identify our major problem as believing in the promise of God. When my friend Mark was dying of cancer, I visited him and asked how he could remain at peace knowing his earthly life would soon be over. He opened a drawer beside his bed and showed me a large sheet of paper. On it were more than a hundred promises. "Whenever I am filled with fear and doubt, I take this sheet and reread the promises of God," he told me. Yes, we have exceedingly great and precious promises. Let us cleave to them accepting the heartaches of life knowing our home is on the other side.

PRAYER

Father, help me to know the promises of Your Word and believe them.
Remind me that peace comes through believing what You promised.

JUST LIKE THAT!

From darkness to light.
ACTS 26:18

D. L. MOODY

I remember one night when the Bible was the driest and darkest book in the universe to me. The next day, it was all light. I had the key to it. I had been born of the Spirit. But before I knew anything of the mind of God in His Word, I had to give up my sin.

ERWIN LUTZER

The miracle of the new birth comes to us from above. It is not self-generated; it is not even a cooperative effort between us and God. It is a direct miracle of creation within us so that, after we have received Jesus Christ as Savior, there was something within us not there previously. It is a miracle of God.

Jesus said to Nicodemus, "Unless one is born again he cannot see the kingdom of God" (John 3:3). The Word of God and the Spirit of God are brought together by God to create within us the *life* of God. This results in a supernatural reality. "If anyone is in Christ, he is a new creation. The old has passed away; behold, the new has come" (2 Corinthians 5:17). After we are born again, the Bible becomes food to us. We need food to grow physically, we also need food to grow spiritually. The Word of God has within it a whole meal; in the Bible, the Word is described as milk, meat, and honey. The new nature needs to be fed; it needs nourishment.

Meditation is to the soul what digestion is to the body.

Thank God that, through the power of the gospel, we are given a new appetite—and a new appreciation for the promises of God. Darkness turns to light.

PRAYER

Father, I thank You for the power of the Spirit
that brought me both life and light.

AS IT SHOULD BE

"A kingdom that shall never be destroyed."
DANIEL 2:44

D. L. MOODY

Napoleon tried to establish a kingdom by the force of arms. So did Alexander the Great and Caesar and other great warriors, but they utterly failed. Jesus founded His kingdom on love, and it is going to stand. When we join this realm of love, then all selfish and unworthy motives will disappear and our work will stand the fire when God shall put it to the test.

ERWIN LUTZER

Some dictators have made promises about their kingdoms; Hitler predicted his empire would last for a thousand years, but it lasted only twelve. Dictators have always promised more than they can deliver; some speak of a coming "utopia" (a word invented by Thomas More in 1516 when he wrote a book by that title). But the idea of a grand kingdom has captivated every generation. We long to be a citizen in a great kingdom. As Moody pointed out, there is an everlasting kingdom coming that cannot and will not be shaken. When Christ returns, He will gather His own and reign for a thousand years, and "shall judge between the nations, and shall decide disputes for many peoples; and they shall beat their swords into plowshares, and their spears into pruning hooks; nation shall not lift up sword against nation, neither shall they learn war anymore" (Isaiah 2:4). After this comes the end when the Son delivers the kingdom to the Father so that God may be all in all (see 1 Corinthians 15:24–28).

The earthy kingdom becomes the heavenly kingdom of which there shall be no end. And we shall reign with Him forever and ever.

PRAYER

Father, help me not to live for the kingdom of this world
but for the kingdom to come.

WAR ZONE

And every work that he undertook . . . he did with all his heart.
2 CHRONICLES 31:21

D. L. MOODY

In all ages, God has used those people who were in earnest. Satan always calls idle men into his service. God calls active and earnest—not indolent men. You remember where Elijah found Elisha ploughing in the field? Gideon was at the threshing floor. Moses was away in Horeb looking after the sheep. None of these were indolent men; what they did, they did with all their might. We want such men and women nowadays. If we cannot do God's work with all the knowledge we would like to have, let us, at any rate, do it with all the zeal God has given us.

ERWIN LUTZER

Moody himself was a man of zeal; a man who seldom was found doing nothing. He understood that the Christian life was a battle and we must be vigilant. "We do not wrestle against flesh and blood, but against . . . the spiritual forces of evil" (Ephesians 6:12). To win in a fight, we need to make a series of wise and difficult decisions. Small victories lead to big victories. But small defeats can eventually lead to huge defeats. Sins we do not conquer will eventually conquer or compromise us.

How do we go about winning battles? We need to stop wasting hours on our computers and smartphones and know that our enemy is not indolent. Satan strategically attacks our weaknesses to bring us down. If you are not in a battle, Satan either doesn't consider you a threat to his kingdom or you can expect an attack tomorrow.

Our spiritual battles are a beautiful blend between human agency and divine intervention. We must pray and we must act. Those who are spiritually lazy don't win battles, they are overrun by evil forces determined to win.

PRAYER

Father, let us actively stand against the forces of evil by prayer, meditation, and connecting with like-minded warriors.

APRIL 26

DIVINE INFLUENCE

For zeal for your house has consumed me.
PSALM 69:9

D. L. MOODY

I heard of someone who was speaking the other day of something that was to be done, and he hoped zeal would be tempered with moderation. Another friend very wisely replied that he hoped moderation would be tempered with zeal. If that were always the case, Christianity would be like a red-hot ball rolling over the face of the earth. There is no power on earth that can stand before the onward march of God's people when they are in dead earnest.

ERWIN LUTZER

Zeal is a character quality many of us lack. Many Christians are zealous for their favorite sports team or zealous for politics, but how many of us are zealous for the gospel? Are we burdened for those around us who do not know Christ?

All of us would like to be a positive influence, the kind of influence that enables us to give people direction, to give them help, to impact their lives forever in the right direction. But, too often, we are not motivated, we lack the conviction to follow through with discipline and consistency.

So I ask, "Do we share Christ's zeal?"

Freely we have received. Freely we must give (see Matthew 10:8). As Jesus Christ's representatives, we have the privilege of introducing men and women to saving faith, to explain the gospel and, being God's link on earth, to pray for their conversion. Let's ask God for the motivation to take some bold steps for the benefit of the lost, for the benefit of His church and, above all, for His glory.

PRAYER

Father, make me passionate with the zeal that motivated Jesus
for His house and His people.

REGULATING YOUR TEMPERATURE

"Would that you were either cold or hot!"
REVELATION 3:15

D. L. MOODY

What we want is to be red hot all the time.

Do not wait until someone hunts you up. People talk about striking while the iron is hot. I believe it was Cromwell who said that he would rather strike the iron and make it hot. So let us keep at our post and we will soon grow warm in the Lord's work.

ERWIN LUTZER

What did Jesus mean when He used the imagery of being hot or cold but not lukewarm?

In Laodicea, there were two kinds of aqueducts. One came from Hierapolis, very hot springs people would bathe in, and believed to provide cures to many ailments. But from the other direction, there was a spring that was very cold and refreshing. People went from one to the other just like people do today when they go to a spa. And so, Jesus was saying, "You can either be hot and passionate, or you can also be cool, refreshing, and invigorating. You can be one or other, but whatever you do, don't be lukewarm."

As for the lukewarm—neither hot nor cold, but tepid—Jesus said, "I will spit you out of my mouth" (see Revelation 3:16). He's talking about Christians who are indifferent; He is speaking about those who have no positive influence because they are carnal and self-satisfied. The lukewarmness of indifference—does that characterize us today?

How do we repent of our lukewarmness? We have to come close to Jesus; His fire, His love, and His passion will become ours. He will invigorate us and give us a passion for Himself, for His gospel, for His word, and for fellowship with Him.

PRAYER

Lord, I repent of my lukewarmness; I repent of my spiritual indifference,
draw me close to You to receive Your love and passion.

READING AHEAD

"He will declare to you the things that are to come."
JOHN 16:13

D. L. MOODY

People talk about news nowadays. The Bible is the only newsworthy book in the world. The newspaper tells us what *has* taken place, but this Book tells us what *will* take place. And for people to be closing it and saying we can be guided without it, is just as reasonable as to shut out the sun by closing our windows because we have the electric light. There is as much reason to say that the sun in the sky is worn out as there is to say that we have gotten beyond the Bible.

ERWIN LUTZER

Weariness seems to be the illness of the day, especially when people describe the state of their heart. Peace and inner rest are in short supply. There is good news for tired Christians. "Blessed is the one who reads aloud the words of this prophecy, and blessed are those who hear, and who keep what is written in it, for the time is near" (Revelation 1:3). As Moody said, the Bible tells us what will take place.

> And I saw what appeared to be a sea of glass mingled with fire—and also those who had conquered the beast and its image and the number of its name, standing beside the sea of glass with harps of God in their hands. And they sing the song of Moses, the servant of God, and the song of the Lamb, saying, "Great and amazing are your deeds, O Lord God the Almighty! Just and true are your ways, O King of the nations! Who will not fear, O Lord, and glorify your name?" (Revelation 15:2–4)

Don't become obsessed with today's news; there will be more news tomorrow. Read the only newspaper that counts, the one which tells us how this world will end. Jesus—King of kings, Lord of lords, will reign forever. That is just the encouragement we need in a world with shouting voices and hollow promises.

PRAYER

Father, help me to look beyond today
and remember that, in the end, Jesus wins!

READY YOUR SWORD

"It is written."
MATTHEW 4:4, 7, 10

D. L. MOODY

Christ overcame Satan by the Word. He simply said: "It is written"; and a second time, and a third time, "It is written"; and that was the arrow that shot right into Satan and drove him away. The devil does not care a bit about our feelings. He can make our feelings good or bad; he can take us up on the mountain or down into the valley, and we can only vanquish him by the sword of the Spirit, which is the Word.

ERWIN LUTZER

The Word does work when it is applied, and that's why we should be memorizing Scripture. We should be able to take that sword and put it into the teeth of the enemy who wants to destroy us. He's after us. "The thief comes only to steal and kill and destroy" (John 10:10). And what makes our battle challenging is that we can't see our enemy with physical sight, nonetheless, I can assure you he is there.

How do we wield the sword? We follow Jesus by directly and specifically using passages of Scripture related to our temptation and our situation. If we continue to stand on God's promises, the enemy will eventually leave us. But believe me, Satan will return with more intoxicating temptations. The battle never ends. We must stand our ground over and over again.

PRAYER

Father, teach me the nature and tactics of the enemy. May I be able to say with Paul, "We are not ignorant of his designs" (2 Corinthians 2:11).

ULTIMATE ENJOYMENT

I know a man in Christ who fourteen years ago was caught up to the third heaven— whether in the body or out of the body I do not know, God knows.
2 CORINTHIANS 12:2

D. L. MOODY

Some people have wondered what the third heaven means. That is where God dwells and where the storms do not come. There sits the incorruptible Judge. Paul, when he was caught up there, heard things that it was not lawful for him to utter, and he saw things that he could not speak of down here. The higher up we get in spiritual matters, the nearer we seem to heaven. There our wishes are fulfilled at last.

ERWIN LUTZER

There are people today who claim to have been taken to heaven and returned to earth to tell us all about what they saw. When this happened to Paul, he kept it quiet; he did not speak of it, lest it tempt him into pride.

In fact, today's verse is actually in the context of his "thorn in the flesh" given to him to keep him humble. And even though he begged God for it to be taken away, God did not, but instead gave Paul a sufficient substitute, namely grace to bear his trial (see 2 Corinthians 12:1–10).

Trials are specifically chosen for us. Paul was given his "thorn" by God; it was what Paul needed. But his thorn was not a detriment to his ministry; it was used by God to enhance his ministry. God's strength was perfected in Paul's weakness.

We will have to wait until we die to have the experience of the "third heaven." But while on earth, we must learn from Paul to accept what we cannot change and that any impediment can be used for the glory of God. God is not indifferent to our needs; He often does not give us what we ask, but He has promised grace to bear whatever He gives us.

Someday, when we arrive at the third heaven, we will see that it has been worth it all.

PRAYER

Father, until I see You face to face, let me say with Bernard of Clairvaux,
"Jesus, the very thought of Thee, with sweetness fills my breast;
but sweeter far Thy face to see, and in Thy presence rest."[6]

MAY 1

A TALE OF TWO KINGDOMS

Our citizenship is in heaven.
PHILIPPIANS 3:20

D. L. MOODY

Someone asked a Scotchman if he was on the way to heaven, and he said: "Why man, I live there; I am not on the way." That is just it. We want to *live* in heaven; while we are walking in this world, it is our privilege to have our hearts and affections there.

ERWIN LUTZER

While Paul was sitting in jail penning the book of Philippians, Nero, who'd had his own mother murdered, was ruling Rome. He was also the one who, when Rome burned, blamed it on the Christians. It is in this context in which Paul explained that we are citizens in two different kingdoms.

A few centuries later, Augustine would define it as two cities: the city of God, and the city of man.[7] The perfect city of God has always existed, but the city of man was born out of the fall. The challenge before us is: How shall we live for the city of God even as we now live in the city of man? The members of the city of God must do all they can to help all who live in the city of man; we must pick up the pieces in a broken culture. We must proclaim the good news that God was in Christ reconciling the world to Himself (see 2 Corinthians 5:18), and that those who believe in Christ can become citizens of the city of God.

Your challenge today as a citizen of heaven: How can you bless those who live in the city of man and help them see beyond this world to the next?

We live for the eternal city, but we must point beyond this world to the beauty, the love, the sacrifice, and the grace of the gospel.

Whatever challenges the city of man poses, our focus must always be on the city of God.

PRAYER

Father, teach me to live with the values of heaven while living here on earth. Give me a desire to lead others to Christ who is the gateway to the Eternal City.

FROM A COCOON TO A BUTTERFLY

The hour has come for you to wake from sleep.
ROMANS 13:11

D. L. MOODY

There are a great many in the church who make one profession, and that is about all you hear of them; and when they come to die, you have to go and hunt up some musty old church records to know whether they were Christians or not. What we want is men with a little courage to stand up for Christ. When Christianity wakes up, and every child that belongs to the Lord is willing to speak for Him, is willing to work for Him, and if need be, willing to die for Him, then Christianity will advance and we shall see the work of the Lord prosper.

ERWIN LUTZER

Moody said it like it is: True conversion results in life-change. But can we really change or are we all stuck with the personality and desires we were given? How does God mold our character? The Lord has given us a certain amount of raw material, and He works with what we are, but we might ask: Does God make far-reaching changes within us, changing our motivations and our attitudes so that we become different people? The answer, of course, is yes!

In the Gospels, we see Peter the cocoon; in the book of Acts, we see Peter the butterfly. Before he was filled with the Holy Spirit, Peter was filled with timidity and fear, but suddenly we see him speaking in boldness because God was standing with him. Just so, God gives us what we need for the moment. Inner transformation is available for those who desire it.

PRAYER

Father, teach me to say no to my sinful desires and weaknesses.
Today, let me receive the strength Your Spirit can give me
to bring about inner transformation.

MAY 3

SURE FOOTING IN THE SPIRITUAL BATTLE

"Truly, truly, I say to you, whoever hears my word and believes him who sent me has eternal life. He does not come into judgment, but has passed from death to life."
JOHN 5:24

D. L. MOODY

I would a thousand times rather stand on that verse than all the frames and feelings I ever had. I took my stand there twenty years ago. Since then, the dark waves of hell have come dashing up against me; the waves of persecution have broken all around me; doubts, fears, and unbelief, in turn, have assailed me; but I have been able to stand firm on this short word of God. It is a sure footing for eternity.

ERWIN LUTZER

Which piece of armor is absolutely necessary? "In all circumstances take up the shield of faith, with which you can extinguish all the flaming darts of the evil one" (Ephesians 6:16). In times when the enemy comes in like a flood, we can only resist him by faith in God's promises.

"Resist the devil, and he will flee from you" (James 4:7). That does not mean he won't be back. Jesus used the Word of God against the devil three times, and it says in the gospel of Luke, "And when the devil had ended every temptation, he departed from him until an opportune time" (Luke 4:13). Don't ever think your battle will be over. Don't ever think you have outgrown spiritual warfare.

Like Moody, all of us have had our seasons of darkness; our fears, our disappointments, and our pain. The person who, in a season of darkness, sees no reason to believe God cares for him and no reason to trust Him, but continues believing on God's Word and promises, has a faith that honors God—that is the shield of faith into which Satan sends his arrows, but they hit the shield and fall to the ground.

PRAYER

Father, today, increase my faith in Your Word;
help me to stand even when cast down by doubt.

ROLE MODELS

"There is joy before the angels of God over one sinner who repents."

LUKE 15:10

D. L. MOODY

"Joy in the *presence* of angels"? Perhaps the friends who have left the shores of time may be looking down upon us; and when they see someone they prayed for while on earth turning to God, it sends a thrill of joy to their very hearts. Even now, some mother who has gone up yonder may be looking down upon a son or daughter, and if that child should say: "I will meet that mother of mine; I will decide for God," the news, with the speed of a sunbeam, reaches heaven, and that mother may then rejoice, as we read, "In the presence of angels."

ERWIN LUTZER

Throughout the world today, I believe there will be tens of thousands of people who will believe on Christ in repentance and faith. And every single one of them is going to cause a cosmic celebration.

We don't know if the joy Jesus referred to in this passage is that of redeemed saints or the angels rejoicing. Although angels will never be heirs of God and joint heirs with Christ, they rejoice in our salvation, totally free of all jealousy, and one-upmanship. You see, angels were created individually. Angels have no relatives; they are not part of a family and will never be a brother to Christ, yet they rejoice in our salvation and are fascinated by our redemption (see 1 Peter 1:10–12).

The angels rejoice at the news of a new convert, but do we also share in that joy? Many Christians are like the elder brother in the story of the prodigal who don't rejoice over a wayward sinner who returns and receives all the blessings and privileges of sonship.

Are you a joyful Christian? Do you rejoice over a sinner who repents?

PRAYER

Father, I give thanks for my brothers and sisters in Christ.
Please give me the joy of introducing a wayward sinner into Your kingdom.

ALL FOR GOD, UNASHAMED

"All . . . All . . . All."

MATHEW 28:18–20

D. L. MOODY

All power is given unto me . . . go . . . teach all nations. Teach them what? To observe all things. There are a great many people now that are willing to observe what they like about Christ, but the things they don't like, they turn away from. But His commission to His disciples was, "Go ye therefore, and teach all nations… to *observe all things* whatsoever I have commanded you" (see Matthew 28:19–20). And what right has a messenger who has been sent of God to change the message?

ERWIN LUTZER

Because of the failure of many high-profile believers, many people today are turned off to Christianity. But we are called to challenge them to look beyond human failure and instead focus on Christ.

We are to witness about Christ by what we say, "Always being prepared to make a defense to anyone who asks you for a reason for the hope that is in you; yet do it with gentleness and respect" (see 1 Peter 3:15). We witness by our words and our attitudes. We must witness with humility, recognizing our own sin even as we point others to Christ. As someone has said, "Evangelism is one beggar telling another where he has found bread."

We also witness by how we speak, and then by how we suffer. We are told to not be surprised but to "rejoice insofar as you share Christ's sufferings, that you may also rejoice and be glad when his glory is revealed" (see 1 Peter 4:13). God wants to build faith in our hearts so when Jesus returns He, is glorified by our faithfulness.

We have to see this world as being under occupation. John says the whole world lies in the power of the evil one (1 John 5:19). We have to know and see beyond the people with whom we are dealing, and to be loving and strong and encouraging in our witness.

PRAYER

Father, I desire to be a part of the great commission; lead me to someone who needs to know about Christ and what He came to do.

MAY 6

WALKING TEMPLES

And they were all filled with the Holy Spirit.

ACTS 2:4

D. L. MOODY

In Exodus, we read that when Moses had finished the tabernacle in the desert, the Shekhinah glory came and filled it with the presence of God—that was the Holy Spirit. The moment the tabernacle was ready, it was filled. And when the temple was built, and the priests and the Levites were there singing with one accord, the cloud came and filled the temple; the moment the temple was ready, it was filled.

These were two of His dwelling places; but where does He dwell now? Ye are the temples for the Holy Spirit to dwell in, and the moment the heart is ready, the Spirit of God will fill it.

ERWIN LUTZER

When an Old Testament high priest entered the Holy Place and went behind the curtain into the Most Holy Place, he sprinkled blood on the ark of the covenant, making intercession for himself and the people. Tradition says a rope was tied around his leg in case he died in there, he could be pulled from behind the curtain without anyone needing to enter the sacred place.

When Jesus died on the cross, the curtain of the temple was ripped down the middle, from top to bottom. This torn veil symbolized the beginning of a new era, and that the entrance into the Most Holy Place was accessible to anyone who would enter through the shed blood of Jesus Christ. We have complete confidence to enter into the holy places (see Hebrews 10:19).

And, yes, as Moody said, the temple of God now exists within every believer, "Do you not know that your body is a temple of the Holy Spirit?" (1 Corinthians 6:19). Today, let us cleanse the temple, through confession and prayer. And let us remember, "In your presence there is fullness of joy" (Psalm 16:11).

PRAYER

Father, cleanse me; let me welcome Your presence in my life today.
Thank You for Your indwelling Spirit.

UNIQUELY POWERFUL

"Do you want to go away as well?"
"Lord, to whom shall we go?"
JOHN 6:67–68

D. L. MOODY

The sun is thousands of years old, but gasoline is new. Shall we then use only gasoline in place of the sun? Block up all the windows of your houses and have nothing to do with the sun! You might as well do that as give up the Bible. Outgrown it! Why, there is no book to be compared with it. No other book will lift up the world. If you could go into a town where men were trying to love without that good book, you would flee from it as they who left Sodom and Gomorrah. Have infidels ever produced a Knox, a Bunyan, or a Milton?[8]

ERWIN LUTZER

I once read a story about a young man who, in a fit of anger, threw the Bible his mother had given him from a train into a passing field. Weeks later, he repented of the sin of desecrating God's Word and returned to the spot, hoping to find his discarded Bible. The story goes that he met a young man who had found the Bible and, as a result, had come to saving faith in Christ.

My point: Moody was right, there is no other book like the Bible. "Thy word is a lamp unto my feet, and a light unto my path" (Psalm 119:105 KJV). Someone has said that the Ten Commandments are like ten lanterns that guard us from wandering into evil. As warning lights, they say to us, "Don't slip into the ditch! Stay on the path." "Moreover, by them is your servant warned; in keeping them there is great reward" (Psalm 19:11).

The Bible warns us and instructs us. And yet, our appetite for God's Word is diluted by our addictions to technology and the struggles of life. We don't take time to let the Word of God feed us, encourage us, and rebuke us. Blessed are those who meditate in the law of God "day and night" (see Psalm 1:1–2).

PRAYER

Father, let me hide thy Word in my heart so I might not sin against You.

MAY 8

BROKEN AND MIGHTY

"Go in this might of yours and save Israel . . . do I not send you?"
JUDGES 6:14

D. L. MOODY

God knows, and you know, what He has sent you to do. God sent Moses to Egypt to bring bondmen up out of the house of bondage into the promised land. Did he fail? It looked, at first, as if he were going to fail. But he fulfilled his calling. God sent Elijah to stand before Ahab, and it was a bold thing for him to say there should be neither dew nor rain: but did God not lock up the heavens for three years and six months?

But did Elijah fail? And you cannot find any place in Scripture where a man was ever sent by God to do a work in which he failed.

ERWIN LUTZER

In today's text, we see God calling Gideon, an ordinary man, to do a great work. Like Moses, Gideon complained to the Lord about his situation, asking questions about why Israel was not delivered. But God saw beyond Gideon's objections and weakness and called him "a mighty man of valor" long before he became one (Judges 6:12). God humbled him before He used him. Weakness in itself is not a barrier to our usefulness. If our weakness drives us to depend on God, we can say as Paul did, "When I am weak, then am I strong" (2 Corinthians 12:10). If we've never been broken, if we've never been humbled, if the sense of pride and self-will has never been dealt with, we will not have the strength to fulfill our calling.

Recently, we spent time with a young couple who were blessed with a child with a disability; taking care of him has been a difficult and unexpected challenge. But as time has passed, their initial anger has turned to joy; their many questions have turned to worship.

To what have you been called? "He who calls you is faithful; he will surely do it" (1 Thessalonians 5:24).

PRAYER

Father, here I am, whatever Your calling is on my life today,
help me to accept it without complaining.

MAY 9

ETERNAL INFLUENCE

By faith Abel offered to God a more acceptable sacrifice than Cain . . . though he died, he still speaks.

HEBREWS 11:4

D. L. MOODY

But there is one thing you cannot bury with a good man; his influence still lives. They buried Daniel, yet his influence is as great today as ever it was. Do you tell me that Joseph is dead? His influence still lives and will continue to live on and on. You may bury the frail tenement of clay that a good man lives in, but you cannot get rid of his influence and example. Paul was never more powerful than he is today.

ERWIN LUTZER

Yes, after we are dead, our influence will continue for good or for ill. We come into this world seeking meaning; we want to do something worthwhile, something that lasts forever. And true meaning can only be found in our love for and service to God.

Imagine the legacy of those who leave an evil impact; those who lived for self, treated others with disdain, and valued only those things that will pass away. They too will be remembered but only for the harm they did, the stingy life they lived, and the broken legacy they left behind.

But for those who lived for Christ, they have sought that which is most precious and endures forever. The good news is that if the glory of God is our goal, we know that the meaning we seek will be found; the impact we hope to have will be realized. And yes, though being dead, we still speak. The judgment seat of Christ is in the future because the good that believers have done keeps having repercussions in the lives of others, often in invisible ways.

I have frequently stood at the grave of D. L. Moody in Northfield, Massachusetts. On his tombstone is written his favorite verse, "He that doeth the will of God abideth forever (1 John 2:17 KJV). Although he died in 1899, he still speaks!

PRAYER

Father, I earnestly pray that the good I do today will have eternal value because it was done in Your name and for Your glory.

MAY 10

LET THE OPPOSITION COME

"No one will take your joy from you."
JOHN 16:22

D. L. MOODY

In the second century, they brought a martyr before a king, and the king asked him to recant and give up Christ, but the man spurned the thought. The king said, "If you don't do it, I will banish you." The man smiled and answered: "You can't banish me from Christ. He says He will never leave me nor forsake me" (Hebrews 13:5). The king got angry and said: "Well, I will confiscate your property and take it all from you." And the man replied: "My treasures are laid up on high; you cannot get them" (Matthew 6:20). The king became still more angry and said: "I will kill you." "Why," the man answered, "I have been dead forty years; I have been dead with Christ; dead to the world. My life is hidden with Christ in God, and you cannot touch it" (see Colossians 3:3).

ERWIN LUTZER

Don't you wish we had the faith of a martyr? In Oxford, England, I stood at the place where three famous martyrs were burned at the orders of Mary Tudor (Bloody Mary). I thought of their heroism, their steadfast faith, and their refusal to recant though facing the terror of the hot flames. And, because sometimes the fire burned slowly, they died a slow, terrible, and excruciating death.

We probably will not have to face such a challenge, but we are faced with the reality of being canceled by friends and relatives, the loss of a job, or the vilification of a hostile culture. Will we ask, "How much will this cost me?" Or simply, "What is the right thing to do?"

We will likely never be martyrs, but we can imitate their faith and example (Acts 5:41).

PRAYER

Father, may I rejoice when I am counted worthy to suffer for You.

NO SMALL PART

"You will be told what you are to do."
ACTS 9:6

D. L. MOODY

A man at sea was once very seasick. If there is a time when a man feels that he cannot do any work, it is then. But he heard that a man had fallen overboard. He couldn't do much, but he laid hold of a light and held it up to the porthole. The light fell on the drowning man's hand, and a man caught him and pulled him into the lifeboat. It seemed a small thing to do to hold up the light, yet it saved the drowning man's life. We can do as much as that. If we cannot do some great thing, we can hold the light for some poor, perishing soul, who is out in the dark waters of sin.

ERWIN LUTZER

Every person can do something for God—no matter how seemingly insignificant. The same Holy Spirit who converted Paul on his way to Damascus is the same Holy Spirit who, two thousand years later, converts people, saves them, transforms them, and then gifts them in the body. Some people are gifted as teachers or leaders, but others are helpers or prayer warriors. As long as you are alive, God has some place for you; there is light you can shine.

A friend of mine who died of cancer invited his neighbors and friends to visit him; at times it was an uncomfortable experience for him as well as for them. Visiting someone near death reminds us of our own mortality. But this dying man knew there was something he could do for God. In his suffering, he shared his faith; this was the light he shone on those who would otherwise die without Christ. Even a dying man has a ministry to fulfill.

Like Moody said, even a man who struggles with seasickness can find something to do. Our challenge: You and I both know someone we can point to the heavenly shore. Let us be a light in the dark, spiritual waters of our culture.

PRAYER

Father, rid me of excuses; help me to shine a light on someone's life today!

MAY 12

THE FAITH TO BELIEVE GOD

"So take heart, men, for I have faith in God that it will be exactly as I have been told."
ACTS 27:25

D. L. MOODY

Faith is a belief in testimony. It is not a leap in the dark. God does not ask any man to believe without giving him something to believe. You might as well ask a man to see without eyes as to bid him believe without giving him something to believe.

ERWIN LUTZER

Faith is not a leap in the dark. There are plenty of reasons to believe in the promises of God, just as Paul did in today's text. Paul's faith was anchored in the character and promises of the Creator. Just as the Romans and sailors trusted Paul, we trust the testimonies about Jesus from the apostles and prophets.

The Bible's dependability has been proven from archaeology, history, and science. Yet, this book is rejected by millions. This rejection typically stems from moral rather than intellectual objections. People prefer to believe that they were born good.

The message of the Bible, however, is that we are born sinners. We don't need good advice; we need good news. It's not enough for us to be helped, we must be rescued; we are not just sick, we are spiritually dead in our trespasses and sins.

The cross, as it is preached, is thought of as foolishness. But redemption in Christ is necessary for everyone. We need to humble ourselves, admit our spiritual helplessness, trusting Christ alone as our sin-bearer. We trust the testimony of God, the true object of our faith: "This is the testimony of God that he has borne concerning his Son" (1 John 5:9).

PRAYER

Father, I thank You that my faith in Christ was not a leap in the dark, but a leap into light. Today, I earnestly pray I might share my faith with someone.

OUR RELATIONAL CREATOR

God is love.
1 JOHN 4:8

D. L. MOODY

If I could only make men understand the real meaning of the words of the apostle John—"*God is love*"—I would take that single text, and would go up and down the world proclaiming the glorious truth. If you can convince a man that you love him, you have won his heart. If we could really make people believe that God loves them, how we should find them crowding into the kingdom of heaven! The trouble is that men think God hates them; and so they are continually turning their backs on Him.

ERWIN LUTZER

Yes, God is love, but today's understanding of love is used to justify that which is evil. Love must be defined by the teachings of the Bible, "This is the love of God, that we keep his commandments" (1 John 5:3) and love "rejoices with the truth" (1 Corinthians 13:6). That being said, Moody's preaching was a great example of someone who preached the love of God in almost every sermon. The love of God was Moody's central theme.

The statement "God is love" reminds us that God is personal; it means that God invites us into fellowship with Him. Love has implications for companionship for the redeemed. In John 17, Jesus prayed that we might know that He loves us even as He is loved by the Father! And as He was loved by the Father in eternity past, so we also have been loved from all eternity.

The Westminster Shorter Catechism has it right. "Man's chief end is to glorify God, and to enjoy him for ever."[9] This is the God who loved His own from all eternity.

And yes, because we have been loved, let us love one another.

PRAYER

Father, thank You for loving me from all eternity. Help me to know what it means to love You with all my heart, soul, and mind (Matthew 22:37).

APART FROM A MIRACLE

The LORD said to him, "What is that in your hand?"
He said, "A staff."
EXODUS 4:2

D. L. MOODY

Here was Moses, a weak, solitary man going down to Egypt to meet a monarch who had the power of life and death. And all he had with which to deliver the people from bondage was this rod! Yet see how famous that rod became. God's servant had but to stretch it out and the water of the country was turned into blood. He had only to lift up the rod and the waters of the Red Sea separated so the people could pass through dry-shod. He lifted this rod and struck the flinty rock; when the water burst forth, they drank and were refreshed. But it was not the rod, it was the God of Moses, who condescended to use it.

ERWIN LUTZER

Yes, the rod of Moses became the rod of God! One day there was a tree growing in the desert, and one of its branches became a staff. This rod accompanied Moses for the rest of his life, becoming a symbol of his relationship with God. The power was not in the rod, but in the God who provided it for His servant.

When Moses was standing at the Red Sea, he faced a crisis. The Egyptians were behind him, the sea was in front of him, and there was difficult terrain on both sides. God led Moses to a tight place; he was exactly where God wanted him. But in that tight place, God provided a way of escape. Moses lifted the object he had acquired in the desert and God parted the sea.

There is a lesson here for us: Just as the staff became a constant reminder to Moses of his life in the desert, so it is with our desert experiences. We learn lessons in the desert that we will carry with us for the rest of our lives. What is in your hand? What did you learn during those hard times that you can use as you move forward in your walk as a Christian?

PRAYER

Father, thank You for being with me in my desert;
help me to be reminded of Your faithfulness.

GRACE THAT KEEPS US

The law was our guardian until Christ came.

GALATIANS 3:24

D. L. MOODY

Doctrines are like a street that leads me to God, just as a city street might lead me to a friend's house for dinner. Doctrine shows me the right path, but if I remain on the street, my hunger will never be satisfied. Feeding on doctrines alone is like trying to live on dry husks; doctrine points the way, but it is not the end of the journey. Lean indeed must be the soul which will not partake of the Bread sent down from heaven.

ERWIN LUTZER

Yes, doctrine is intended to lead us to Christ. In today's text, Paul emphasized that the law was not an end in itself, but rather points us to Christ. One day, William Randolph Hearst who loved paintings, insisted on having a certain work of art. His employees were asked to search for it and he would pay whatever the price might be. After several weeks he was told, "We have found what you want, and you don't have to pay a single dime for it." He was surprised. They said, "We found it in your own warehouse."

We have the riches of Christ already in our possession. In Galatians, Paul keeps underscoring that we are not justified by the works of the law but by faith. Throughout the book, he keeps clarifying that the law was only a path, it was not the end of the journey. We are to walk in grace. We take strides against the devil in grace. We receive joy and hope through the grace given to us in Christ. To put it simply: The grace that saves us is the grace that keeps us.

So, again and again, we run to the only Person who is able to save us amid our need—Jesus Christ. "And because of him you are in Christ Jesus, who became to us wisdom from God, righteousness and sanctification and redemption" (1 Corinthians 1:30). Our "warehouse" is filled with the riches of Christ.

PRAYER

Father, help me to enter the grace given to me in Christ;
teach me to claim the riches I already have in Him.

MAY 16

DYING TO LIVE

"Death shall be no more."
REVELATION 21:4

D. L. MOODY

Someone said to a person dying: "Well, you are in the land of the living yet." "No," said he, "I am in the land of the dying, but I am going to the land of the living; they live there and never die." Here and now is the land of sin and death and tears, but up yonder they never die. It is perpetual life; it is unceasing joy.

ERWIN LUTZER

Death is not really the enemy it appears to be on this side of the curtain. Is it mysterious and fearful? Yes! Entering that vast unknown? Yes! Hamlet wrestled with the possibility of suicide. And then he concluded, "For in that sleep of death what dreams may come, when we have shuffled off this mortal coil."[10] What he's saying is, "I'd like to commit suicide, but perhaps what lies on the other side is worse than what I'm experiencing here."

Contrast this with the words of Paul, "For to me to live is Christ, and to die is gain" (Philippians 1:21). Hamlet said, "Live or die, I lose." Paul said, "Live or die, I win."

What lies on the other side for the believer? Death is fearsome; it is still our enemy. It ruptures relationships. It brings tears. It brings loneliness. It brings heartache. That's on this side of the curtain. On the other side, there is happiness, bliss, being with Christ, being in His presence forever.

All of us want to live as long as we possibly can, but when God's number strikes, when the moment comes for believers to enter into eternity, He will be there to meet us. He has gone ahead to prepare a place for us, and thus, death has lost its sting.

PRAYER

Father, when the time comes, give me the grace to die
with the hope and anticipation of seeing You face to face.

MAY 17

GOD IN US

From of old no one has heard or perceived by the ear,
no eye has seen a God besides you, who acts for those who wait for him.
ISAIAH 64:4

These things God has revealed to us through the Spirit.
1 CORINTHIANS 2:10

D. L. MOODY

Most people say, "Eye hath not seen, nor ear heard," and they stop there. But see what the New Testament says, "God hath revealed them unto us by his Spirit." You see, the Lord has revealed them unto us: "For the Spirit searcheth all things, yea, the deep things of God."

ERWIN LUTZER

Let's not interpret the above verse to say that we as individuals should expect to receive special revelations about our future heaven by the Holy Spirit. Rather, God, by His Spirit, revealed to Paul the glories of Christ which he then recorded for us in Scripture. But we as believers often do not enter into the blessings of the Spirit that are ours by faith.

If we had a better grasp of what awaits us in glory, if we could, for a moment, see the unseen and understand the glory that shall be revealed in us, we would live differently. Paul wrote the above words to encourage us, reminding us that we see through a glass darkly; but the day is coming when we shall see Him face to face (see 1 Corinthians 13:12).

Until then, Jesus has given us the gift of His presence. He said, "It is to your advantage that I go away, for if I do not go away, the Helper will not come to you. But if I go, I will send him to you" (John 16:7). He went on to explain, "Right now, the Spirit is with you, but soon He is going to be in you." Do you need guidance? The Spirit is there to guide you. Do you need strength to make it through today? Do you need an advocate with the Father? These needs and others are met by the Holy Spirit of God.

Take advantage of the Spirit's availability and by faith receive His fullness for today.

PRAYER

Father, forgive me for all the times I have grieved the Holy Spirit.
Today, enable me to walk in the hope that awaits me.

DESPERATE, DELIGHTFUL PRAYER

"Until now you have asked nothing in my name. Ask, and you will receive."
JOHN 16:24

D. L. MOODY

It is related of a king that he gave one of his generals, who had pleased him, permission to draw any sum from his treasury. When the draft came in, the treasurer was incredulous, and yet fearfully paid the amount. Later, the treasurer conferred with the king, who confirmed the amount and replied, "Don't you know that the general has honored me and my kingdom by making a large draft?" So we honor God by making a large draft on Him.

ERWIN LUTZER

D. L. Moody loved to quote verses having to do with prayer. He himself prayed with regularity and consistency. He knew that, for many people, only desperation drives us to prayer. God doesn't always answer our prayers immediately; persistence is important. "Ask, and it will be given to you; seek, and you will find; knock, and it will be opened to you" (Matthew 7:7). We are to keep on knocking. What God is saying is, "I want to stretch your faith. I want to develop your faith. I want to give you lots of needs so that you end up coming to me, realizing you need me more than you need answers to your needs."

You and I know God sometimes says no to our prayers. At times like that, let us say with Job, "Though he slay, I will hope in him" (Job 13:15). I'll trust Him when I get answers to prayer; I'll also trust Him when I don't get answers to prayer. And when we don't see the answers, let us not become bitter, but rather find delight in God. Don't ever interpret the silence of God as the indifference of God.

PRAYER

Father, help me to lift my requests to You in faith and be satisfied with Your response. What You give and what You withhold is Your decision.

ALREADY YOURS

The promised Holy Spirit, who is the guarantee of our inheritance.
EPHESIANS 1:13–14

D. L. MOODY

A poor woman once told Rowland Hill that the way to heaven was short, easy, and simple; comprising only three steps—out of self, into Christ, and into glory. We have a shorter way now—out of self and into Christ. That way is the kingdom of heaven begun below—a little of what awaits us in glory.

ERWIN LUTZER

D. L. Moody's preaching was characterized by simplicity, directness, and deep conviction. He used visual imagery, challenging both the unsaved and the Christians of his day. As far as he was concerned, we could have the assurance of heaven at this moment. The Bible agrees.

The full passage of Ephesians 1:13–14 says, "In him you also, when you heard the word of truth, the gospel of your salvation, and believed in him, were sealed with the promised Holy Spirit, who is the guarantee of our inheritance until we acquire possession of it, to the praise of his glory."

At conversion, the Holy Spirit seals us. The imagery comes to us from ancient times when a king would seal a document by having it rolled up and then hot wax poured on it where the end of the parchment met the rolled paper. Then the king's signet ring would be pressed into the hot wax to form the seal. The only one allowed to break the seal was either the king or the intended recipient of the document. In our case, the Holy Spirit is both the one who seals us and the only one who could break the seal. But He will not break the seal because we are "sealed for the day of redemption" (Ephesians 4:30).

Are you struggling spiritually? Thank God right now for the sealing of the Spirit, and trust Him to bring a bit of sunshine into your restless heart.

PRAYER

Father, thank You for sealing me with Your Spirit, and grant me
the assurance of my eternal destiny.

MAY 20

GROWING CHEER

Gracious words are like a honeycomb,
sweetness to the soul and health to the body.
PROVERBS 16:24

D. L. MOODY

I remember hearing of a man in one of the hospitals who received a bouquet of flowers on behalf of the Flower Mission. He looked at the beautiful bouquet and said: "Well, if I had known that a bunch of flowers could do a fellow so much good, I would have sent some myself when I was well." If people only knew how they might cheer some lonely heart and lift up some drooping spirit, or speak some word that shall be lasting in its effects for all coming time, they would be up and about it.

ERWIN LUTZER

James says, "The tongue is a fire, a world of unrighteousness" (James 3:6). The devil wants to control our tongues, to slander and lie. And Jesus reminds us, that "out of the abundance of the heart the mouth speaks" (Matthew 12:34). Our tongues can either speak with the anger of a fiery hell or the encouragement of our hope of heaven.

We must give God our tongues, which really means we are to give Him our hearts—the fountain where it all begins. Let us say, "God, you gave me this tongue. Help me to use it for wholesome words, words that build up, words that help, words that heal wounds rather than cause the wounds. Oh God, I surrender my tongue to you." As Scripture says, "Let no corrupt communication proceed out of your mouth, but that which is good to the use of edifying" (Ephesians 4:29 KJV).

We should use words that encourage and provide wise counsel. What words will you speak today? Words that help or words that hurt? Words that heal or words that tear apart?

PRAYER

Lord, forgive me for misusing my tongue; give me a peaceful and pure heart so that my tongue would speak words that bless and not curse.

THE FATHER'S LOVE

"Our Father."
MATTHEW 6:9

D. L. MOODY

If you ask me why God should love us, I cannot tell. I suppose it is because He is a true Father. It is His nature to love; just as it is the nature of the sun to shine.

ERWIN LUTZER

What Moody doesn't tell us here is that his own father was an alcoholic who died when Moody was about nine years old. Perhaps this is why the fact that God is our heavenly Father was so precious to Moody. He didn't have a father on earth who loved him, but he did have a Father in heaven. As believers, God is indeed our Father. And as His children, we need discipline. Discipline doesn't just mean *punishment*, it also means *training*. There are three different kinds of discipline. The first is *preventative* discipline. None of us realizes how many things God has prevented us from doing. How many traps along our path have we avoided because He has brought some trial or diversion along our way? We could call the second type *instructive* discipline as in the case of Job. It's the hardships of life that teach us to trust God no matter what.

The third kind of discipline is *retributive*. That means we are taught through the consequences of our disobedience; we are, in effect, reaping what we have sown. We are learning the lesson that "the way of transgressors is hard" (Proverbs 13:15 KJV).

Why are we disciplined? God wants us to be more like His Son, Jesus Christ. As Hebrews 12:6 says, "For the Lord disciplines the one he loves, and chastises every son whom he receives."

PRAYER

Father, thank You for your love which means You care for me,
and discipline me for my good and for Your glory.

KEEPER OF THE KEYS

"I will place on his shoulder the key of the house of David. He shall open, and none shall shut; and he shall shut, and none shall open. And I will fasten him like a peg in a secure place, and he will become a throne of honor to his father's house."

ISAIAH 22:22–24

D. L. MOODY

There is one nail fastened in a sure place; and on it hang all the pitchers and all the cups. "Oh," says one little cup, "I am so small and so black, suppose I were to drop!" "Oh," says the pitcher, "there is no fear of you; but I am so heavy, so very weighty, suppose I were to drop!" And a little cup says, "Oh, if I were only like the gold cup there, I should never fear falling." But the gold cup answers, "It is not because I am a gold cup that I keep up, but because I hang upon the nail."

ERWIN LUTZER

Christ is the nail that can hold up the greatest of sinners; He is also the one with the keys who determines the destiny of all who stand before Him for judgment.

While on a trip to Europe, my wife and I waited at a huge door in a castle. We could have tried to look through the keyhole or kick down the door. But then a man arrived with a big key. What we could not do, the keeper of the keys did in a few seconds. Yes, Christ is the One with authority to open and to close; to save and to judge. He holds the master key; all doors open, all doors close by His authority.

For Jesus, there are no closed doors. He can bring people to Himself even in closed countries. There is no room in the universe where Jesus Christ is excluded. There is no square inch on planet earth where Jesus Christ cannot come if He wills to do it.

Jesus is the Keeper of the keys. He is also the nail that is strong enough to hold all of His treasures.

PRAYER

Father, thank You for Jesus; help me to rest my life on Him
for He is mighty in strength.

MAY 23

POINT TO JESUS

"Let your light shine before others, so that they may see your good works and give glory to your Father who is in heaven."

MATTHEW 5:16

D. L. MOODY

If a man has not grace to keep his temper, he is not fit to work for God. If he cannot live uprightly at home, he is not fit for God's service; and the less he does the better. But if he *can* keep his temper, he *can* live uprightly at home, by the grace of God.

ERWIN LUTZER

Moody was concerned about our testimony before others. Yes, if we are short-tempered, we could drive people away from Christ rather than nudge them toward Him. We are to let our light shine in a dark world. The early church attracted some people because of their love, but their commitment to holiness repelled others. Jesus said that men, by nature, love darkness rather than light (John 3:19).

Some people will make up their minds about Christ based on their interaction with us. Christians must guard their testimony. Light gives us perspective. As a child on a farm, I would frequently run out in the fields after dark. I would often take a flashlight because I'd imagine things that weren't there. Darkness can be terrifying, misleading, and dangerous.

Our world needs light. Today's culture calls darkness light and light darkness. We have the privilege and responsibility of showing others that there is a light they can confidently follow—a light leading us to the reality of forgiveness and hope. Suicide is on the rise because of hopeless despair. Sadly, at the same time, many Christians are hiding their light, fearful of being canceled, ridiculed, or otherwise thought to be odd.

Let's honestly answer these questions: Are we good representatives of Christ's light in the lives of those who walk in darkness? What sin is keeping us from letting our light shine? Are we fearful, hesitant, and unprepared? Or, as Moody would say, "of a bad temper?"

PRAYER

Father, may I represent Christ without shame and without rancor.
Let my temperament and attitude be pleasing in Your sight.

MAY 24

RUNNING TOWARD JESUS

I have fought the good fight.
2 TIMOTHY 4:7

D. L. MOODY

Rome never had such a conqueror as Paul within her walls. Rome never had such a mighty man as Paul within her boundaries. Although the world looked down upon him, and perhaps he looked very small and contemptible, yet in the sight of heaven, he was the mightiest man who ever trod the streets of Rome. Probably there will never be another one like him travelling those streets. The Son of God walked with him like the fourth man in the fiery furnace (see Daniel 3:24–25).

ERWIN LUTZER

Soon after Paul wrote 2 Timothy, he was beheaded by Nero, reminding us that death does not end all. Not only that, but decisions and victories won in this world may be very different in the life to come.

Then I think of Dietrich Bonhoeffer. He turned against Hitler, becoming part of the resistance movement, and was eventually hung in Flossenbürg. What impresses me is that on the morning of his hanging (and that wouldn't be a nice way to die, would it?), a biographer says that he was stripped, taken to the gallows, and was allowed to pray. And he prayed these words. He said, "This is the end . . . for me the beginning of life."[11] And with that, he walked to the gallows and was hung. Dr. H. Fischer-Hüllstrung who saw him said he had never seen anyone die "so entirely submissive to the will of God."[12] "This is the end. . . . For me the beginning of life."

Things are not what they appear to be, and at the end of the day, what we need is Jesus so that we can say, "For to me to live is Christ, and to die is gain" (Philippians 1:21).

PRAYER

Father, teach me faithfulness in matters both small and weighty
until I make it all the way to the finish line.

MAY 25

NOTHING BUT THE BLOOD

The blood of Jesus his Son cleanses us from all sin.

1 JOHN 1:7

D. L. MOODY

You may pile up your sins till they rise like a dark mountain, and then multiply them by ten thousand, taking into account those you cannot think of: and after you have tried to enumerate all the sins you have ever committed, just let me give you one verse, "The blood of Jesus his Son cleanses us from all sin," and that mountain will melt away.

ERWIN LUTZER

We all have within us a sin factory, manufacturing truckload after truckload of sin. Jesus said that evil thoughts (stubbornness, self-will, murder, violence, revenge, adultery, sexual immorality, theft, false witnesses, and slander, to name just a few), exist within the human heart (Mark 7:21). The seeds are there in all of us. What an indictment!

Yet, paradoxically, we read, "Have confidence to enter the holy places [the very throne room of God!] by the blood of Jesus" (Hebrews 10:19). That means there is no sin you can ever commit, no sin so great that could devalue the blood of Christ. I frequently receive letters from people who think they have committed the unpardonable sin. True, there is an unpardonable sin, but it is always committed by unbelievers who say no to God too long and too often. It is not that they cannot be forgiven, but they are determined to not accept God's forgiveness.

To put it clearly: The issue is never the greatness of our sin, but rather the wonder of the gift of righteousness given to us when we believe the gospel. The blood gives us the right to be called children of God (see John 1:12).

PRAYER

Father, thank You for the blood of Christ,
which cleansed me from my sins.

MAY 26

NOBODY LIKE JESUS

Only the high priest goes, and he but once a year, and not without taking blood, which he offers for himself and for the unintentional sins of the people.

HEBREWS 9:7

D. L. MOODY

Look at the Roman soldier as he pushed his spear into the very heart of the God-man. What a hellish deed! But what was the next thing that took place? Blood covered the spear! Oh! Thank God, the blood covers sin. The very crowning act of sin brought out the crowning act of love; the crowning act of wickedness was the crowning act of grace.

ERWIN LUTZER

We again see Moody's ability to use imagery, simplicity, and a sense of immediacy when he says the blood covered the spear, signifying that the soldier too could be saved. Moody was convinced that many people believed they had sinned too greatly to be forgiven, so in his messages, he constantly emphasized the expansive work of God's grace.

At the cross, the dissidence between God's love and God's justice was resolved. God's love wanted to redeem humanity, but His justice wouldn't allow it. God has all of His attributes in equilibrium and in right proportions. Where do we see the clearest evidence of God's love? At the cross. Where is the clearest evidence of God's justice? At the cross.

Before the cross, the Old Testament saints were saved on credit; God had fellowship with them on the basis of a sacrifice that was still to come; in our case, our fellowship is based on the glorious fact that the sacrifice has already come. In both cases, the sacrifice of Christ is the basis of salvation.

Yes, even those who crucified Christ, including the soldier who pierced His side, could have been forgiven if they came in humble faith to the Man they nailed to the cross. Let us proclaim this message of hope to a world lost in hopelessness.

PRAYER

Father, I love You because You first loved me.
Thank You that the blood of Christ is sufficient to cover all of my sin!

MAY 27

IDOL HUNTING

Nor idolaters . . . will inherit the kingdom of God.
1 CORINTHIANS 6:9–10

D. L. MOODY

It is clear that idolaters are not going to enter the kingdom of God. I may make an idol of my business; I may make an idol of the wife of my bosom; I may make idols of my children. I do not think you need go to heathen countries to find men guilty of idolatry. Anything that comes between me and God is an idol—anything—I don't care what it is; business is all right in its place, and there is no danger of my loving my family too much if I love God more; but God must have the first place; and if He has not, then the idol is set up.

ERWIN LUTZER

John Calvin, a Swiss Reformer, said that the mind was an idol factory.[13] We are constantly erecting idols in our hearts (Ezekiel 14:3). By nature, we are idolaters; we don't have idols of wood and stone, but we do have idols of fame, fortune, and pleasure. The idol of technology has stolen our hearts and distracted us from what is most important. Our smartphones have taken us places on the internet where we would have never thought we'd go.

It's easy to find out what your idol is. Number one: What do you think about most of the time when you have free time to think? And secondly: Who do you desire most to please? The answers to those questions may well be the idol(s) of your heart God needs to pluck from you.

The dearest idol I have known, Whate're that idol be,
Help me to tear it from thy throne, And worship only thee.[14]
—William Cowper

PRAYER

Father, let not an idol steal my affection for You;
come to my aid and deliver me from its power!

MAY 28

MIRACLE OF ADOPTION

But to all who did receive him, who believed in his name,
he gave the right to become children of God.
JOHN 1:12

D. L. MOODY

By receiving Him, you get power, and not otherwise. Many persons have tried to be Christians and have failed. A man may as well try to jump over the ocean to Europe as to try to serve God before he is born of God. He has not the power. But when he receives Christ, Christ is the power of God unto salvation. We take Him: and He is our salvation.

ERWIN LUTZER

What Moody wrote is true, of course. But we also have to recognize that from the earliest days of the church, there have been those who have claimed supernatural power quite apart from God. In Acts 8, we are introduced to Simon the magician who amazed people with his miraculous wonders. Later, when he saw the gifts of the Holy Spirit, he thought he could purchase them for money, using them to enhance his powers. In effect he said, "Peter and Paul, give me a course in miracles so I can do what you can do." They basically replied, "Be condemned along with your money. Your heart is not right with God." True miracles come from God; fake miracles come from Satan.

It is the power of Jesus that gives us unique, resurrection life. Faith in Christ makes us children of God and saves us from our sin. "If anyone is in Christ, he is a new creation. The old has passed away; behold, the new has come" (2 Corinthians 5:17). That is the true miracle; it is the power of God to transform a human heart, change our desires, and give us the assurance of eternal life.

PRAYER

Father, thank You for making me a new creation;
thank You for doing what only You can do in me, a sinner.

WE HIDE, GOD SEEKS

"I will seek the lost."
EZEKIEL 34:16

D. L. MOODY

I do not believe there is a man that the Spirit of God has not striven with at some period of his life. Every man who has ever been saved through these six thousand years was sought after by God. No sooner did Adam fall than God sought him. He had gone away frightened, and hid himself away among the bushes in the garden, but God sought him; and from that day to this, God has always taken the initiative to seek the lost.

ERWIN LUTZER

We've all heard a testimony where someone says, "I found Christ as my Savior." We understand what they mean, but we don't actually find Christ until Christ has found us. Paul says in Romans 3, "No one seeks for God" (v. 11). As Moody said, the best imagery of human nature is Adam and Eve in the Garden. They were not looking for God. They were hiding themselves in the trees of the garden trying to get away from Him. They were seeking ways to run from a holy God to whom they had to give an account. It is God who finds them and initiates the plan of salvation.

Christ came "to seek and to save the lost" (Luke 19:10). As far as I know, sheep never go seeking a shepherd. The shepherd has to find the sheep. If you are saved today, it's because the Good Shepherd came looking for you and drew your heart toward Him. We can only contemplate the mystery of divine sovereignty and human responsibility, we cannot understand it fully. Jesus said, "No one can come to me unless the Father who sent me draws him" (John 6:44).

Perhaps a more God-honoring way to give a testimony would be to say, "God found me." Meanwhile, we urge people to believe, but we do so in total dependence on God who sent Christ to seek and to save the lost.

PRAYER

Father, thank You for seeking me even when I was not seeking You.
I rejoice that You found me!

EYES ON THE PRIZE

"O you of little faith, why did you doubt?"
MATTHEW 14:31

D. L. MOODY

Someone has said: "There are three directions to look. If you want to be wretched, look within; if you wish to be distracted, look around; but if you would have peace, look up." Peter looked away from Christ and he immediately began to sink. He had God's eternal Word, which was a sure footing, and better than either marble, granite, or iron; but the moment he took his eyes off Christ, down he went into the water.

ERWIN LUTZER

So far as we know, throughout history, there have only been two people who have ever walked on water: the Lord Jesus Christ and Peter. As has been said, anybody who tells you that they have walked on water are the people who know where the rocks are. For a brief moment, Peter is participating in a miracle with Christ. As long as he was looking at the Lord Jesus Christ, as long as he was looking into the eyes of his Savior, he was walking above the waves. But as soon as he glanced at the wind, he thought, "I can't believe what I'm doing! I'm going to drown!" Then he went under.

How long did it take for Peter to begin to sink when he took his eyes off of Jesus? A second? How long does it take for us to take our focus from Christ before we collapse and fall into sin? The answer is, "Not very long."

Let us look at Christ by meditating on His promises.

PRAYER

Father, let me recall the promises of Christ, keeping my focus on Him rather than my circumstances.

ALL LIGHTS NEEDED

You shine as lights.
PHILIPPIANS 2:15

D. L. MOODY

If we cannot be a lighthouse, let us be a candle. In the old times, people used to come to the evening meetings, bringing their candles with them. The first one would not make a great illumination, but as more people came, there was more light. Suppose all Christians today were burning with a candlelight, would not God be more glorified? If we cannot be a lighthouse, let us be a candle.

ERWIN LUTZER

We are called light. Jesus didn't say, "Now, you'll be the light of the world after you get mature in walking with me." No. Early on, He said to His disciples, "You *are* the light of the world" (Matthew 5:14). We might be a dim light or a hidden light or a flickering light, but we already *are* the light of the world. We often underestimate our importance within the framework of God's plan. We are His representatives; we represent Christ to our families, to our neighbors, and to the wider culture.

Let's think of ourselves as the moon in it's relationship to the sun. The moon has no light of its own, but it does reflect the sun's light. Just so, our dependence on Christ should help others see the light they need to navigate their spiritual and moral darkness.

Do you feel that being a light to those around you is a task beyond you? Jesus went on and said we should live in such a way that others would see our good works and glorify our Father in heaven (see Matthew 5:14–16).

Do a sacrificial deed, say a word of encouragement, open the door to a conversation about Christ—you are on your way to let your light shine.

PRAYER

Father, help me to reflect the light of Christ and teach me how to do it well.

YOUR ETERNAL REWARD

"Behold, I am coming soon, bringing my recompense with me, to repay each one for what he has done."
REVELATION 22:12

D. L. MOODY

If I understand things correctly, whenever you find men or women who are looking to be rewarded here for doing right, they are unqualified to work for God; because if they are looking for the applause of men, looking for reward in this life, it will disqualify them for the service of God.

ERWIN LUTZER

God doesn't have a pay scale in heaven by which He evaluates us like people do on earth. It isn't an employer-employee relationship at all. It would be wrong to think, "Well, thirty years of service, therefore thirty crowns; twenty-five years of service, twenty-five crowns."

Paul says we should be "filled with the fruit of righteousness," which refers not only to our works done for the glory of God, but also our attitudes while doing them (Philippians 1:11). If we give a cup of cold water in His name, we will not lose our reward (Matthew 10:42) because Jesus makes such works perfect. The only person God is really satisfied with is Christ. And God is satisfied with us because we are in Christ, and so our works are made acceptable because of Jesus.

Jesus said, "Abide in me, and I in you. As the branch cannot bear fruit by itself, unless it abides in the vine, neither can you, unless you abide in me" (John 15:4). Now notice! Apart from Christ, we can do nothing. Christ is not saying we can't do anything without Him. He is saying we cannot do anything that will really last without Him. Ultimately, God rewards us for the work He does in and through us.

So, as Moody said, we do not look to be rewarded in this life, but rather in the life to come.

PRAYER

Father, keep me faithful and give me the desire to seek Your approval, not the praise of men.

JUNE 2

THE CHRISTIAN RELAY

"Lay up for yourselves treasures in heaven. . . .
For where your treasure is, there your heart will be also."
MATTHEW 6:20–21

D. L. MOODY

Very few people are satisfied with earthly riches. Often the richer the man, the greater the poverty. Somebody has said that getting riches brings care; keeping them brings trouble; abusing them brings guilt; and losing them brings sorrow. It is a great mistake to make so much of riches as we do. But there are some riches we cannot praise too much: riches that never pass away. They are the treasures laid up in heaven for those who truly belong to God.

ERWIN LUTZER

How much power does the human mind have? Is it possible for us to talk ourselves into being winners when, in point of fact, we are losers? The apostle Paul frequently used the imagery of games, particularly the Olympic games of his day, as an example of how to live the Christian life. He reminded us that those winners received a corruptible crown, but we who serve Christ have an incorruptible crown. Paul used this imagery as an example of winning and of losing, a contrast of winning on earth versus winning in heaven.

I want to repeat: Paul said, "They do it to obtain a corruptible crown" (1 Corinthians 9:25 KJV), but we do it for an incorruptible crown, a crown that will last forever, a crown that will endure. Not only that, but it won't be presented to us by the Olympic Committee. It's presented to us by Christ. Imagine hearing the words, "Well done, good and faithful servant!" (Matthew 25:23).

PRAYER

Father, please help me to run the race well, causing none to stumble.
Lord, I long to hear "Well done" from Your lips at the finish line!

JUNE 3

UNFAZED FAITH

[Abraham] grew strong in his faith.
ROMANS 4:20

D. L. MOODY

Real, true faith is man's weakness leaning on God's strength. It is the Shepherd's business to keep the sheep. Whoever heard of the sheep keeping the shepherd? People have an idea that they have to keep themselves and Christ too. It is a false idea. It is the work of the Shepherd to look after them and take care of those who trust Him. An Irishman said, on one occasion, that he often trembled, but his Rock never did.

ERWIN LUTZER

How do we keep believing in God when He doesn't do what we think He should?

Abraham is a good example of somebody who died in faith. He not only trusted God to fulfill the promise of an heir but also the land promises. One day, God said to him, "I am the Lord who brought you out from Ur of the Chaldeans to give you this land to possess" (Genesis 15:7). Yet when Sarah, his wife, died, what did Abraham have to do? Of all things, he had to purchase a burial plot for her in the very land God promised him. He died in faith, not having seen everything that was promised (Hebrews 11:8–10).

Many of the heroes of faith listed in Hebrews 11 did not see any miracles, but they kept believing God's promises despite contrary evidence. This explains why they were honored in the catalog of the heroes of faith. What they said was, "Life is hard, but I'm not going to blame God and I'm not going to conclude He doesn't love me just because things don't turn out my way."

From my heart to yours: Keep on believing. Don't abandon your faith; our Father tests us so that He might bless us. Let us resolve that we will die in faith, not having seen everything that has been promised us.

PRAYER

Father, my faith is weak; invigorate me.
Help me to continue in faith rooted in Your promises, rooted in Christ.

HEAVEN OR HELL

Arise and go, for this is no place to rest.
MICAH 2:10

D. L. MOODY

Though some think of this world as heaven, it is the home of sin, a hospital of sorrow, a place that has nothing to satisfy the soul. Men go all over the world to get out of it all they can—and yet are unsatisfied. People soon grow tired of the best pleasures it has to offer. Someone has said that the world is a stormy sea whose every wave is strewed with the wrecks of mortals that perish in it. Every time we breathe, someone is dying. We all know we are going to stay here but a very little while. Only the other life is enduring.

ERWIN LUTZER

A number of years ago, I was asked to take a funeral. I didn't know the family, and when I went to the funeral home the son said to me, "I want you to know that we are not religious. We don't believe in God. The only reason you are here is because some member of the family thought that a minister should be present." He said, and I quote, "Anything you say will not be too short." I said to him, "Why is it you want it to be so short?" "Well," he said, "we feel uncomfortable because we don't believe in God." So I made a deal with him. I said, "Look, I'll tell you what. I will be brief, but I do need to have the opportunity to tell you what I think about death in general, and Christ in particular." He reluctantly agreed. Despite the beautiful things said about the man whose body lay in the casket, what he was experiencing in those moments was the beginning of eternal agony. This world makes promises it cannot keep. It may present itself like a form of heaven, but for the unbeliever, hell awaits. May I emphasize that your eternal destiny is determined in this life, not in the life to come. Who in your life can you witness to about their eternal destiny?

PRAYER

Lord Jesus, I long to live for the life to come, not this fleeting world.
Bring into my life someone who needs to know You
so they might flee from the wrath to come.

GET OFF THE FENCE

Who is on the LORD's side?
EXODUS 32:26

D. L. MOODY

When I was in England in 1867, a friend happened to introduce me to a man from Dublin. Alluding to me, the latter said, "Is this young man all O O?" Said the London man, "What do you mean by O O?" Replied the Dublin man, "*Is he Out-and-Out for Christ?*" I tell you it burned down into my soul. It means a good deal to be O O for Christ.

ERWIN LUTZER

After the people of Israel worshiped the golden calf at Mount Sinai, Moses burned the gold and made the sons of Israel drink the water with the powder and ashes within it. He wanted them to feel the negative effects, the backwash of their idolatry. Eventually, the very thing they craved had a bitter taste. Moses stood in the gate of the camp and said, "Who is on the LORD's side? Come to me."

Through Moses, God was saying, "You can't be on the fence; either your heart belongs to me or to an idol." This represents the source of conflict within the human soul. We are idol lovers and God is an idol hater. God deals severely and drastically with our idols. Our temptation is to think we can actually serve our idols and God at the same time.

Not one of us is capable of turning away from our idols. We must come to God who is the one and only idol smasher. We come to the true and the living God who has trampled on all idols, and we come to a Savior who has been raised from the dead and taken to heaven as proof of His absolute total triumph.

Being number two in life is the essence of life if God is number one. Please take an unhurried moment and ask God to show you your number one idol. Fight against it by turning to God in repentance and faith. As Moody said, let us be O and O for Christ!

PRAYER

Father, in the presence of my idols, I am helpless. Deliver me from idols for Your name's sake, not just today, but each day of my life.

OUR BRIDEGROOM

For now we see in a mirror dimly, but then face to face.
1 CORINTHIANS 13:12

D. L. MOODY

For now, we see God, as it were, in a mirror, but then, face to face.

Suppose we knew nothing of the sun except what we saw of its light reflected from the moon? Would we not wonder about its immense distance, about its dazzling splendor, about its life-giving power? But all that we see, the sun, the moon, the stars, the ocean, the earth, the flowers, and above all, man, are a grand mirror in which the perfection of God is imperfectly reflected.

ERWIN LUTZER

Yes, Paul said that we do see through a mirror "dimly" but, thank God, we do see! God has a Son, Jesus, and He is known as the last (or second) Adam (1 Corinthians 15:45). Whereas the first Adam took the image of God and messed it up, Jesus Christ, the second Adam, is the perfect image of the invisible God. He is not just a replica of God; He is very God of very God.

And God says in effect, "I'm going to begin a new humanity. Adam is still going to be the head of the human race, but I'm going to begin a redeemed race with Christ as the head, the second Adam." And so, just as God created Eve to be a helper for Adam, He has redeemed the church to be a bride for Christ as an eternal companion.

At the marriage supper of the Lamb, we shall be wedded with Christ forever. For now, we see God dimly, and His best representation on earth is the bride of Christ.

PRAYER

Father, grant me the ability to see beyond all the superficial things to those which are eternal. I pray that we who are the bride of Christ might represent You well. May others see a glimmer of Your love through us.

A BETTER WAY

You are not under law but under grace.
ROMANS 6:14

D. L. MOODY

When Moses was in Egypt, to punish Pharaoh, he turned the waters into blood. When Christ was on earth He turned the water into wine. That is the difference between law and grace. The law says, "Kill him"; grace says, "Forgive him." Law says, "Condemn him"; grace says, "Love him." When the law came out of Horeb, three thousand men were destroyed (Exodus 32:28). At Pentecost, under grace, three thousand men found life (Acts 2:41). What a difference! When Moses came to the burning bush, he was commanded to take the shoes from off his feet (Exodus 3:5). When the prodigal came home after sinning, he was given a pair of shoes to put on his feet (Luke 15:22). I would a thousand times rather be under grace than under the law.

ERWIN LUTZER

Reread what Moody said. He used vivid imagery and always pointed to grace and love, not condemnation and law. However, we need to keep in mind that the God of Calvary is also the God of Sinai. Yes, there is a difference between the Old Testament teaching and the New. We have a better demonstration of grace in the New Testament and Christ is the clearest picture of grace.

We come before God with all of our needs, with all of our sins, and it is God who acquits us and basically says, "In Christ you are righteous legally, even though you may continue to be a sinner and struggle with sin in your experience."

During the process of sanctification, we should not only sin less, we should become more aware of how sinful we are. This helps us appreciate God's undeserved blessing of grace. Christ pleased the Father and is our only grounds of acceptance before a holy God.

PRAYER

Father, thank You that my salvation is by grace through faith.
Give me a grateful heart for Your gift of righteousness.

THE SWEETEST FRUIT

And the ransomed of the Lord shall return and come to Zion with singing; everlasting joy shall be upon their heads.

ISAIAH 35:10

D. L. MOODY

I think there is a difference between happiness and joy. *Happy*-ness is caused by things which *happen* around me, and circumstances will mar it, but joy flows right on through trouble; joy flows on through the dark; joy flows in the night as well as in the day; joy flows all through persecution and opposition; it is an unceasing fountain bubbling up in the heart; a secret spring which the world can't see and doesn't know anything about. The Lord gives His people perpetual joy when they walk in obedience to Him.

ERWIN LUTZER

There was a pastor who was baptizing a new convert. This new believer had the kind of joy that we, who are older converts, ought to have; and this convert, after being baptized, shouted, "I am so full of joy, I will never be tempted again." The pastor wisely said to him, "In order for you to have that blessing, I would have had to keep you under the water a little longer." Yes, that's right. Someday, we'll never be tempted again, but not right now.

We must ever realize that when we get saved, God does a great miracle. He creates something within us that wasn't there before: a new nature. "If anyone is in Christ, he is a new creation" (2 Corinthians 5:17). God makes a place in our lives where His Holy Spirit, whom we love and whose companionship we crave, can dwell within us. And He births within us qualities that are supernatural, things that are totally contrary to the flesh. When we walk in the Spirit and obey God's Word, we grow in Christ's likeness. The result is that we bear fruit, including the fruit of "joy that is inexpressible and filled with glory" (1 Peter 1:8).

PRAYER

Father, thank You for the joy of my salvation.
Grant me the healing fruit of a joyful heart.

THE LAST THING

Arise, shine, for your light has come. . . . And nations shall come to your light, and kings to the brightness of your rising.

ISAIAH 60:1, 3

D. L. MOODY

Love must be active, just as light must shine. As someone has said: "A man may hoard up his money; he may bury his talents in a napkin; but there is one thing he cannot hoard up, and that is love." You cannot bury it. It must flow out. It cannot feed upon itself; it must have an object.

ERWIN LUTZER

Isaiah was talking about God showering Israel with His glory and love, and the nations being drawn in as a result. God's love for us, and our love for others can be a testimony to a watching world. Let me give you a parody of the famous love chapter, 1 Corinthians 13. "Though I sing in the choir, though I volunteer for Sunday school, though I am willing to be on the parking committee and thereby miss a Sunday morning church service, and though I volunteer for many projects, if I have not love, I am nothing."

Paul writes, "So now faith, hope, and love abide, these three; but the greatest of these is love." Why is love the greatest? The day is going to come when our faith in Christ is going to be unnecessary because we will see Him. Hope is going to be unnecessary, because hope will be reality. But love will abide forever. Love is what God says is the more excellent way (1 Corinthians 12:31). Love is at the heart of it all.

Paul is talking about a supernatural kind of love that is contrary to our nature. That's why it is so important to realize that love is the distinguishing mark of the church; it is unique, it is a gift from God.

May God rebuke us for our lack of love.

PRAYER

Father, help me to love others as you do.
May others see Christ's love in me.

A DAILY WITNESS

"Will you not tell us what these things mean for us?"
EZEKIEL 24:19

D. L. MOODY

We may not be able to do any great thing, but if each of us will do *something*, however small it may be, a good deal will be accomplished for God. For many years I have made it a rule not to let any day pass without speaking to someone about eternal things. I commenced it way back years ago, and if I live the life allotted to man, there will be more than eighteen thousand persons who will have been spoken to personally by me. How often we as Christians meet with people when we might turn the conversation into a channel that will lead them to Christ.

ERWIN LUTZER

Ezekiel tells them what it all means. He warns them that their sinful rebellion will result in destruction. That's the same message we have today. Don't you wish we had the same burning desire to witness as Moody had? Those who knew him personally said Moody appeared flighty; he was a restless man, but a man with a mission. His agenda was clear. He talked to as many people about Christ as he could.

Witnessing to unbelievers was a task God left to the church. When we speak of the church, we are not speaking of a building. The church is the body of Jesus Christ. The church is people. The church is the people whom God has called out of the world and now sends back into the world to represent Him in the midst of each generation. The church must be burdened to see people come to know Christ as Savior through the proclamation of the gospel.

Would you pray right now that God would lead you to someone who needs the hope of the gospel? I've learned that when I do so, God leads me, doors open, and hearts are more receptive than I imagine they would be. Let's ask God for the passion of Moody.

PRAYER

Father, I pray that I would have a heart for Your church and for a lost world.
Lead me to people whose hearts you have prepared to hear
the good news of the gospel.

GLORIOUS TREASURE. ORDINARY VESSEL

God chose what is low and despised in the world.
1 CORINTHIANS 1:28

D. L. MOODY

Notice that all the men whom Christ called around Him were weak men in a worldly sense. They were all men without rank, without title, without position, without wealth or culture. Nearly all of them were fishermen and unlettered men, yet Christ chose them to build up His kingdom. When God wanted to bring the children of Israel out of bondage, He did not send an army, He sent one solitary man. So in all ages, God has used the weak things of the world to accomplish His purposes.

ERWIN LUTZER

Can you and I open anybody's eyes to the glories of the gospel? Of course not. But we are coworkers together with God. Paul says in 2 Corinthians 4:7, "But we have this treasure in jars of clay, to show that the surpassing power belongs to God and not to us." Paul is saying that the treasure we have is the knowledge of the glory of God in the face of Jesus Christ. In other words, the treasure is the good news of the gospel. God says, "I'm going to use imperfect people, just common jars of clay, to spread the message of hope and forgiveness to a very hurting world."

What a word of encouragement. It's okay for you and I to be weak in the world's eyes. We may have limited gifts and continue to struggle with sin—we are just ordinary people, but we have an extraordinary message. Do you realize how freeing this is? Clay pots were everywhere during the time this was written, and Paul says, "That's all you are, but that's all you have to be."

We are imperfect people pointing people to a perfect Savior.

PRAYER

Father, may I never lose sight of Your wonder.
Thank You, Lord, for using me in my ordinariness.

THE BLESSED GIFT

"And the faith that is through Jesus has given the man this perfect health in the presence of you all."
ACTS 3:16

D. L. MOODY

Faith is the hand that takes the blessing. But don't look too much at the hand. Suppose I ask a man who has just received a thousand dollars from a friend: "Did he give it to you with his right hand?" He would reply: "What do I care about which hand? I've got the money."

ERWIN LUTZER

Faith takes the gift of salvation from the hands of Christ. Our problem is that our sin is so great and God is so holy, we can do nothing to bridge the gap. Martin Luther, a German monk from over five hundred years ago, began his quest for perfection by taking advantage of all of the means of grace that were afforded him in the monastery. He lived a life of strict discipline. He wore coarse clothing, hoping this discomfort would help mortify the flesh. He sometimes fasted so long that some of his friends saw his emaciated body and worried that he might die.

Then Luther saw something in the Bible he hadn't realized before. There was not only a righteousness of God, but there was a gift of righteousness given to needy sinners. When we believe in Jesus as our Lord and Savior and believe that God raised Him from the dead, God places upon Christ all of our iniquities and all of our sins and, in return, we receive Christ's righteousness to stand before God.

So, we receive salvation freely from the hand of God.

PRAYER

Father, thank You for the blessed gift of Christ's righteousness purchased by the wounded hands of Christ.

JUNE 13

AMBASSADORS OF GLORY

"For the Son of Man is as a man taking a far journey, who left his house, and gave authority to his servants, and to every man his work."

MARK 13:34 KJV

D. L. MOODY

If you notice that verse carefully, it does not read "to every man some work," or "to every man a work," but "to every man his work." And I believe that every man and woman living has a work laid out for them to do; that every man's life is a plan of the Almighty, and that way back in the councils of eternity, God laid out a work for every one of us. There is no man living who can do the work God has for me to do, no one but myself. And if any man's work is not done, he will have to answer for it when he stands before the bar of God.

ERWIN LUTZER

Paul clearly notes that God has entrusted us with the ministry of reconciliation (2 Corinthians 5:18). As Moody said, we each have a different work, but we work together for the good of the gospel. The church in Corinth was imperfect, but they were still called to be ambassadors. They were called to represent Christ, and if they did it in humility, even their imperfections would not stand in the way.

An ambassador is to convey the message of his king to the place he is appointed to serve. He is a conduit, taking the message of one kingdom and giving it to another. The kingdom we represent is invisible, but it's very real; we bring the message of that kingdom to earth. We have a message that says, "Heaven is interested in you, heaven is available to you, and grace can be extended to you." Jesus said, "As the Father has sent me, even so I am sending you" (John 20:21).

Another characteristic of an ambassador: He is commissioned; he represents his kingdom, not himself. Finally, an ambassador looks to his king for resources. God has given us the Holy Spirit; we have all we need to be ambassadors of hope to a hopeless world.

PRAYER

Father, remind me each morning as I wake that I am an ambassador for reconciliation, ready to introduce people to my King.

JUNE 14

UNDER NEW MANAGEMENT

The LORD will give grace and glory.

PSALM 84:11 KJV

D. L. MOODY

There is not such a great difference between grace and glory after all. Grace is the bud, and glory the blossom. Grace is glory begun, and glory is grace perfected. To people who are serving God down here, glory will not come hard when they go up yonder to heaven. They will change places, but they will not stop serving.

ERWIN LUTZER

The word *glory* has a variety of meanings. When applied to God, it means majesty, worthiness, and eternality. We too will enjoy glory, though not of our own doing but because of what Christ has done for us. Jesus prayed, "The glory that you have given me I have given to them" (John 17:22).

We can't comprehend what that really means. After all, our eyes cannot see and our hearts cannot grasp the wonder of our salvation and our eternal bliss. All we can be certain of is that everything we have is because of the undeserved grace of God. I told my wife, Rebecca, that if, for the first thousand years in heaven, I will be on my face thanking and worshiping Jesus, that would be fine with me. Being reunited with my relatives and friends can come later.

Meanwhile, we have a battle we must win. Until we see Jesus, we must realize we are in a war. Galatians 5:16–17 says, "But I say, walk by the Spirit, and you will not gratify the desires of the flesh. For the desires of the flesh are against the Spirit, and the desires of the Spirit are against the flesh, for these are opposed to each other, to keep you from doing the things you want to do."

The Holy Spirit not only wants to subdue the sinful flesh, He seeks to birth in us the fruit of the Spirit. And, I believe that the greater our victories on earth, more glory that awaits us in heaven.

For us who believe, we receive grace today and glory tomorrow!

PRAYER

Father, help me to keep eternal glory in mind
and daily kill the desires of the flesh.

TEMPORARY SUFFERING, ETERNAL VICTORY

For the things that are seen are transient, but the things that are unseen are eternal.
2 CORINTHIANS 4:18

D. L. MOODY

The heir to some great estate, while a child, thinks more of a dollar in his pocket than all his coming inheritance. Just so, even some professing Christians are more elated by a passing pleasure than they are by their title to eternal glory.

ERWIN LUTZER

A mark of maturity, we are told, is delayed gratification. Some people live for the pleasures of this fleeting world without much thought about their eternal existence. And when suffering comes, they find themselves unable to look beyond it to God.

Satan's intention is to use our suffering to distract us and make us so miserable and cynical that we no longer trust God. So, Satan wins *temporary* victories in our lives. I say "temporary" because the Christian's future is secure, however, the enemy can still win in this life by making us forget about our life to come. God's own purpose for suffering is very different. It is to break us, to humble us, and to develop our relationship with Him. We should see suffering as a divine gift, coming from God's hand for God's purposes. To put it clearly, suffering is actually God putting His arms around us.

Remember what Paul endured: a thorn in the flesh, people trying to undermine him, he was beaten, stoned, and left for dead. Yet despite all of that and more, he said, "For this light momentary affliction is preparing for us an eternal weight of glory beyond all comparison" (2 Corinthians 4:17).

The key to life is not to be absorbed by the things that are seen but rather the things unseen.

PRAYER

Father, show me Your grace even in my affliction;
help me to focus on eternity and not just time.

AGAINST THE CURRENT

Faith apart from works is useless.
JAMES 2:20

D. L. MOODY

You may very often see dead fish floating with the stream, but you never saw dead fish swimming against it. Well, such a fish is a false believer. Profession is just floating down the stream, but confession is swimming against it, no matter how strong the tide.

ERWIN LUTZER

I like Moody's phrase, "*profession* is floating down the stream, *confession* is swimming against it." Confessing Christ as Lord brings with it a transformation of the heart, a transformation of values. We begin to hate what we once loved and love what we once hated.

Yet the cultural currents are swirling around us. Solzhenitsyn recounts a chilling tale from Russia: A deputy's fervent praise of Stalin led to a standing ovation that went on for minutes without end. After a factory director dared to sit after eleven long minutes, he was imprisoned for a decade. Solzhenitsyn's point? Freedom dies with "thunderous applause."[15]

We cannot go along with the cultural currents that conflict with our Christian convictions—especially if evil is accepted and applauded. We need heroes who are willing to stand against the culture. Just because you are under pressure does not mean you should ever violate your conscience. The Bible says, "Whatever does not proceed from faith is sin" (Romans 14:23).

Churches need to stand against the current of society, even if we become known as counter-cultural for what we stand for.

Let us be faithful to our conscience and to the Word of God, swimming against the stream of the sins and confusion of our culture.

PRAYER

Father, I seek not just profession but confession,
with my faith firmly rooted in You.

JUNE 17

OUR EXAMPLE

Blessed are you when others revile you and persecute you.

MATTHEW 5:11

D. L. MOODY

Listen to Paul in the jail at Philippi. "If God wants me to go to heaven by way of this prison," he says, "it is all the same to me; rejoice and be exceeding glad, Silas. I thank God that I am accounted worthy to suffer for Jesus' sake." And as they sang their praises to God, the other prisoners heard them; but, what was far more important, the Lord heard them, and the old prison shook. Talk about Alexander the Great making the world tremble with his armies, here is a little tentmaker who makes the world tremble without any army!

ERWIN LUTZER

The better the world understands Christ, the more they will come to hate Him. Paul and Silas were not in prison for doing evil, but for doing good. The authorities rejected the gospel, the one message that could show them their sin and the way of forgiveness. The gospel is so contrary to the lust of the flesh, the lust of the eyes, and the pride of life that its message can only be accepted by the convicting work of the Spirit.

Jesus told His disciples, "'A servant is not greater than his master.' If they persecuted me, they will also persecute you" (John 15:20). Jesus tells us to expect hatred from the world. That is why Paul and Silas could sing in prison: they knew they were there by divine appointment.

We think we are suffering for Christ when someone cancels us on social media. But historically, the church has often experienced horrendous personal, physical, and emotional suffering for the gospel. Blessed are those who can sing in the midst of such trials.

PRAYER

Father, teach me to sing Your praises today, no matter how my day goes.

JUNE 18

BORROWED LIGHT

"I am the light of the world."
JOHN 8:12

D. L. MOODY

I heard of an unbeliever once who said, "Look at your convert; it is all moonshine [total lies]." The young convert replied to him, "I thank you for the compliment. We are perfectly willing to be called that. The moon borrows the light from the sun, and so we borrow ours from Christ."

ERWIN LUTZER

Again, we are reminded that the moon has no light of its own, it only reflects the light of the sun. Just so, we have no spiritual light apart from our dependence on Christ. The moon is four hundred times smaller than the sun. but it appears to us as just as big as the sun because it is also four hundred times closer to earth. My point: When there is an eclipse of the sun, it's because the moon blocks the light of the sun, but the sun itself isn't affected—it's just as powerful as ever. Just so, when we experience spiritual darkness, God is unaffected; He remains powerful and remains the God of light.

Moody's point emphasizes that we do indeed receive our light from God even as the moon receives its light from the sun. We read, "For at one time you were darkness, but now you are light in the Lord. Walk as children of light" (Ephesians 5:8). Jesus talked about the unbelieving world walking in darkness, and here Paul talks about believers walking in the light.

We walk in the light because of what we know and have experienced. We walk in the light by what we think and say. In context, Paul tells us to not let any unwholesome talk come out of our mouth. And of course, we have to abstain from sensuality and anger so that we don't grieve the Holy Spirit (see Ephesians 4:17–31).

Do you feel weary today? Tired because of the demands of life? Tell the Lord how you feel; remind yourself that your light comes from Him. And give God praise that He be glorified.

PRAYER

Father, today, I confess that I have no light of my own.
I trust You to be light and life in me.

PAID AT THE CROSS

That though he was rich, yet for your sake he became poor,
so that you by his poverty might become rich.
2 CORINTHIANS 8:9

D. L. MOODY

This poor world is groaning and sighing for sympathy—human sympathy. I am quite sure it was that in Christ's life which touched the hearts of the common people. He made Himself one with them. He who was rich for our sakes became poor. He was born in the manger so that He might put Himself on a level with the lowest of the low.

ERWIN LUTZER

Jesus became poor and became the victim of dishonor. In heaven, everyone knew who He was. On earth, He was no longer honored—He was shouted at, spat upon, viciously attacked, and falsely accused. He did not believe that being equal with God meant He had to insist on keeping His high position; He took on the form of a servant (Philippians 2:5–8). He still retained God's attributes. He was God in the flesh, but He gave up the use of those attributes and depended totally on the Father. That's why He spent so much time in prayer.

No illustration is sufficient to illustrate the mystery of the incarnation, but think of it this way: If someone were a millionaire and still worked and lived with the poorest of the poor, if he could live in a palace but chooses a hut—that choice helps us understand a little bit about the Incarnation and the tremendous price Jesus paid to redeem us. He humbled Himself and became a servant. Nobody has ever been that high who has willingly stooped that low. But through His poverty, we have become rich.

Are we willing to accept poverty that God be glorified?

PRAYER

Father, break me of my selfishness and stinginess
and make me giving and generous for Your honor and glory.

THE GOSPEL THROUGH YOU

"Take away the stone."
JOHN 11:39

D. L. MOODY

Before the act of raising Lazarus could be performed, the disciples had their part to do. Christ could have removed the stone with a word. It would have been very easy for Him to have commanded it to roll away, and it would have obeyed His voice, as the dead Lazarus did when He called him back to life. But the Lord would have His children learn this lesson: that they have something to do toward raising the spiritually dead. The disciples had not only to take away the stone, but after Christ had raised Lazarus, they had to "loose and let him go."

ERWIN LUTZER

When Jesus was in the world, He was the one who exposed people's sin and their need for God's righteousness. It is impossible for people to come to saving faith in Christ unless they are drawn by the Holy Spirit. In fact, Jesus said, "No one can come to me unless the Father who sent me draws him" (John 6:44). That's why He says, "It is to your advantage that I go away" (John 16:7). The Spirit is going to convict the world (John 16:8). But let's remember that we have a part to play in God's plan of redemption; we are commanded to share the gospel. To use Moody's analogy: we are to take away the stone. Jesus said He will send the Holy Spirit to believers (John 16:13–16). And when the Spirit is sent to us, it is *through us* that the world is convicted of its sin. The Holy Spirit does not work in a vacuum. The Spirit uses our obedience to share the gospel, showing the world its need for God.

What stones do we need to remove for someone to believe the gospel? The answer might be different for each person, but we can direct all the people we meet to Christ who can raise them to spiritual life.

PRAYER

Father, because I love You, may I play my part in the lives of others so that they might believe and be saved.

BUILT ON PEACE

"But the wicked are like the tossing sea; for it cannot be quiet, and its waters toss up mire and dirt."
ISAIAH 57:20

D. L. MOODY

The only thing that can keep us from peace is sin. God turns the way of the wicked upside down. "There is no peace unto the wicked," says God (Isaiah 48:22). They are like the troubled sea that cannot rest, casting up filth and mire all the while; but peace with God by faith in Jesus Christ, peace through the knowledge of forgiven sin is like a rock—the waters go dashing and surging past, but peace remains.

ERWIN LUTZER

Everybody wants peace, but there are certain thieves that rob us of our peace. I'm talking about guilt, self-hatred, anger, and jealousy; those inner sins of the spirit steal our peace. Then there are outward things like financial struggles and conflict with people that also rob us; perhaps you even have a person in mind right now who has robbed you of peace. Bitterness robs us of peace.

We need to renew our faith in the gospel of peace. "But now in Christ Jesus you who once were far off have been brought near by the blood of Christ. For he himself is our peace" (Ephesians 2:13–14). It's not just that He brings peace. He *is* peace. You see, the good news of the gospel is, "since we have been justified by faith, we have peace with God through our Lord Jesus Christ" (Romans 5:1). Jesus brings peace because He is peace; He is also the only one who can bring peace between you and God. Moody frequently returned to the topic of peace, and for a good reason: We need to be reminded that peace is available to those who come to God. Our burdens must be transferred from our shoulders to Christ who cares for us.

PRAYER

Father, may I be given grace to cast my burdens unto
Your shoulders and receive the gift of peace.

JUNE 22

THE GREATEST IN HEAVEN

"Do good . . . expecting nothing in return."
LUKE 6:35

D. L. MOODY

Love never looks to see what it is going to get in return. I have generally found that those workers who are looking to see how much they are going to get from the Lord are never satisfied. But love does its work and makes no bargain.

ERWIN LUTZER

All of us have aspired to greatness. We would like to be remembered for doing something significant. That desire for significance is actually God-given because God put eternity in our hearts. In our fallenness, we look for significance in all the wrong places—and that's a problem.

Mark records, "James and John, the sons of Zebedee, came up to him and said to him, 'Teacher, we want you to do for us whatever we ask of you.'" "And they said to him, 'Grant us to sit, one at your right hand and one at your left, in your glory'" (Mark 10:35, 37).

It's very interesting to notice that, when the other ten disciples heard it, they began to be indignant at James and John. Jesus called His disciples to Him and reminded them that greatness in the kingdom of heaven is measured by service. To be first in God's kingdom is to be last. "For even the Son of Man came not to be served but to serve, and to give his life as a ransom for many" (Mark 10:45).

Let's admit that, like James and John, we find it difficult to rejoice over those who seemingly have been blessed more than we have. From my heart to yours, let us rejoice for any part we have been given in the vineyard of the Lord, however small it might be; and if others receive greater rewards, let us rejoice as if their reward is our own. Let us serve with joy, not for what we shall receive in return but for the privilege of serving the One we love.

PRAYER

Father, grant me opportunities to serve others in humility and love,
and to rejoice for victories achieved by others.

THE OLD IS PAST, THE NEW HAS COME

Since you have been born again, not of perishable seed but of imperishable.
1 PETER 1:23

D. L. MOODY

God has not only adopted us, but we are His by birth: We have been born into His kingdom. My boy was as much mine when he was a day old as now that he is fourteen. He was *my son*; although it did not appear what he would be when he attained manhood. He is mine; although he may have to undergo testing under tutors and governors. The children of God are not perfect; but we are perfectly His children.

ERWIN LUTZER

The topic of God's special relationship to you is the best news you will ever hear. Since all who trust Christ belong to God, there are many promises we can claim. Just as Moody mentioned, we belong to God because we are born again. Let's take just one promise given to us as His child and consider what it means for us.

You've read it before, but reread it, "And we know that for those who love God all things work together for good, for those who are called according to his purpose." Read the verses that follow and you will discover that we are a part of God's eternal purposes. Paul says God foreknew us, He calls and justifies us, and in His mind, we are already glorified (see Romans 8:28–30). God says, "It's a finished process." In the meantime, He is conforming us to the image of Christ.

There are times when we need to put away all distractions and quietly concentrate on who we are in Christ. We don't have to understand all of God's ways in order to know that we belong to Him, and anything He ordains for us is just and good. To be a son or daughter of God is the highest privilege; it is to join a family on earth that will be glorified in heaven.

PRAYER

Father, thank You for remembering me; You know my name.
Thank You for adopting me into Your family.

JUNE 24

NO ONE MORE TRUSTWORTHY

Now faith is the assurance of things hoped for, the conviction of things not seen.
HEBREWS 11:1

D. L. MOODY

This is the biblical definition of *faith*. The best definition I ever saw outside the Bible is: Dependence on the veracity of another. In other words, Faith says *Amen* to everything that God says. Faith takes God without any "If's." If God says it, Faith says, "I believe it;" Faith says Amen to it.

ERWIN LUTZER

Virtually every test we encounter in the Christian life comes down to two questions. First: "Is God trustworthy?" The second question is: "Will I sincerely trust Him?" Our temptation is to trust ourselves rather than God. We tell ourselves that sinning is preferable to obedience; we tell ourselves that God will not help us, so we have to bear our own burdens. Everything comes down to a matter of trust. Let's face it: There are very few events we are able to control. God has our future in His hands, we don't. Can we trust Him?

Abraham was told by God that he would not only receive the land, it would be his and his offspring's forever. Abraham and Sarah were already beyond the point to bear a child and so they were driven by this question: "How is God going to do it?" Abraham wavers; he can't wait for the child of promise. So, he has a child by their Egyptian servant named Hagar—which had devastating consequences for four thousand years (Genesis 16:1–6). Yet despite those lapses in faith, we read that Abraham believed God, and it was credited to him as righteousness (Romans 4:3). Ultimately, Abraham was absolutely convinced that whatever God said, God could perform. Sometimes we have to believe even though we don't know how God is going to do it.

PRAYER

Father, thank You that You keep Your covenants
and are faithful when I am not. When my faith wavers, uphold me.

JUNE 25

FROM FIRST BEST TO SECOND BEST

So we see that they were unable to enter because of unbelief.
HEBREWS 3:19

D. L. MOODY

When the Israelites first came out of Egypt, God would have led them right up into the land of Canaan if it had not been for their accursed unbelief. But they desired something besides God's Word, so they were turned back and had to wander in the desert for forty years. I believe there are thousands of God's children wandering in the wilderness still. The Lord has delivered them from the hand of the Egyptian and would, at once, take them through the wilderness right into the promised land if they were only willing to follow Christ. Christ has been down here and has made the rough places smooth and the dark places light and the crooked places straight. If we will only be led by Him right into the land of promise, all will be peace and joy and rest.

ERWIN LUTZER

When the Israelites refused to obey God and were condemned to wander in the wilderness, they later regretted their decision. They experienced what we could call the "second best." Does this mean God forsook them and said, "Well, you know, you made your own bed, you have to lie in it"? No, God blessed them even while they were being disciplined in the desert. God still gave them guidance through the cloud and the pillar of fire. He also gave them manna every morning.

Have you made a bad decision in the past and still experience the painful consequences? God is able to meet us in our wilderness, in the midst of a waisted life, or a life that has been ruined by others. God comes to help, to encourage, and to forgive.

Cry up to God in your wilderness; call upon Him, for He is near. He does not forsake us in the desert, but provides an oasis, a place of rest and blessing. You can't redo the past, but your future can still be blessed. God is the God of second chances.

PRAYER

Father, help me in my unbelief; graciously provide an oasis
in the desert of my experience.

JUNE 26

JOYFUL HARVEST

For I rejoiced greatly when the brothers came and testified to your truth, as indeed you are walking in the truth.

3 JOHN 1:3

D. L. MOODY

There is more than one kind of joy; there is the joy of one's own salvation. I thought, when I first tasted that, it was the most delicious joy I had ever known and that I could never get beyond it. But I found, afterward, there was something more joyful than that: the joy of the salvation of others. Oh, the privilege, the blessed privilege, to be used of God to win a soul to Christ, and to see a man or woman being led out of bondage by the gospel we shared. To think that God should condescend to allow us to be coworkers with Him! It is the highest honor we can have. It surpasses the joy of our own salvation, this joy of seeing others saved, and walking in the truth.

ERWIN LUTZER

As a pastor, I have heard reports from people who have gone into a neighborhood to share the gospel. When they return, they excitedly tell of how they led someone to Christ. Even though they've had a busy day, their countenance reflects their joy. They themselves are so thrilled when they realize that God used them to share a message of transformation with a needy sinner. One of the blessings I had as a pastor was to baptize others. I was exhilarated when I saw new converts weep with joy, hugging one another and sharing their newfound sense of belonging in the family of God.

Moody often spoke of the joy he experienced when he saw sinners converted. These new converts renewed his determination to preach only the gospel. What a blessing it is to be used by God to bring others to Him.

PRAYER

Father, I make myself available for You to use to advance the gospel.
I long for the special joy of leading others to faith in Christ.

RUNAWAY FEAR

Those who look to him are radiant.
PSALM 34:5

D. L. MOODY

If you want to scatter your doubts, look at the blood; and if you want to increase your doubts, look at yourself. You will get doubts enough for years by being occupied with yourself only a few days.

ERWIN LUTZER

Conflict with doubt. Have you ever noticed how easy it is for us to slide into despair? And when we're in despair, it's very easy for us to make a mistake or a wrong decision in a panic. In the Old Testament, David is painted very realistically. In fact, there are lessons we have to learn from his life because of his failures and his backslidings.

Visualize this: David is on the run from Saul when he comes to Ahimelech the priest and lies to get some food (1 Samuel 21). He told Ahimelech that he was on assignment for the king. He then asks for a weapon that he might do the king's will. The priest believes the lie and then David acts on that lie. He actually takes up residence in the territory of the Philistines! Think of it: Here is David, the man who killed Goliath, choosing to make his bed in enemy territory. Fear made him backslide.

The point: Discouragement and fear can weigh us down and destroy our faith. We risk the danger of ending up in enemy territory if we look around us rather than look upward to God. Giant slayers have fallen into sin because they stopped trusting and started running in the wrong direction.

PRAYER

Father, keep my eyes focused on You.
Let my faith in You cast out fear as I meditate on Your promises.

HEAVEN, THE CHOIR ROOM OF GOD

We always thank God, the Father of our Lord Jesus Christ . . .
because of the hope laid up for you in heaven.
COLOSSIANS 1:3, 5

D. L. MOODY

A great many persons imagine that anything said about heaven is only a matter of speculation. They talk about heaven much as they would about the air. Now there would not have been so much in Scripture on this subject if God had wanted to leave the human race in darkness about it. "All scripture," we are told, "is given by inspiration of God, and is profitable for doctrine, for reproof, for correction, for instruction in righteousness: That the man of God may be perfect, thoroughly furnished unto all good works" (2 Timothy 3:16–17). What the Bible says about heaven is just as true as what it says about everything else. The Bible is inspired. What we are taught about heaven could not have come to us in any other way than by inspiration. No one knew anything about it but God, and so if we want to find out anything about it we have to turn to His Word.

ERWIN LUTZER

There is much we could say about heaven, but I will focus on one aspect: In heaven, the worship of God will be ongoing. We can prepare for heaven while on earth by worshiping the Lord. "Ascribe to the Lord the glory due his name" (1 Chronicles 16:29). Just read the book of Revelation and you will find praise and worship directed to God sung by angels and yes, sung by us. So, prepare for heaven now by worshiping God today. If you are looking for help, just read Revelation 5:9–14.

Let me repeat: The best preparation for heaven is to worship God well on earth.

PRAYER

Father, may I praise and glorify Your name today
through my submission and worship.

PARADISE EXPRESS

And to the one who does not work but believes in him who justifies the ungodly, his faith is counted as righteousness.
ROMANS 4:5

D. L. MOODY

The thief had nails through both hands, so he could not work; and a nail through each foot, so he could not run errands for the Lord. He could not lift a hand or a foot toward his salvation, and yet Christ offered him the gift of God, and he took it. He threw him a passport, and took him with Him into paradise.

ERWIN LUTZER

Look again at this remarkable conversion story—the thief on the cross. One of the criminals who hung there, hurled insults at Jesus. "Aren't you the Christ? Save yourself and us!" But the other criminal rebuked him. "Don't you fear God," he said, "since you are under the same sentence? We are punished justly for we are getting what our deeds deserve, but this man has done nothing wrong" (see Luke 23:39–41 NIV). It's no accident Jesus hung on the middle cross between two thieves.

He hung there as a dividing symbol of the whole human race between those who believe and those who mock. The thief who believed was probably as wicked as the thief who did not, but that was not important in his dying moment. The issue was which one looked to Christ as Savior. Can you imagine this thief arriving in heaven to dine with Christ that very evening! If he is asked how he got there, all he can say is, "The man on the cross gave me permission to come." As Moody said, Jesus threw him a passport and took him with Him to Paradise! And that is all that we can say when we arrive at heaven's doorstep: The man on the cross gave us permission to enter the divine sanctuary of eternity. What a Savior!

PRAYER

Father, I thank You for the gift of saving faith. I thank You that this thief, in his dying moments, looked to Christ as King, and though his faith was meager, it was sufficient. Grant me such a gift of faith that I too might be welcomed into Your presence.

THE FRUIT OF FRIENDSHIP WITH JESUS

But the fruit of the Spirit is love, joy, peace, patience, kindness, goodness, faithfulness, gentleness, self-control; against such things there is no law.
GALATIANS 5:22–23

D. L. MOODY

The fruit of the Spirit begins with love.

There are nine graces spoken of, and of these nine, Paul puts love at the head of the list; love is the first thing, the first in that precious cluster of fruit. Someone has said that all the other eight are an outflow from love. Joy is love exulting; peace is love in repose; long suffering is love on trial; gentleness is love in society; goodness is love in action; faith is love on the battlefield; meekness is love at school; and temperance is love in training. So it is love all the way; love at the top, love at the bottom, and all the way along down this list of graces. If we only just brought forth the fruit of the Spirit, what a world we would have! Men would have no desire to do evil.

ERWIN LUTZER

Are you a fruit-bearing Christian? One day, I was talking to a man going blind. He was angry at people, but most of all, he was angry at God. He bitterly told me, "I have always been a self-made man. And now I am going to have to depend upon others." I tried to encourage him, but later I thought, God can't use "self-made men." God only uses "God-made" men. God has to take us as self-made men and women and prune us in order to make us fruit-bearing Christians.

The result of friendship with Jesus is fruit-bearing. Jesus said, "You did not choose me, but I chose you and appointed you that you should go and bear fruit and that your fruit should abide" (John 15:16). As Moody reminds us, the fruit that should be most evident is love. And we love Him because He first loved us. With that kind of love, we can even love our enemies!

PRAYER

Father, thank You for calling me Your friend and calling me to be a fruit-bearing Christian. May I bring You glory by developing a more intimate relationship with You and loving others even as You love me.

JULY 1

IF YOU BELIEVE IT, LIVE IT!

But be doers of the word, and not hearers only, deceiving yourselves.

JAMES 1:22

D. L. MOODY

A man may preach with the eloquence of an angel, but if he doesn't live what he preaches, and doesn't act upon his faith in his home and his business, his testimony goes for naught, and the people say it is all hypocrisy; it is all a sham. Words are very empty if there is nothing back of them. Your testimony is poor and worthless if there is not a record back of it consistent with what you profess.

What we need is to pray to God to lift us up out of this low, cold, formal state we have been living in, that we may live in the presence of God continually, and that the Lord may lift upon us the light of His countenance, and that we may shine in this world, reflecting His grace and glory.

ERWIN LUTZER

Greek scholars tell us that the word *hearers*, which James uses in today's verse, is a word used for *auditors*. An auditor is someone who comes to class but doesn't do any of the assignments, and if he audits all of his classes, he won't graduate. He's there just in case there is something interesting for him to learn. Auditors confuse *knowing* and *believing*, and are oftentimes deceived because they think to themselves, "I've heard the lecture and I've attended the class," and foolishly think they have met all the requirements for success.

Jesus said many would claim to know Him, even citing miracles to prove it, but His response was that He never knew them (see Matthew 7:21–23). Keep in mind, these people actually thought the door of heaven would swing open for them, but instead they discovered it was closed because, though they heard the word, they didn't really believe it; they had no saving faith. They were only auditors.

Let us be hearers and, for the glory of God, also be doers of the Word.

PRAYER

Father, help me to love Your word and be changed by it.
May I listen and live what I profess.

UNSHAKEN FAITH

And those who know your name put their trust in you, for you, O LORD, have not forsaken those who seek you.

PSALM 9:10

D. L. MOODY

A man will not trust strangers. I want to get acquainted with a man before I put my confidence in him. I have known God for forty years, and I have more confidence in Him now than I ever had before; it increases every year. In the Bible, some things that were dark ten years ago are plain today; and some things that are dark now will be plain ten years hence.

We must take things by faith. You take the existence of cities on the testimony of men that have been in those cities; and we ask men to take our testimony, who have found joy in believing.

ERWIN LUTZER

There is compelling evidence that the Bible is the Word of God, but that being said, there are difficulties in the Bible we struggle to understand. As Blaise Pascal would say, there is enough evidence for Christianity for those who are open to belief but also enough darkness for those who are committed to disbelief.[16]

But for those of us who accept the Bible as God's Word and have come to know Christ, as Moody said, our faith grows year by year. We look back and see what God has done for us; we have experienced His forgiveness and guidance.

I can do no better than to quote the words of David: "One thing have I asked of the LORD that will I seek after: that I may dwell in the house of the LORD all the days of my life, to gaze upon the beauty of the LORD" (Psalm 27:4). Day by day and year by year, the longer we walk with God the more we trust Him.

PRAYER

Father, increase the faith and love I have for You.
Let my faith in You be unshaken.

HANDS IN HARMONY

"I give them eternal life, and they will never perish, and no one will snatch them out of my hand. My Father, who has given them to me, is greater than all, and no one is able to snatch them out of the Father's hand. I and the Father are one."

JOHN 10:28–30

D. L. MOODY

These are precious verses to those who are afraid of falling, who fear they will not hold out. It is God's work to hold. It is the Shepherd's business to keep the sheep. Whoever heard of the sheep going to bring back the shepherd? People have an idea that they have to keep themselves and Christ too. It is a false idea. It is the work of the Shepherd to look after them and to take care of those who trust Him. He has promised to do it.

A sea captain, when dying, said, "Glory to God, the anchor holds." He trusted in Christ. His anchor had taken hold of the solid Rock.

ERWIN LUTZER

Years ago, I preached a sermon based on John 10 titled, "Held in God's Hands." We are in the hands of *both* the Son and the Father, and no one can snatch God's sheep out of those hands. "But," you say, "what about free will? Can't I pluck myself out of His hands?" It cannot be done, because we are not only held by dual hands, but even more precious, we are His hands! We become "members of his body" (Ephesians 5:30).

God's sheep are secure, belonging to Him forever. He will see to it that they arrive home to be with Him forever. True children of God might backslide, but they return to the Father having seen the high price they are paying for their sin. No good shepherd arrives at the sheepfold in the evening with fewer sheep than he left with in the morning. The bottom line is this: The basis of our own security is His faithfulness and promises—not our own.

PRAYER

Father, please comfort me by reminding me that I am one of Your sheep. Grant me the gift of assurance.

BELIEVING IS SEEING

And he did not do many mighty works there, because of their unbelief.
MATTHEW 13:58

D. L. MOODY

Unbelief is as much an enemy to the Christian as it is to the unconverted. It will keep back the blessing now as much as it did in the days of Christ. We read that in one place Christ could not do many mighty works because of unbelief. If Christ could not do this, how can we expect to accomplish anything if the people of God dare unbelieving? I contend that God's children are alone able to hinder God's work. Infidels, atheists, and skeptics cannot do it. Where there is union, strong faith, and expectation among Christians, a mighty work is always done.

ERWIN LUTZER

Today we say, "To see is to believe," but in the Bible, the opposite is sometimes necessary: "To believe is to see." For example, David would have despaired but he said, "I shall look upon the goodness of the LORD in the land of the living!" (Psalm 27:13). It was faith that caused the psalmist to see the blessing of God despite the circumstances around him. And remember the words of Christ to Mary and Martha at the grave of Lazarus, "Did I not tell you that if you believed you would see the glory of God?" (John 11:40). Believing came before seeing.

Of course, we are not speaking about blind faith, this is faith based on God and His Word. Without faith, we are not able to please God and we forfeit experiencing His power in impossible circumstances. To paraphrase Charles H. Spurgeon, a great preacher in London who met with Moody when he visited England, is known to have said, "A little bit of faith will take your soul to heaven, but a great deal of faith will bring heaven to your soul."

Let me quote it again, "Without faith it is impossible to please God" (Hebrews 11:6).

PRAYER

Father, increase my faith. I repent of my unbelief.

DISCIPLINED TOWARD REPENTANCE

"If the wicked restores the pledge, gives back what he has taken by robbery, and walks in the statutes of life, not doing injustice, he shall surely live; he shall not die. None of the sins that he has committed shall be remembered against him. He has done what is just and right; he shall surely live."

EZEKIEL 33:15–16

D. L. MOODY

If you have ever taken money dishonestly, you need not pray God to forgive you and fill you with the Holy Ghost until you make restitution. If you have not got the money now to pay back, you must will to do it, and God accepts the willing mind.

Many a man is kept in darkness and unrest because he fails to obey God on this point. If the plough has gone deep, if the repentance is true, it will bring forth fruit. What use is there in my coming to God until I am willing, like Zacchaeus, to make it good, if I have done any man wrong or have taken anything from him falsely? Confession and restitution are the steps that lead up to forgiveness.

ERWIN LUTZER

Obviously, Ezekiel 33 is not teaching salvation by works, it is referring to civil penalties that can be avoided if the offender makes restitution. But I cannot overemphasize the need for restitution; we should not pray for the fullness of the Spirit until we have returned what we have stolen and asked forgiveness from those we have hurt.

Years ago, there was a genuine revival in western Canada. Christians were experiencing deep and abiding repentance. They were returning money they had misappropriated from their taxes; they were asking forgiveness of each other. Such humble actions were blessed by God and people came to saving faith in Christ. God wants His children to be fully right with Him and also have a clear conscience in regard to others. If we are willing to pay any price to be fully right with God, we will experience the fullness of the Spirit in many blessed ways.

PRAYER

Father, search my heart. Convict me of any sin I have hidden.
Let me make restitution wherever appropriate—no matter the cost.

TRUSTING IN "GODS" THAT CANNOT SAVE

"You shall have no other gods before me."
EXODUS 20:3

D. L. MOODY

You don't have to go to heathen lands today to find false gods. America is full of them. Whatever you make most of is your god. Whatever you love more than God is your idol. Rich and poor, learned and unlearned, all classes of men and women are guilty of this sin. "The mean man boweth down, and the great man humbleth himself" (Isaiah 2:9).

A man may make a god of himself, of a child, of a mother, of some precious gift God has bestowed upon him. He may forget the Giver and let his heart go out in adoration toward the gift. "Thou shalt have no other gods before me."

ERWIN LUTZER

Somebody gave me a *Chicago Tribune* article showing a bus with a slogan, "In the beginning, man created God." That slogan would be correct if they had changed the last word—if they had made it lower case and pluralized it. "In the beginning, man created *gods*." That would be true. We are always developing new idols. Our culture is awash with idols of sexuality, money, and fame. The gospel confronts these idols and casts them down as we worship God alone.

I believe that only God can show us our idols. We are so steeped in our idols of the heart that we are unaware of all the attention we give to them. We spend time and energy seeking what is good for ourselves without even asking, "What does God want me to have?" Like a magnet, our thoughts are drawn to something or someone other than God and His Word.

We are often unaware of our spiritual idolatry.

PRAYER

Father, reveal to me my idols that I may I confess and forsake them.
"Search me, O God" (Psalm 139:23).

BE RID OF THE PAIN

Then Peter came up and said to him, "Lord, how often will my brother sin against me, and I forgive him? As many as seven times?" Jesus said to him, "I do not say to you seven times, but seventy-seven times."

MATTHEW 18:21–22

D. L. MOODY

Peter did not seem to think that *he* was in danger of falling into sin; his question was, "How often should I forgive *my brother*?" But very soon we hear that Peter has fallen. I can imagine that when he did fall, the sweet thought came to him of what the Master had said.

The voice of sin may be loud, but the voice of forgiveness is louder.

ERWIN LUTZER

Jesus was essentially commanding unlimited forgiveness if your brother sins against you. I don't need to tell you that we live in a hurting world. Many of those hurts come from within our own families. And yes, we are often hurt by the wider family of God. Aren't you sometimes shocked at what Christians do to one another?

But let me clarify: There is a difference between forgiveness and reconciliation. If someone sins against us, we must forgive them; if we do not forgive, we will live in our own torture chamber. Bitterness has deep and dark roots. We do ourselves a favor when we confess and forsake bitterness.

This doesn't mean we have to be reconciled to people who repeatedly sin against us. Trust, once shattered, cannot easily be restored. Reconciliation is difficult, and in some instances, impossible.

Moody also applied this verse to God's relationship with us. Yes, it is true that God has forgiven us seventy times seven . . . and in His case, He does receive us back to Himself.

Whatever you don't forgive, you pass on. Release your bitterness to Christ.

PRAYER

Father, help me to be willing to forgive just as, in Christ, You forgave me.

GARDEN OF LIFE

So is it with the resurrection of the dead. What is sown is perishable; what is raised is imperishable. It is sown in dishonor; it is raised in glory. It is sown in weakness; it is raised in power. It is sown a natural body; it is raised a spiritual body. If there is a natural body, there is also a spiritual body.

1 CORINTHIANS 15:42–44

D. L. MOODY

As I go into a cemetery, I like to think of the time when the dead shall rise from their graves. We read part of this chapter in what we call the "burial service." I think it is an unfortunate expression. Paul never talked of "burial." He said the body was sown in corruption, sown in weakness, sown in dishonor, sown a natural body. If I *bury* a bushel of wheat, I never expect to see it again, but if I *sow* it, I expect results. Thank God, our friends are not buried; they are only sown! I like the Saxon name for the cemetery—"God's acre."

ERWIN LUTZER

Years ago, Rebecca and I visited Herrnhut in eastern Germany. Herrnhut ("God's watch" or "God's care") housed Moravian Christians in the early eighteenth century. The cemetery features a tower with a 360-degree balcony—depicting God watching over their dead. The people were buried according to their choir positions so, at resurrection, they would be ready to sing praises to God!

Christians respect the body because of our fervent belief in a bodily resurrection. As Paul said, the body is like a seed placed in the ground that will eventually grow (be resurrected) into a new, indestructible, and eternal body (1 Corinthians 15:35 –58).

Like Christ, whose body was placed in a tomb, just so, we also anticipate that God will raise up our bodies, recreated in the likeness of Christ. Yes, God watches over the dead, for someday, the trumpet will sound and the dead will live!

So when death comes calling for you, what will your legacy be?

PRAYER

Father, thank You that I can live in hope of the resurrection.

AN HONEST EVALUATION

There is no distinction: for all have sinned and fall short of the glory of God.
ROMANS 3:22–23

D. L. MOODY

That is one of the hardest truths man has to learn. We are apt to think that we are just a little better than our neighbors, and if we find they are a little better than ourselves, we go to work and try to pull them down to our level. If you want to find out who and what man is, go to the third chapter of Romans, and there the whole story is told, "There is none righteous, no, not one. . . . For all have sinned, and come short of the glory of God" (Romans 3:10, 23). All! Some men like to have their lives written before they die. If you would like to read your biography, turn to this chapter, and you will find it already written.

ERWIN LUTZER

The third chapter of Romans is a convicting indictment of the human race. There we find God looking into the human heart and seeing its corruption and capacity for evil.

Ponder that for a moment. What is God's standard for entry into heaven? It is His own glory and righteousness. Anything less and we will be cast into the lake of fire. We dare not judge ourselves by others, thinking we are better than they; we cannot improve ourselves to reach God's standard. If we are to be saved, God must give us what we don't have, namely, the gift of His own righteousness.

The issue is not the depth of our sin but the glorious truth of the wonder of God's righteousness given to us through Christ. On the cross, Jesus got what He didn't deserve—our sin. We, in turn, got what we don't deserve—His righteousness. This is the "great exchange."

PRAYER

Father, thank You for Jesus who bore my sin
and gave His righteousness to me when I believed on Him.
In Him, I see the glory of God.

JULY 10

THE LOAD-BEARING SAVIOR

"Come to me, all who labor and are heavy laden, and I will give you rest."
MATTHEW 11:28

D. L. MOODY

Some years ago, a gentleman asked me which I thought was the most precious promise of all those that Christ left. I took some time to look over the promises, but I gave it up. I found that I could not answer the question. Like a man with a large family of children, he cannot tell which he likes best, he loves them all. But if not the best, this is one of the sweetest promises of all:

"Come unto me, all ye that labour and are heavy laden, and I will give you rest. Take my yoke upon you, and learn of me; for I am meek and lowly in heart: and ye shall find rest unto your souls. For my yoke is easy, and my burden is light" (Matthew 11:28–30).

ERWIN LUTZER

Rest.

Most of us have little time for rest. Addicted to distractions, our anxieties, and our apprehensions, we are too preoccupied to seriously rest in the Lord. But there is rest for the people of God.

Imagine if, an hour into an international flight, I were to ask a flight attendant to check if the pilots were awake. If I expected the attendant to repeatedly reassure me that the pilots were awake, they would become exasperated: "You are insulting this airline!" And I would be.

Yet, we insult God every day; we give Him a burden then investigate whether He has done something about it. But, just as I should rest on the plane, so we should rest once a matter has been given to God. We do not collapse into laziness or presumption, but we rest while we work. The pressure, the worries, and the cares of this world no longer plague us.

Choose to transfer your burdens to Christ right now and come to Him, finding rest for your weary, overly distracted soul. He has strong shoulders; just deal with the sins He brings to your attention and trust Him to take you all the way home!

PRAYER

Father, may I cast my burdens on You and trust in You.

HIDDEN SIN LIVES AGAIN

Whoever conceals his transgressions will not prosper,
but he who confesses and forsakes them will obtain mercy.
PROVERBS 28:13

D. L. MOODY

"He that covereth his sins shall not prosper." He may be a man in the pulpit, a priest before the altar, a king on the throne; I don't care who he is. Man has been trying it for six thousand years. Adam tried it and failed. Moses tried it when he buried the Egyptian whom he killed, but he failed. "Be sure your sin will find you out" (Numbers 32:23). You cannot bury your sin so deep but it will have a resurrection by and by, if it has not been blotted out by the Son of God. What man has failed to do for six thousand years, we had better give up trying to do.

ERWIN LUTZER

The story of David committing adultery with Bathsheba is well-known. She became pregnant, and then he had her husband, Uriah, killed. For a while, David thought his sin was covered, he had done what he needed to do to get out of the mess and salvage his reputation. But the cover-up didn't work very well. It never does.

Whether we were brought up in a strict or lenient home, we all have a conscience. And there's nothing we can do about the stain of sin upon our conscience. Time will never obliterate our sin. We need God to do that for us.

Are we willing to come honestly and openly and say, "Jesus, here I am, exposed in your presence"? We begin there, and then we go to those whom we have wronged and we say, "At all costs, I want to be right before God and man."

We can't hide our sin from God, nor from ourselves, and usually not from others.

PRAYER

Father, search my heart. Convict me of my hidden sins
so I can confess and repent of those sins.

UNDERSTAND YOUR FIGHT

For we do not wrestle against flesh and blood, but against the rulers, against the authorities, against the cosmic powers over this present darkness, against the spiritual forces of evil in the heavenly places.
EPHESIANS 6:12

D. L. MOODY

The reason why so many Christians fail all through life is just this—they underestimate the strength of the enemy. We have a terrible enemy to contend with. Don't let Satan deceive us. Unless we are spiritually dead, it means warfare. Nearly everything around tends to draw us away from God. We do not step clear out of Egypt on to the throne of God. There is the wilderness journey, and there are enemies in the land.

ERWIN LUTZER

Millions of Americans are coming to the conclusion that there is a spiritual realm to the universe. The problem is that many of them simply assume the spiritual realm is always a friendly place, and that if you open up your life and connect with this spiritual realm, it will always do you good. The spiritual realm, however, is seldom friendly—it is filled with evil spirits.

Keep in mind: Just because this spiritual world is unseen doesn't mean it's unreal. Demons and angels exist. Let's not think that only that which we see has reality. As Christians, we must confess that we are in an invisible war. But remember, we're standing on territory conquered by Christ. We read, "He disarmed the rulers and authorities and put them to open shame, by triumphing over them in him" (Colossians 2:15). Satan's sentence in the eternal flames has already been pronounced even though he is allowed out on bail. In the words of Martin Luther:

> For lo, his doom is sure:
> One little word shall fell him.[17]

That word is *Christ.*

PRAYER

Father, You have won the war through Your Son.
Help me to take full advantage of His victory and apply it to my life.

STARVING PRIDE

Clothe yourselves, all of you, with humility toward one another, for "God opposes the proud but gives grace to the humble."

1 PETER 5:5

D. L. MOODY

A man can counterfeit love, he can counterfeit faith, he can counterfeit hope and all the other graces, but it is very difficult to counterfeit humility. You soon detect mock humility. They have a saying among the Arabs that as the tares and the wheat grow they show which God has blessed. The ears that God has blessed bow their heads and acknowledge every grain, and the more fruitful they are, the lower their heads are bowed. The tares lift up their heads erect, high above the wheat, but they are only fruitful of evil.

If we only get down low enough, God will use us to His glory.

ERWIN LUTZER

Yes, God is at war with the proud. The proud person has to be the center of attention, seeing people as "ego supply," evaluating how others can serve them. They do not seek wise counsel, believing they have, within themselves, all the wisdom needed to navigate life. They do not learn from their mistakes; they blame others.

Jesus embodies true humility. The proud disadvantage others to serve themselves, the truly humble disadvantage themselves for the sake of others. Read these words: "Do nothing from selfish ambition or conceit, but in humility count others more significant than yourselves. Let each of you look not only to his own interests, but also to the interests of others. Have this mind among yourselves, which is yours in Christ Jesus" (Philippians 2:3 –5).

Jesus stooped to wash His disciples' feet; He voluntarily went to the cross, tortured for the benefit of others. He came to serve, not to be served. As Moody said, you cannot fake humility. When I meditate on this, I am personally convicted of my own pride, selfishness, and self-seeking. Let us humble ourselves, asking God to forgive this great sin.

PRAYER

Father, forgive my pride and give me the mind of Christ.

WHY SERVE?

For the love of Christ controls us.
2 CORINTHIANS 5:14

D. L. MOODY

I am getting sick and tired of hearing the word *duty, duty, duty*. You hear so many talk about it being their duty to do this and do that. My experience is that such Christians have very little success. Is there not a much higher platform than that of mere duty? Can we not engage in the service of Christ because we love Him? When that is the constraining power it is so easy to work.

It is not hard for a mother to watch over a sick child. She does not look upon it as any hardship. You never hear Paul talking about what a hard time he had in his Master's service. He was constrained by love to Christ, and by the love of Christ to him. He counted it a joy to labor, and even to suffer, for his blessed Master.

ERWIN LUTZER

There are many reasons we should be motivated to serve God. The word love should be at the top of the list. That's a wonderful motivation, and it is absolutely true that God would be worthy of worship and adoration and service even if we receive no rewards.

There are other motivations that are biblical and legitimate. One is fear. Yes, you read correctly, I said *fear*. We read, "For we must all appear before the judgment seat of Christ." Paul, speaking to Christians, adds, "Therefore, knowing the fear of the Lord, we persuade others" (2 Corinthians 5:10–11). Even believers will be judged by what we did with what we were given. Let us never take for granted that Christ's love for us will cancel His honest evaluation of our works and service done here on earth.

But love remains our primary motive; we should love God more than we love our sin. "We love because he first loved us" (1 John 4:19).

PRAYER

Father, help me to fear You and to love You more than I love my sin.

GOD ALONE

For Christ also suffered once for sins, the righteous for the unrighteous, that he might bring us to God, being put to death in the flesh but made alive in the spirit.

1 PETER 3:18

D. L. MOODY

Here we see that Christ was raised up from the grave by the Spirit, and the power exercised to raise Christ's dead body must raise our dead souls and quicken them. No other power on earth can quicken a dead soul but the same power that raised the body of Jesus Christ out of Joseph's sepulchre. And if we want that power to quicken our friends who are dead in sin, we must look to God, and not be looking to man to do it. If we look alone to ministers, or Christ's disciples to do this work, we shall be disappointed; but if we look to the Spirit of God and expect it to come from Him and Him alone, then we shall honor the Spirit, and the Spirit will do His work.

ERWIN LUTZER

The unconverted are not only spiritually dead, they think they are alive! Of course, they are alive physically, but they don't know they're dead spiritually. If I might paraphrase Martin Luther, "The natural man is blind and deaf and dead, but he perceives himself to be able to see, and to be able to hear, and he sees himself as being alive." In other words, sin blinds us from seeing ourselves as we are in God's presence.

Why share the gospel? The Word of God, combined with the Spirit of God, breathes into the human heart the life of God. Our privilege is sharing the Word; only God can take those words and create life. Our God is a God of resurrection!

PRAYER

Father, help me to trust Your Word to breathe life into those who hear.

JULY 16

WORKING TOGETHER FOR YOU

For there are three that testify:
the Spirit and the water and the blood; and these three agree.
1 JOHN 5:7–8

D. L. MOODY

I find clearly presented in my Bible, that the one God who demands my love, service, and worship, has there revealed Himself, and that each of those three names of Father, Son, and Holy Ghost has personality attached to them. It has been remarked that the Father plans, the Son executes, and the Holy Spirit applies. But I also believe they plan and work together.

ERWIN LUTZER

Moody's comments are drawn from the larger teaching of Scripture. The Father, Son, and Holy Spirit work in harmony with one another, with divine work ascribed to each member of the Trinity, but they have distinct roles (see John 14 and 17). Jesus stated that when the Holy Spirit would come, He would testify of Jesus (John 15:26).

In the context of 1 John 5, John is focused on the testimony about the Son. We read, "The Spirit is the one who testifies, because the Spirit is truth" (v. 6). Then, in verse 8, it says the Spirit, water, and blood agree. What does that mean? The Holy Spirit of God testifies to the truth of Jesus who came by water (He was baptized) and by blood (He shed his blood for us). These represent the beginning and end of His earthly ministry. The Spirit, who is truth, testifies to both events, confirming Jesus' identity at His baptism and His completed work at the cross.

Bottom line: The Father sent the Son out of love, the Son paid the price for sin out of obedience, and the Spirit seals us for the day of salvation to bring glory to the Father and Son.

May I leave you today with deep gratitude for our salvation wrought by the triune God.

PRAYER

Father, thank You for loving me and sending Christ to pay for my sin.
Thank You for Jesus' obedience, and thank You for the ministry
and fellowship of the Spirit.

JULY 17

PRAYING FROM MORNING TO NIGHT

Pray without ceasing.
1 THESSALONIANS 5:17

D. L. MOODY

It was in November or December when those men of Judah arrived at Shushan (Nehemiah 1:1–2), and Nehemiah prayed on until March or April before he spoke to the king. If a blessing doesn't come tonight, pray harder tomorrow, and if it doesn't come tomorrow, pray harder, and even then, if it doesn't come, keep right on, and you will not be disappointed. God in heaven will hear your prayers, and will answer them. He has *never failed*, if a man has been honest in his petitions and honest in his confessions. Let your faith beget patience. God is never in a hurry, said St. Augustine, because He has all eternity to work.[18]

ERWIN LUTZER

How can we pray without ceasing? It should be a recurring part of our lives, praying even as we are busy. The apostle Paul is talking about a soul continuously open to God. Day by day, we begin by giving ourselves to God, committing ourselves and opening our lives to Him. We walk with a sense of dependence. Because we can't get through the day without the Lord, we begin it with Him, inviting the Holy Spirit to help us.

Sometimes, when I am asked questions in an interview or asked to decide about some matter, I am inwardly claiming a promise like, "If any of you lacks wisdom, let him ask God, who gives generously to all without reproach, and it will be given him. But let him ask in faith, with no doubting" (James 1:5–6). Such promises can be in the back of my mind even while I am wrestling through some topic, some trial, or occupied with some task.

Why is it so difficult for us to pray without ceasing? Perhaps it's because we are out of agreement with God; confession and dealing with sin puts us in agreement with Him. Honestly seeking His will and what He wants for us is essential to be in a continual attitude of prayer.

PRAYER

Father, help me to pray prayers of dependence and confession regularity.

JULY 18

GOD: BATTING A THOUSAND

"God is not man, that he should lie, or a son of man, that he should change his mind. Has he said, and will he not do it?"

NUMBERS 23:19

D. L. MOODY

Suppose a man, directing me to the post office, gives me ten landmarks, and that in my progress, there I find nine of them to be as he told me. I should have good reason to believe that I was coming to the post office. And if, by believing, I get a new life and a hope, a peace, a joy, and a rest to my soul that I never had before; if I get self-control, and find that I have a power to resist evil and to do good, I have pretty good proof that I am on the right road to the "city which hath foundations, whose builder and maker is God" (Hebrews 11:10). And if things have taken place, and are now taking place as recorded in God's Word, I have good reason to conclude that what yet remains will be fulfilled. And yet people talk of doubting! Faith is to take God at His word, unconditionally.

ERWIN LUTZER

While there are many good reasons to believe the Word of God, Moody noted one compelling reason: the Holy Spirit's transforming work in our lives. If we discover a hatred for sin and a desire to love God within ourselves, then we know those desires have come to us from God.

I have counseled many who doubt their salvation. I try to be very careful for I fear giving false assurance to someone who is actually not converted. On the other hand, I know Christians who show fruit of the Spirit and a love for God and give a clear testimony of when they trusted Christ as Savior, yet they doubt if their conversion is genuine.

The very desire we have for assurance is a good sign we are converted. The unconverted may speak of their conversion as an intellectual curiosity but have no holy desire to make certain they are among the redeemed. The truly saved are those who pursue God, grow in their faith, and eventually come to "the full assurance of faith" (see Hebrews 10:22). God's Word accomplishes all of His purposes, even in you.

PRAYER

Father, help me to trust You to finish all You said You would do.

SITTING ON CHRIST'S THRONE

I will set him on high.
PSALM 91:14 KJV

D. L. MOODY

God is able to do it. Up above the angels, up above the archangels, up above the cherubim and seraphim, on the throne with His own Son.

We are called to be sons and daughters of the eternal God. Do you know, the Prince of Wales cannot sit on the throne with Queen Victoria? But it is not so yonder. Christ has gone up and taken His seat at the right hand of the Father, and every son and daughter of God is to be lifted up to the throne. Think of the promise. Isn't it rich, isn't it sweet? "I will set him on high."

ERWIN LUTZER

The truth that every son and daughter of God is seated with Christ is mind-boggling. Just take time to ponder: Right now, our position spiritually in Christ is "seated…with him in the heavenly places" (Ephesians 2:6). Jesus promises, one day, "The one who conquers, I will grant him to sit with me on my throne, as I also conquered and sat down with my Father on his throne" (Revelation 3:21).

That's one reason we need not fear death. We already have residence in heaven. Yet Christ doesn't just save us; the purpose of salvation is not just to keep you from hell, though, praise God, it does! The purpose of salvation is to prove what He is able to do through sinners and for sinners who don't deserve anything at all. God raises us up and, someday, we will reign with Jesus Christ forever.

How big is the throne of Christ? I don't know, but it must be big enough to seat all His overcomers! Figuratively speaking, God picks us up from our muck and enables us to sit with Him on marble; He takes us up from the grave and makes us sit with Him on a golden throne. Never before have created beings come from so low and been exalted so high.

PRAYER

Father, I thank You for making me one of Your children—an heir—through Christ's sacrifice. Thank You for the privilege of reigning with You forever.

RESTORATION

And the Lord turned and looked at Peter. And Peter remembered the saying of the Lord, how he had said to him, "Before the rooster crows today, you will deny me three times." And he went out and wept bitterly.

LUKE 22:61–62

D. L. MOODY

The Master might have turned and said to Peter, "Is it true, Peter, that you have forgotten me so soon? Do you not remember when your wife's mother lay sick of a fever that I rebuked the disease and it left her? Do you not call to mind your astonishment at the draught of fishes so that you exclaimed, 'Depart from me; for I am a sinful man, O Lord'? Do you remember when in answer to your cry, 'Lord, save me, or I perish,' I stretched out my hand and kept you from drowning in the water? Have you forgotten when, on the Mount of Transfiguration, with James and John, you said to me, 'Lord, it is good to be here: let us make three tabernacles.' Have you forgotten being with me at the supper table, and in Gethsemane? Is it true that you have forgotten me so soon?" The Lord might have upbraided him with questions such as these, but He did nothing of the kind. He cast one look on Peter, and there was so much love in it that it broke that bold disciple's heart, and he went out and wept bitterly.

ERWIN LUTZER

After Jesus was raised, He appeared first to Peter, then the other apostles (see 1 Corinthians 15:5). Why Peter? Jesus was saying in effect, "You sinned, but you are forgiven; you denied me, but I have not left you."

Later, Jesus will give Peter three opportunities to confess his love to His Savior and Lord (John 21). The same lips that denied Christ are now the same lips by which Peter confessed his love. The failure is past, the restoration is complete, and it is time to serve the sheep.

Let us be encouraged by Jesus' restoring work. When we sin, if we are willing to confess, He is willing to forgive. Christ's forgiveness increases our love for Him and proves His love for us.

PRAYER

Father, thank You for restoring me to You.

FADING INTO THE BACKGROUND

"He must increase, but I must decrease."
JOHN 3:30

D. L. MOODY

Dr. Bonar, once remarked that he could tell when a Christian was growing.[19] In proportion to his growth in grace he would elevate his Master, talk less of what he was doing, and become smaller and smaller in his own esteem until, like the morning star, he faded away before the rising sun. Jonathan was willing to decrease that David might increase; and John the Baptist showed the same spirit of humility.

ERWIN LUTZER

Many sought John the Baptist's baptism for blessings but not with a heart of repentance. Over time, John's crowds dwindled as people flocked to Jesus, whose disciples were baptizing nearby (John 4:1–2). As Jesus' popularity grew, John's disciples said in effect, "Jesus is taking away your converts and your ministry appears to be over." But John made two powerful statements, "A person cannot receive even one thing unless it is given him from heaven" (John 3:27). We're called to stop comparing ourselves with one another and to be content with the gifts and talents (or lack of them) God has given us. This one remark should forever cure us of all envy.

But then comes John's refreshing confession of humility, "He must increase, but I must decrease." Ministry of any kind is never about us, it is always about Christ. We must step back from any glory or praise; all praise directed toward us should immediately be passed along to Christ. In summary: Our gifts or possessions are gifts deserving no credit from us, so we gladly pass the thanks to Jesus. We must fade into the background and exalt Christ in every way possible.

PRAYER

Father, I refuse to take the credit for any success I have had,
and I give You all the praise!

TROUBLE CLARIFIES

I will be with him in trouble.
PSALM 91:15

D. L. MOODY

We are apt to think young people do not have any trouble, but if they haven't, there is one thing they can make sure of: they are going to have trouble later. "Man is born unto trouble, as the sparks fly upward" (Job 5:7). Trouble is coming. No one is exempt. God has had one Son without sin, but He has never had one without sorrow. Jesus Christ, our Master, suffered as few men ever suffered, and He died very young. Ours is a path of sorrow and suffering, and it is so sweet to hear the Master say: "I will be with you in trouble."

Don't think for a moment that you can get on without Him. You may say now, "I can get on; I am in good health and prosperity," but the hour is coming when you will need Him.

ERWIN LUTZER

"Cancer clarifies."

That was the crisp message spoken by my friend who was recently diagnosed with cancer. When you hear that word, you no longer care about who wins the big game. Cancer brings us to grips with our mortality; we are not meant to live eternally in this world. At that moment, we desperately need God's promise, "I will be with him in trouble."

When times are good, with good health, plenty of money, and everything falling your way, it is easy to believe in any god that suits your fancy. We hear people say, "I am into spirituality, but I don't believe any specific doctrines." That sounds good until you are in deep trouble or diagnosed with a terminal disease. Yes, cancer clarifies.

Yet, it is a mistake to wait for a death sentence before we focus on pursuing God. Eternity awaits us all, whether we suffer from cancer, die of a heart attack, or have an accident. Let us not wait for the day of trouble before we get our priorities in the right order.

PRAYER

Father, teach me to walk with You so that I will be ready
when trouble knocks on my door.

POWER UNTO LIFE

For I am not ashamed of the gospel, for it is the power of God for salvation to everyone who believes.

ROMANS 1:16

D. L. MOODY

I remember some meetings being held in a locality where the tide did not rise very quickly, and bitter and reproachful things were being said about the work. But one day, one of the most prominent men in the place rose and said: "I want it to be known that I am a disciple of Jesus Christ, and if there is any odium to be cast on His cause, I am prepared to take my share of it."

It went through the meeting like an electric current, and a blessing came at once to his own soul and to the souls of others.

ERWIN LUTZER

Moody lived long before the internet gave people the ability to say hurtful and harmful things about one another in a public forum. In Moody's day, if "harmful and reproachful" things were said about God's servants, it would have stayed within the local community. In our day, needless dirt is often thrown on the bride of Christ and spread globally. Of course, skeptics use the same outlets to heap scorn on Christianity.

Even in today's culture, Paul's words cut like a knife to the heart of our Christian witness. We should not be ashamed of the gospel; we dare not pull back, hide, or be silent in the midst of our confused world. We must stand for Christ and consider criticism as a badge of honor.

As for shame, we can be glad that Christ "shamed shame" on our behalf. We should be "looking to Jesus, the founder and perfecter of our faith, who for the joy that was set before him endured the cross, despising the shame, and is seated at the right hand of the throne of God" (Hebrews 12:2).

How can we possibly be ashamed to be identified with Jesus? Though we risk criticism, let us stand with our Savior and, as best we can, represent Him in a confused world.

PRAYER

Father, thank You for saving me. May I never be ashamed of Your gospel.

GOD: OUR SHIELD AND REWARD

After these things the word of the LORD came to Abram in a vision: "Fear not, Abram, I am your shield; your reward shall be very great."
GENESIS 15:1

D. L. MOODY

Abram might have thought that the kings he had defeated might get other kings and other armies to come; and he might have thought of himself as a solitary man, with only three hundred and eighteen men, so that he might have feared lest he be swept from the face of the earth. But the Lord came and said: "Abram, fear not."

That is the first time those oft-repeated words "Fear not" occur in the Bible.

"Fear not, for I will be your shield and your reward."

I would rather have that promise than all the armies and all the navies of the world to protect me—to have the God of heaven for my Protector! God was teaching Abram that He was to be his Friend and his Shield if he would surrender himself wholly to His keeping and trust in His goodness. That is what we need—to surrender ourselves up to God, fully and wholly.

ERWIN LUTZER

If we remember the context of this promise, we can understand why it was so important and such a comfort for Abram (later, Abraham). The king of Sodom was so grateful to Abraham for bravely rescuing the people from his city, he said Abraham could keep the plunder. To his everlasting credit, Abraham refused this offer saying he didn't want the king of Sodom to be able to say that he made Abraham rich.

So God made these promises: The Lord would make Abraham rich and He would protect Abraham from the rogue nations that wanted to steal Abraham's wealth. God would be both Abraham's shield and his reward.

Let's take that promise for ourselves. Let our wealth be honestly acquired, and let us trust God to protect us.

PRAYER

Father, shield me from harm and keep me from greed
as You did with Abraham.

THE ONE WHO LOVED ENOUGH TO DIE

For God so loved the world, that he gave his only Son,
that whoever believes in him should not perish but have eternal life.
JOHN 3:16

D. L. MOODY

I have never been able to preach from that text. I have often thought I would, but it is so high that I can never climb to its height, I have just quoted it and passed on. Who can fathom the depth of those words: "God *so* loved the world"? We can never scale the heights of His love or fathom its depths. Paul prayed that he might know the height, the depth, the length, and the breadth of the love of God, but it was past his finding out.

ERWIN LUTZER

Yes, God loves the world, but what is even more remarkable is the special love He has for those who are His—the Father's very gift to the Son. Jesus prayed, "The glory that you [the Father] have given me I have given to them. . . . I desire that they also, whom you have given me, may be with me where I am, to see my glory that you have given me because you loved me before the foundation of the world" (John 17:22, 24). Loved from before creation, loved from the eons of eternity! Believers are loved unconditionally; both in eternity past and eternity future.

Not so the rest of the world. We must also remember the last verse of John 3, "Whoever believes in the Son has eternal life; whoever does not obey the Son shall not see life, but the wrath of God remains on him" (v. 36). If we say God loves the unconverted unconditionally, we would negate the wrath of God.

Where do we see the clearest display of the love of God? At the cross. Where do we see the clearest display of the wrath of God? At the cross. There, Jesus sacrificially bore the wrath of God for all who would believe on Him. This should motivate us to share the gospel, urging people to come to Christ.

PRAYER

Father, thank You for Your boundless love through Jesus.
May I share the gospel so others find refuge in Him.

HEAVEN IS JUST A BONUS

"Let me die the death of the upright, and let my end be like his!"
NUMBERS 23:10

D. L. MOODY

The sanctified man and the unsanctified one look at heaven very differently. The unsanctified man simply chooses heaven in preference to hell. He thinks that if he must go to either one, he would rather try heaven. It is like a man with a farm who has a place offered him in another country where there is said to be a gold mine; he hates to give up all he has and take any risk. But if he is going to be banished and must leave, and has his choice of living in a wilderness or digging in a coal pit, or else take the gold mine, then there is no hesitation. The unregenerate man likes heaven better than hell, but he likes this world the best of all. The true believer prizes heaven above everything else, and is always willing to give up the world. Everybody wants to enjoy heaven after they die, but they don't want to be heavenly-minded while they live.

ERWIN LUTZER

I had not seen Moody's point clearly before: If the unregenerate person must choose, he'd prefer heaven over hell, but loves the world most of all. After all, humans are driven by our fallen desires, which are most easily satisfied by the world; we prefer our natural state. The unconverted love the world, thinking they are in charge when, in fact, they are slaves to it. But blessed are those whose desires have been transformed into a love for God and His gift of salvation. We desire heaven over the world, and shun hell's suffering because we would miss God's presence for eternity. No matter how beautiful heaven might be, without the presence of God, it could never satisfy us. Eternal fellowship with God makes heaven a place of uninterrupted bliss and fulfillment.

Do we prefer this world to heaven? Do we love God as much as Paul, who preferred to die and be with Christ than to live in this world? (Philippians 1:21–23).

PRAYER

Father, shift my desires to prepare for the life to come,
living with thanksgiving and worship.

A DIM LIGHT IS BETTER THAN NONE

"Let your light shine before others, so that they may see your good works and give glory to your Father who is in heaven."
MATTHEW 5:16

D. L. MOODY

If every one of us was illuminated by the Spirit of God, how we could light up the churches! But to have a lantern without any light, would be a nuisance. Many Christians carry along lanterns and say, "I wouldn't give up my religion for yours." They talk about religion. The religion that has no fire is like painted fire. These are artificial Christians.

Do you belong to that class? You can tell. If you can't, your friends can.

ERWIN LUTZER

I heard about a man charged with negligence for not using his lantern to warn a train conductor approaching a critical crossing. In court, he testified he did wave his lantern, and was acquitted. Later, he told a friend, "It's true, I did wave my lantern; I'm just glad they didn't ask me if it was lit."

I sympathize with people who work in an environment surrounded by attitudes and words exuding the irreverent and foul deeds of the world. Some believers have to change jobs. But we should also thank God for believers who choose to stay—who not only wave their lantern, but keep it lit. "Artificial Christians" have form but no substance, the cloak of religion but no heart change. What Jesus said to His disciples applies to us: "You are the light of the world" (Matthew 5:14).

Even if you don't think you're a very good light, you're probably the best light these people will ever meet. Be faithful, represent Jesus. If you fall back into the darkness, confess your sins and begin walking in the light anew, praying and seeking God. You might be surprised about the impact you have. Right where you are, right where God has planted you, you represent Him in an evil time. In the darkest night, keep your lamp burning.

PRAYER

Father, help me to represent Your Son well;
may those who are in darkness see the Son's light reflected in my life.

HOLD NOTHING BACK

"She has done what she could; she has anointed my body beforehand for burial."
MARK 14:8

D. L. MOODY

I imagine when Mary died, if God had sent an angel to write her epitaph, he couldn't have done better than to put over her grave what Christ said: "She hath done what she could."

I would rather have that said over my grave, if it could honestly be said, than to have all the wealth of the Rothschilds. Christ raised a monument to Mary that is more lasting than the monuments raised to Caesar or Napoleon. Their monuments crumble away, but hers endures. Her name never appeared in print while she was on earth, but today it is famous in three hundred and fifty languages.

We may never be great; we may never be known outside our circle of friends; but we may, like Mary, do what we can. May God help each one of us to do what we can! Life will soon be over; it is short at the longest. Let us rise and follow in the footsteps of Mary of Bethany.

ERWIN LUTZER

Isn't it wonderful that God doesn't expect us to achieve beyond our abilities? We should, however, hone our skills and develop our gifts, but in the end, our epitaph should read that we have done what we could. Having done that, we are still "unworthy servants" (Luke 17:10).

That being said, we should not be satisfied with mediocrity or laziness. The apostle Paul uses the illustration of the athlete in a race to remind us we need discipline, dedication, and determination if we are to succeed (1 Corinthians 9:24–27).

Mary gave her finest treasure, the expensive oil, to Jesus. But cost didn't matter. She gave all she had to Jesus, holding nothing back. Pouring it on His feet was not a waste; it was an unimaginable investment.

Let it be said of us: "We have done what we could." Nothing less and nothing more.

PRAYER

Father, I stumble, and sometimes I cause others to stumble.
Enable me, Lord, to run well and to hear Your "Well done."

JULY 29

MORE PRECIOUS THAN BIRDS

"Give us each day our daily bread."
LUKE 11:3

D. L. MOODY

If God could set a table for His people in the wilderness, and feed three million Israelites for forty years, can He not give us our daily bread? I do not mean only the bread that perisheth, but also the Bread that cometh from above. If He feeds the birds of the air, surely He will feed His children made in His own image! If He numbers the very hairs of our head, He will take care to supply all our temporal wants.

ERWIN LUTZER

Jesus gave us three reasons why we should not worry. First, He says we should not worry because of who we are. "Look at the birds of the air: they neither sow nor reap nor gather into barns, and yet your heavenly Father feeds them. Are you not of more value than they?" (Matthew 6:26). If He takes care of the birds, will He not take care of us? Don't miss Jesus' point: When we worry, we diminish our value!

Second, we should not worry because it's useless; it cannot add to our stature. Worry is like putting on the brakes and stepping on the gas simultaneously. It would be worth it if it added to the length of our life, but in fact, it might diminish it.

Third, we should not worry because of our testimony. When we worry, we act like the pagans who don't know the heavenly Father. Two people get cancer, one is a Christian, the other is not. How tragic if the Christian accepts it no better than the pagan!

Yes, we need to look daily to the Lord to receive what He has promised.

PRAYER

Father, I know You love me and desire what is best for me.
Help me to not carry tomorrow's burdens today;
tomorrow will take care of itself. Thank You for caring for me.

JULY 30

OUR DAILY GRACE

For it is all for your sake, so that as grace extends to more and more people it may increase thanksgiving, to the glory of God. So we do not lose heart. Though our outer self is wasting away, our inner self is being renewed day by day.

2 CORINTHIANS 4:15–16

D. L. MOODY

A man can no more take in a supply of grace for the future than he can eat enough today to last him for the next six months, or take sufficient air into his lungs at once to sustain life for a week to come. We must draw upon God's boundless stores of grace from day to day, as we need it.

ERWIN LUTZER

The moment we are born, we are born to die. We are born and our bodies begin to disintegrate. Death, in this life, is not only continuous, it's also visible and irreversible. In the end, death gets us. Death always wins.

That's the outer body. But the inner soul is being renewed day by day. Your soul is being perfected for eternity. Your soul is under construction because you are going to live forever. Eventually, your body will live forever too, but that will be a little later (2 Corinthians 5:1–4). Your soul is going to eternity when you die, but in the meanwhile, it's being renewed day by day in strength, in faith, in purity, and in holiness. In all these different ways, the inner person is being renewed, as we are responding to God.

As for old age, "The path of the righteous is like the light of dawn, which shines brighter and brighter until full day" (Proverbs 4:18).

PRAYER

Father, may I daily find the grace I need in You.
By Your power, sustain me to glorify You.

IN HEAVEN FOR YOU

"And I assign to you, as my Father assigned to me, a kingdom, that you may eat and drink at my table in my kingdom and sit on thrones judging the twelve tribes of Israel."
LUKE 22:29–30

D. L. MOODY

Think of the Lord stooping down and taking a poor drunkard right up and out of the gutter and putting his feet on the rock, and a new song in his mouth, and lifting him up above powers and principalities, above angels and archangels, seraphim and cherubim, up, up, up, onto the throne with Himself! Do you suppose that an angel flying over the nations of the earth would look at any throne? What a great time they had a few years ago putting the Czar on to the throne of Russia! Nation after nation sent representatives to assist at the ceremonies. But Christ's is more than that. His is an everlasting kingdom. His is a throne that is going to endure forever, and He says, "Ye shall sit with me on my throne" (see Matthew 19:28). Man, look up! Look at the stars tonight! Our inheritance is above.

ERWIN LUTZER

Moody is the best example of someone who was motivated by eternity, not just the events that transpire here on earth. He was busy, a man in a hurry, going from one place to another, encouraging believers, and winning souls.

He was driven by promises such as 1 Peter 1:4 that says our inheritance is "kept in heaven." He knew it was guarded in heaven for him and for all believers. Some think Jesus is still preparing it since He told His disciples that He would prepare a place for them. But that preparation was completed in just a moment of time.

Do you realize there's a room in heaven only you can enter and a crown only you can wear? A believer's place in heaven is assured and guarded for us. So, look at the stars and know that our inheritance is beyond it.

PRAYER

Father, thank You for redeeming me through Christ, making me one of Your children who inherits Your promises.

EVERY KNEE BOWS

"So shall my word be that goes out from my mouth; it shall not return to me empty, but it shall accomplish that which I purpose, and shall succeed in the thing for which I sent it."

ISAIAH 55:11

D. L. MOODY

Sometimes it looks as if God's servants fail. When Herod beheaded John the Baptist, it looked as if John's mission was a failure. But was it? The voice that rang through the valley of the Jordan rings through the whole world today. You can hear its echo upon the mountains and the valleys yet, "He must increase, but I must decrease" (John 3:30). He held up Jesus Christ and introduced Him to the world, and Herod had no power to behead Him until His lifework had been accomplished.

Stephen never preached but one sermon that we know of, and that was before the Sanhedrin; but how that sermon has been preached again and again all over the world! Out of his death probably came Paul, the greatest preacher the world has seen since Christ left this earth. If a man is sent by Jehovah, there is no such thing as failure.

ERWIN LUTZER

God never allows us to see all the good we have done in the world. John the Baptist, Stephen, and thousands of other believers died not knowing their future impact. That also is true of us; we too will die, oblivious to the impact we have had. That is why I frequently quote Revelation 14:13, which speaks of the blessedness of the departed saints and says, "Their deeds follow them!"

Yes, God is able to take what appears to be failure and turn it into good; and most of the time in this life, we do not know what the good actually is or how evil will be turned into good.

Don't underestimate the eternal effect of an ordinary life lived for the glory of God.

PRAYER

Father, today, I trust You to use me in ways that might seem insignificant to me, but bring You glory and bless others.

ONE PROMISE, MANY BLESSINGS

"And I will make of you a great nation, and I will bless you and make your name great, so that you will be a blessing."

GENESIS 12:2

D. L. MOODY

There is no name in history so well known as the name of Abraham. The Muslims, the Persians, and the Egyptians make a great deal of Abraham. His name has been, for centuries and centuries, favorably known in Damascus. God promised him that great lineage through his offspring. Was there ever a nation that has turned out such men? Think of Elijah and Daniel and Isaiah, and all the other wonderful Bible characters that have sprung from this man! Then think of John the Baptist, Peter, James, John, and Paul—a mighty army. No one can number the multitude of wonderful men and women that have descended from this one man who was called out of the land of the Chaldeans. He probably was an unknown idolater when God called him; and yet, literally, God has fulfilled His promise that through him, He would bless all the nations of the earth—all because he surrendered himself fully and wholly to let God bless him.

ERWIN LUTZER

We call Abraham our father, but we do not inherit all the promises God gave him. For example, Christians are not promised the land whose boundaries God gave to Abraham's physical descendants. But through Abraham, we are spiritually blessed; after all, Christ is the ultimate seed of Abraham. Thus, we are all the children of Abraham by faith in Christ Jesus (Galatians 3:26, 29).

But Moody's point is important for us today: God sovereignly called Abraham, but Abraham proved his calling by his obedience, even willing to slay his precious son, Isaac. God calls us, but we are expected to prove our calling through our surrender and obedience.

Let us ask God to show us what that obedience means for us today.

PRAYER

Father, You have called me. Let me rejoice in that calling
and grant me the strength to prove that calling in all I do today.

FAITH FOR A FRIEND

And when they could not get near him because of the crowd, they removed the roof above him, and when they had made an opening, they let down the bed on which the paralytic lay.

MARK 2:4

D. L. MOODY

These four friends were terribly in earnest.

They let the bed on which the man was lying, down into the room. They laid their friend right at the feet of Jesus Christ; a good place to lay him, was it not?

Perhaps you have a skeptical son or an unbelieving husband, or some other member of your family, that scoffs at the Bible and sneers at Christianity. Lay them at the feet of Jesus, and He will honor your faith.

ERWIN LUTZER

Jesus was always using His miracles as a teaching opportunity. He always illustrated something other than the physical healing, and that is clearly seen in this passage. We read, "And when Jesus saw their faith, he said to the paralytic, 'Son, your sins are forgiven'" (Mark 2:5). Jesus used the occasion not just for a physical healing, but also a spiritual healing of forgiveness. Notice in verse 6, it was evidently the faith of his friends that prompted Jesus to respond to this man's need. There are those among us who are distracted, skeptical, and often bound by sin. In a sense, we have to believe for them as well as ourselves. Yes, we have to go to Jesus on behalf of others, and we should have the determination of these four men who spared no effort to get their friend to Him.

Let me emphasize that we need to think of ways to share the good news of the gospel with others; we need to help those bound by the paralysis of sin to see that there is someone who can set them free. Let us intercede for them, befriend them, and be willing to expend effort to lead them to Jesus.

We all know someone we can help get to Jesus.

PRAYER

Father, for the sake of Your glory, bring to mind those I must help come to Jesus through my efforts, my witness, and my love.

OTHERWORLDLY REST

Vanity of vanities, says the Preacher; all is vanity.
ECCLESIASTES 12:8

D. L. MOODY

The worship of pleasure is slavery. (Solomon tried pleasure and found bitter disappointment, and down the ages has come the bitter cry, "All is vanity.")

There is no rest in sin. The wicked know nothing about rest. The Scriptures tell us the wicked "are like the troubled sea, when it cannot rest" (Isaiah 57:20). Man, like the sea, has no rest. He has had no rest since Adam fell, and there is none for him until he returns to God again, and the light of Christ shines into his heart.

Rest cannot be found in the world but, thank God, the world cannot take it from the believing heart! Sin is the cause of all this unrest. It brought toil and labor and misery into the world.

ERWIN LUTZER

Think of how revolutionary it was when Jesus cried out to all who would listen, "Come to me, all who labor and are heavy laden, and I will give you rest . . . you will find rest for your souls" (Matthew 11:28–29). Imagine the authority of Jesus—who else could make such a promise?

In the book of Hebrews, the author challenges his readers to ask whether they have actually entered into rest (Hebrews 4:1–4). In the next verses, he uses the Israelites who died in the wilderness as an example of those who refused to enter into the rest (which is described as the land of Canaan). And then the author continues by pointing out how Christ is our rest.

Like I mentioned in a previous entry, whenever I hear of a Christian who has died, I extend comfort to the bereaved by quoting Revelation 14:13, "'Blessed are the dead who die in the Lord from now on.' 'Blessed indeed,' says the Spirit, 'that they may rest from their labors, for their deeds follow them!'"

The ultimate rest is the everlasting rest of all the saints. Rest indeed!

PRAYER

Father, help me to cease striving with You; let me rest in the Lord.

COUNTERFEIT BLESSINGS

Or do you not know that the unrighteous will not inherit the kingdom of God? Do not be deceived: neither the sexually immoral, nor idolaters, nor adulterers, nor men who practice homosexuality, nor thieves, nor the greedy, nor drunkards, nor revilers, nor swindlers will inherit the kingdom of God.

1 CORINTHIANS 6:9–10

D. L. MOODY

Notice that the covetous are named between thieves and drunkards. We lock up thieves and have no mercy on them. We loathe drunkards, and consider them great sinners against the law of God as well as the law of the land. Yet there is far more said in the Bible against covetousness than against either stealing or drunkenness.

ERWIN LUTZER

In the Bible, money is always presented as the most seductive competitor for our hearts. It competes with God for our loyalty, commitment, and security. Money makes all of the same promises that God does. Money says, "I will be with you during hard times. I'll be there when you are sick and when you are well; I'll be there to feed you, to clothe you, to give you an inheritance so you can have a wonderful retirement."

Yet, as Moody said, because covetousness is primarily an internal matter of the heart, there are no penalties against it. It's easy for this particular sin to grow in our hearts without us detecting it. There is only one way to overcome it: be a generous giver (2 Corinthians 9:7). We should be generous because Christ has been merciful and generous to forgive us, to make us heirs of God and joint heirs with Himself. After all, it is not our money, we are only stewards of what God gave us.

PRAYER

Father, help me to acknowledge that all I have belongs to You.
May I hold all that I have in an open generous hand, asking You to root covetousness from my heart.

DISCIPLES MAKE DISCIPLES

And after the meeting of the synagogue broke up, many Jews and devout converts to Judaism followed Paul and Barnabas, who, as they spoke with them, urged them to continue in the grace of God.

ACTS 13:43

D. L. MOODY

How much would Paul and Barnabas have accomplished if they had pronounced the benediction and sent these people home? It is a thing to weep over that we have got thousands and thousands of church members who are good for nothing toward extending the kingdom of God. They understand markets, and fairs, and sewing circles; but when you ask them to sit down and show a man or woman the way into God's kingdom, they say: "Oh, I am not able to do that. Let the deacons do it, or someone else."

It is all wrong. The church ought to be educated on this very point. There are a great many church members who are just hobbling about on crutches. They can just make out that they are saved, and imagine that is all that constitutes a Christian. As far as helping others is concerned, that never enters their heads. They think if they can get along themselves, they are doing amazingly well. They have no idea what the Holy Ghost wants to do through them.

ERWIN LUTZER

In days gone by, Christians would bring their unbelieving friends to church hoping they would hear the gospel and be saved. But a large segment of today's population is skeptical about the church and would never attend. We must realize that we have the personal responsibility of building bridges and witnessing to their need for faith in Christ. Moody would say to us, "Today, begin to seek the lost."

PRAYER

Father, bring to mind unbelievers, neighbors, friends, and relatives.
May I take seriously Your command to help the lost find their way.

AUGUST 7

DESPERATE FOR GRACE

"On that day many will say to me, 'Lord, Lord, did we not prophesy in your name, and cast out demons in your name, and do many mighty works in your name?' And then will I declare to them, 'I never knew you; depart from me, you workers of lawlessness.'"

MATTHEW 7:22–23

D. L. MOODY

It has been said that there will be three things which will surprise us when we get to heaven—one, to find many whom we did not expect to find there; another, to find some not there whom we had expected; a third, and perhaps the greatest wonder, to find ourselves there!

ERWIN LUTZER

"I was capable of anything. I had not the least fear of God before my eyes . . . I not only sinned with a high hand myself, but made it my study to tempt and seduce others."[20] Those are the words of John Newton, an atheist who, after surviving a great storm at sea, came to faith in Christ and would later write the words to the hymn "Amazing Grace."

The way in which you perceive yourself will depend on the way in which you view grace. The better you think yourself to be, the less grace you think you need. But the Bible tells us that we were all dead in our trespasses and sins (Ephesians 2:1). We've all met people who live a decent, moral life, but they are not saved; they will not be in heaven because they think they do not need much grace. But when God reveals their sin to them and their desperate need for grace, they then can believe the gospel and be saved.

I think Moody's point is that we often cannot tell who is saved and who is not. When Jesus told the disciples that one of them would betray Him, despite three years together, the disciples didn't know it was Judas because he had played the game so well. They asked the question all of us should ask: "Is it I?"

So I ask, "Is it you?"

PRAYER

Father, search my heart, let me examine myself.
Reveal to me the true state of my heart.

PRESIDENT OF MY HEART

"The wind blows where it wishes, and you hear its sound, but you do not know where it comes from or where it goes. So it is with everyone who is born of the Spirit."

JOHN 3:8

D. L. MOODY

You might just as well tell me there is no such thing as wind, as tell me there is no such thing as a man being born of the Spirit. I have felt the Spirit of God working in my heart just as really and as truly as I have felt the wind blowing in my face. I cannot reason it out. There are a great many things I cannot reason out, but which I believe. I never could reason out the creation. I can see the world, but I cannot tell how God made it out of nothing. But every man will admit there was a creative power.

ERWIN LUTZER

Moody is emphasizing that the Holy Spirit not only regenerates us, but also "bears witness with our spirit that we are children of God" (Romans 8:16). The Scripture makes it very clear that, if you are a believer in Jesus, God resides within you by the Holy Spirit. And He is going to birth holiness within us; He's there to prompt us toward holiness and put us on a different trajectory. The Spirit has been given not just to be resident, but to be president and lead us all the way to our heavenly home.

Jesus described the gift of the Spirit as one who is a comforter, an advocate, a helper (John 14:16, 26). In His body, Jesus could only be in one place at one time but, by His Spirit, He can be with us and in us, regardless of where we are geographically. All believers are united in one body, and this unity should be displayed for the world to see.

Confusion about the work of the Spirit has often made believers wary of the work of the Spirit in our lives. But let us develop a relationship with this Friend that Jesus promised to all who believe. May we know the Spirit, enjoy the Spirit, and depend upon the Spirit for all things.

PRAYER

Father, today, I pray that the Holy Spirit will transform me and give me assurance.

AWAKE AND BRIGHT

"Awake, O sleeper, and arise from the dead, and Christ will shine on you."
EPHESIANS 5:14

D. L. MOODY

If the lost are to be reached by the gospel of the Son of God, Christianity must be more aggressive than it has been in the past. We have been on the defensive long enough; the time has come for us to enter on a war of aggression. When we as children of God wake up and go to work in the vineyard, then those who are living in wickedness all about us will be reached; but not in any other way. You may go to mass meetings and discuss the question: "How to reach the masses," but when you have done with discussion, you have to go back to personal effort. Every man and woman who loves the Lord Jesus Christ must wake up to the fact that he or she has a mission in the world, in this work of reaching the lost.

ERWIN LUTZER

I find it refreshing that Moody, who spoke to crowds of thousands of people without a microphone, would say what all of us know: The best method of evangelism is personal evangelism. One-on-one relationships are most often used to build bridges for the gospel. Mass evangelism has its place, but it should never be a substitute for friendship, interaction, and a sacrificial commitment to the needs of others. It is not just words, but deeds and personal credibility.

Remember, the unconverted are walking in darkness but think they're walking in light. The gospel shows us who we really are, just like sunlight which illuminates reality. Everything exposed by the light becomes visible for it is light that makes everything visible.

As believers, we should walk in the light of God's truth not only for ourselves, but to witness to others. Jesus spoke of letting our lights shine so that others might see our good works (Matthew 5:16). That cannot be done very well in a mass meeting. It always comes down to individual relationships.

PRAYER

Father, I ask that my light may shine brightly. Let me make connections and form relationships that will have eternal consequences.

TIME TO LIVE

Jesus said, "Leave her alone, so that she may keep it for the day of my burial."

JOHN 12:7

D. L. MOODY

I can imagine Mary thought that if she waited until Jesus was dead she might not have a chance to anoint His body, and so she came before His death to anoint Him. There is a lesson there. How very kind and thoughtful we are to a family that has lost some member, and what kind words are said after the person is dead and gone! Would it not be better to say a few of those good things before they go? Wouldn't it be well to give some of your bouquets before a man dies, and not go and load down his coffin?

ERWIN LUTZER

You might be surprised how difficult it is for people to commend their family and friends while they are alive. It might be due to unacknowledged resentment, feeling that no one has given us words of support and praise. One of the saddest stories I heard was of a father whose son died. At the funeral, the father put a note in his dead son's hand that read simply, "I love you." I wonder how many times the father said that to his son when he was alive?

As Moody pointed out, Mary, at great personal cost, expressed her love for Christ while He was alive, that is, before His crucifixion. Thankfully, we can express our love for Him even now since He was raised from the dead and is in heaven today. In fact, bow your head and do that right now. And then ask God to bring someone to mind today that you can bless with a word of appreciation and encouragement. Don't wait until they die.

Let me, like Mary, through the gloom, Come with a gift to Thee;
Show to me now the empty tomb, Lead me to Calvary.[21]

PRAYER

Father, I love You, but I do long to love You more.
Increase my love for You and others.

STANDING IN EXILE

But Daniel resolved that he would not defile himself with the king's food, or with the wine that he drank. Therefore he asked the chief of the eunuchs to allow him not to defile himself.

DANIEL 1:8

D. L. MOODY

I can imagine men saying to Daniel, "Look here, young man, you are too puritanical. Don't be too particular; don't have so many religious scruples. Bear in mind you are not now in Jerusalem. You will have to get over these notions here in Babylon. You are not now surrounded by friends and relatives. You are not a Jerusalem prince now. You have been brought down from your high position. You are now a captive. And if the monarch hears about your refusing to eat the same kind of meat he eats, and to drink the same kind of wine he drinks, your head will soon roll from off your shoulders. You had better be a little politically acceptable." But this young man had piety and religion deep down in his heart; and that is the right place for it; where it will grow; where it will have power; where it will regulate the life. Daniel had not joined the company of the faithful few in Jerusalem because he wanted to get into "society," and attain a position, it was because of the love he had toward the Lord God of Israel.

ERWIN LUTZER

As exiles, the Jews in Babylon reflect us, the church, living in today's world. And as such, we must learn from men like Daniel and his friends how to be *in* a culture, but not *of* the culture. They had a price to pay for faithfulness; we also must be willing to pay the price of faithfulness. Daniel continued to pray with his window open even though he was threatened with the lion's den.

Sometimes we find ourselves in difficult circumstances threatening to divert our allegiance away from Christ. In those moments, we need to emulate Daniel.

PRAYER

Lord, fortify my resolve to stand strong for You, no matter the outcome.

ACKNOWLEDGING THE DIVINE PRESENCE

Then Jacob awoke from his sleep and said, "Surely the LORD is in this place, and I did not know it." And he was afraid and said, "How awesome is this place! This is none other than the house of God, and this is the gate of heaven."

GENESIS 28:16–17

D. L. MOODY

When people come into the house of God, they put on a sober appearance. They act as if there was something very strange about the house of God. I would not say a word to detract from the holiness of the house of God. But let us bear in mind that every place ought to be holy to a child of God; in every place we ought to be true to God. We ought to be as true to Him in our place of business as we are in the church. When Jacob said, "This is the house of God, and this is the gate of heaven," he was under the canopy of high heaven. That was where God met him; but God will meet us in the street as well as in the place of worship. He will meet us at home. He is also with us in our closets.

Every place is holy because God is there. Putting on another air and a sanctimonious look when we come into the house of God, and laying it aside when we go out, thinking that this is going to be acceptable to God, is all wrong. Every place ought to be holy to a true child of God.

ERWIN LUTZER

God says, "You shall be holy, for I am holy" (1 Peter 1:16). But this is not just a "sanctimonious look," as Moody described it. To be holy is to be set apart. The Bible says, "For if you live according to the flesh you will die, but if by the Spirit you put to death the deeds of the body, you will live" (Romans 8:13). You have to kill sin or sin will kill you.

The fact that God is present everywhere should be a deterrent for willful sin. As Jacob learned, even the wilderness is "the gate of heaven" (Genesis 28:17). What is revival? It is the manifest presence of God among His people.

PRAYER

Father, like Jacob, make me to be aware of Your presence.
May I remember You are with me as You were with him.

ARE WE THERE YET?

But, as it is written, "What no eye has seen, nor ear heard, nor the heart of man imagined, what God has prepared for those who love him"—these things God has revealed to us through the Spirit. For the Spirit searches everything, even the depths of God.

1 CORINTHIANS 2:9–10

D. L. MOODY

It is said by travelers that in climbing the Alps, the houses of far distant villages can be seen with great distinctness, so that sometimes the number of panes of glass in a church window can be counted. The distance looks so short that the place to which the traveler is journeying appears almost at hand, but after hours and hours of climbing, it seems no nearer. This is because of the clearness of the atmosphere. By perseverance, however, the place is reached at last and the tired traveler finds rest.

So sometimes we dwell in high altitudes of grace; heaven seems very near, and the hills of Beulah are in full view. At other times, the clouds and fogs caused by suffering and sin cut off our sight. We are just as near heaven in the one case as we are in the other, and we are just as sure of gaining it if we but keep in the path that Christ has pointed out.

ERWIN LUTZER

Moody's devotional blesses all of us. It's true that the eye of faith cannot see heavenly realities. As Paul said, we are unable to comprehend the glories that await us (Romans 8:18). And sometimes, because of the darkness of despair, the spiritual battles we face, and the pressures of life, we forget about the certainty of the future and think only of the present.

The Holy Spirit is a pledge that there is more to follow. Today we have the shadow, but the true substance is coming. As someone has said, today we get the flower, but someday we will get the garden—our eternal home.

Are you physically burdened today? Remember a new body and a new home are on their way!

PRAYER

Father, help me embrace the future awaiting me.
Guide me to live for eternity, not for today.

THE "MEASLY" 300

And the LORD said to Gideon, "With the 300 men who lapped I will save you and give the Midianites into your hand, and let all the others go every man to his home."
JUDGES 7:7

D. L. MOODY

It would be a good thing for the church of God if all the fearful and faithless ones were to step to the rear, and let those who are full of faith and courage take their empty pitchers and go forward against the enemy. The little band of three hundred men who were left with Gideon routed the Midianites, but it was not their own might that gave them the victory. It was "the sword of the LORD, and of Gideon" (Judges 7:18). If we go on in the name of the Lord, and trusting to His might, we shall succeed.

ERWIN LUTZER

What kind of a person does God use? Consider: Gideon was outnumbered four hundred and fifty to one! A person of faith, not fear. A person of focus, not carelessness!

You can't be too small for God to use. God delights in taking that which is despised, small, and unassuming, and using our weaknesses for His glory. Often it is not a matter of giftedness or talent that He honors; He honors humility. Though you can't be too small for God to use, you can be too big. The Scripture says God is able to save by many or by few (1 Samuel 14:6). Let us never forget that the battle is the Lord's!

God uses imperfect and weak saints who never forget that the battle is the Lord's! Apply that to your personal battle today!

PRAYER

Father, today, I transfer the weight of my personal battle to Your shoulders.

THE FRUIT OF JOY

"These things I have spoken to you, that my joy may be in you, and that your joy may be full."
JOHN 15:11

D. L. MOODY

People should look for joy in the Word, and not in the world. They should look for the joy, which the Scriptures furnish, and then go to work in the vineyard, because a joy that doesn't send me out to someone else, a joy that doesn't impel me to go and help the poor drunkard, a joy that doesn't prompt me to visit the widow and the fatherless, a joy that doesn't cause me to go into the Mission Sunday school or other Christian work, is not worth having, and is not from above. A joy that does not constrain me to go and work for the Master is purely sentiment and not real joy.

ERWIN LUTZER

People are able to fake love, peace, and patience, but they cannot fake joy. Joy is the one fruit of the spirit that cannot be superficially duplicated by the unconverted; it's not a matter of positive thinking. In fact, Jesus explains, "Whoever abides in me and I in him, he it is that bears much fruit, for apart from me you can do nothing" (John 15:5). Then later He adds these marvelous words in verse 11, "These things I have spoken to you, that my joy may be in you, and that your joy may be full." The bottom line: You cannot please Christ without being a fruit-bearing Christian, and if you are bearing fruit, you should do so with the divine gift of joy. To abide in Christ is to live with a clear conscience with daily and hourly dependence on Him. All of us have many different tasks and challenges each day but if, in the morning, we spend time in God's presence in full fellowship and obedience, we will exhibit the fruit of the Spirit, including joy.

No one alive today personally knew D. L. Moody, but those who worked with him described him as full of vigor, passion, and unbounded joy. Let us follow his example.

PRAYER

Father, may Your gift of joy overflow in my service for others.

SUPERNATURAL WITNESS

"But you will receive power when the Holy Spirit has come upon you, and you will be my witnesses in Jerusalem and in all Judea and Samaria, and to the end of the earth."

ACTS 1:8

D. L. MOODY

If these early Christians had gone out and commenced preaching then and there without the promised power, do you think that scene would have taken place on the day of Pentecost? Peter would have stood up and beat against the air, while the Jews would have gnashed their teeth and mocked him. But they tarried in Jerusalem; they waited ten days.

"What!" you say, "with the world perishing and men dying! Shall I wait?"

Do what God tells you. There is no use in running before you are sent; there is no use in attempting to do God's work without God's power. A man working without this unction, a man working without this anointing, a man working without the Holy Ghost upon him is losing time after all. We shall not lose anything if we tarry till we get this power.

ERWIN LUTZER

Why do we need the Holy Spirit to share the gospel's power? We face two obstacles: First, the human heart resists the gospel's exposure of sin and its call to trust Christ as Savior. Second, Satan blinds minds, distracts thoughts, and hardens hearts. Only God's power overcomes these!

But we do not have to wait for the power of the Holy Spirit in the same way the disciples did. The coming of the Spirit at Pentecost ushered in the new era of the church, and after that event, all believers everywhere are indwelt with the Holy Spirit. But we do have to wait before the Lord in repentance and faith so that we experience the filling of the Holy Spirit. Only then can we have an effective witness for the gospel.

PRAYER

Father, help me to take time today to seek You for the filling of the Holy Spirit.

DISCERNING FALSEHOOD

"To the teaching and to the testimony! If they will not speak according to this word, it is because they have no dawn."
ISAIAH 8:20

D. L. MOODY

Any man or any woman who comes to us with any doctrine that is not according to the law and the testimony, let us understand that they are from the evil one and are enemies of righteousness. They have no light in them. You will find those people who are consulting familiar spirits from the first to the last, attacking the Word of God. They don't believe it. If it was a message from God, do you think you would have to go into a dark room and put out all the lights? God is not in that movement, and we want, as children of God, to keep ourselves from this evil.

ERWIN LUTZER

The occultism of today is usually more hidden and subtle than in Moody's time. The New Age movement, which exists under many different names and different practices, uses the same basic message: You are your own god and have the power to access other powers in the spirit world. There is no need for repentance of sin or a change of lifestyle. Your problem is not sin, it's ignorance. If you learn how to control "the powers," you will achieve greatness.

The Bible condemns this in all of its forms.

Today, discernment is more important than ever. We cannot simply imbibe false teaching, no matter its source. The Bible alone is the basis for all we need to know about our relationship with God, angels, demons, and eternal matters. False teachers who claim direct communication from God by saying, "The Lord said to me . . ." must be shunned.

God takes His revelation seriously. It is so much better to be divided by truth than to be united in error.

PRAYER

Father, I ask that You'll make me a discerning Christian
in an age with so much confusion.

SPIRITUAL SURGERY

Nathanael said to him, "Can anything good come out of Nazareth?" Philip said to him, "Come and see."

JOHN 1:46

D. L. MOODY

After all, we do not gain much by discussion. Let objectors or inquirers only get one personal interview with the Son of God, and that will scatter all their darkness, all their prejudice, and all their unbelief. The moment that Philip succeeded in getting Nathanael to Christ, the work was done.

ERWIN LUTZER

My brothers and sisters, when the Holy Spirit of God does His work to show us our sin and our need of Christ, it is a great work. According to the Bible, you cannot believe without the action and direct intervention of the Holy Spirit because it isn't just an intellectual issue, it is a heart issue. Even when everything within us says, "No, no, no," God has to overcome that resistance through the action of the Holy Spirit (see John 16:8–10; 1 Corinthians 2:10–13).

Jesus said the Holy Spirit of God would convict a person of their sin, but notice also the one standard given: the standard of righteousness. The Bible says there are two different kinds of righteousness. There is the righteousness of man and the righteousness of God—and what a difference there is between the two. God uses His Word and usually brings that Word through one of His people. The Spirit comes to you. Through you, He will convict the world of sin and righteousness and judgment. And so the gift of the Spirit is poured out upon the church, not just for ourselves, but for the benefit of the wider community that needs to know the good news of the gospel, and believe, and be saved.

PRAYER

Father, I pray that You might overcome everything that would keep others from You.

AUGUST 19

BROUGHT INTO LIGHT

Jesus answered him, "Truly, truly, I say to you, unless one is born again he cannot see the kingdom of God."

JOHN 3:3

D. L. MOODY

You can look abroad and see many beautiful trees, but the tree of life you shall never behold unless your eyes are made clear by faith in the Saviour. You may see the beautiful rivers of the earth, you may ride upon their bosoms, but bear in mind, your eye will never rest upon the river which bursts out from the throne of God and flows through the upper kingdom unless you are born again. You may see the kings and lords of the earth, but the King of kings and Lord of lords you will never see except you are born again. When you are in London, you may go to the Tower and see the crown of England, which is worth thousands of dollars and is guarded by soldiers; but bear in mind, your eye will never rest upon the crown of life except you are born again.

It is God who says it. You may see ten thousand beautiful things in this world, but the city that Abraham caught a glimpse of and, from that time, became a pilgrim and sojourner—you shall never see unless you are born again (Hebrews 11:8, 10–16). You may often be invited to marriage feasts here, but you will never attend the marriage supper of the Lamb except you are born again. It is God who says it.

ERWIN LUTZER

Reread Moody's devotional above. His sermons had a sense of immediacy and imagination capturing the experiences of life interwoven with the gospel. Everyone can identify with the images he uses to help us understand that if we want to look beyond this world, we must be born again. This new birth is a birth from above; it refers to the work of the Holy Spirit giving us transformed desires and a new identity. This comes about by repentance and faith.

PRAYER

Father, thank You for the birth from above;
I affirm this miracle through faith in Christ.

FIGHT THE DEVIL WITH THE BIBLE

Therefore let anyone who thinks that he stands take heed lest he fall.
1 CORINTHIANS 10:12

D. L. MOODY

Twenty-five years ago—and for the first five years after I was converted—I used to think that if I were able to stand for twenty years, I need fear no fall. But the nearer you get to the cross, the fiercer the battle. Satan aims high. He went amongst the twelve and singled out the treasurer, Judas Iscariot, and the chief apostle, Peter.

Most men who have fallen have done so on the strongest side of their character. I am told the only side upon which Edinburgh Castle was successfully assailed was where the rocks were steepest and where the garrison thought themselves secure. If any man thinks he is strong enough to resist the evil at any one point, he needs special watch there, for the tempter comes that way.

ERWIN LUTZER

What do you do when you want to kill a bear? You use a trap with bait. You let the trap and the bait do your work. Satan has as many lures as we have interests, and he concentrates on where we are most vulnerable. Behind the trap is the trapper, and behind the lie is the liar. The moment we no longer fear sin, we are vulnerable; we wrongly think we can handle temptation, and it's at that moment when falling into deep sin is almost inevitable. One concession to sin leads to another and then another. The history of the church is strewn with the wreckage of men and women whose testimony was destroyed through toying with temptation.

The devil's purpose in temptation always is to draw us away from God. The way we resist temptation is the same way Jesus did, by the power of God's Word (Matthew 4:1–11). When we know and submit to God's Word, we can resist temptation. If you are not reading your Bible regularly and memorizing the Word of God, you are not going to be ready for the devil when he comes.

PRAYER

Father, I rebuke the devil's wiles.
Help me submit to Your Word and walk in Christ's victory.

AUGUST 21

LITTLE DISCIPLES

And they were bringing children to him that he might touch them, and the disciples rebuked them.

MARK 10:13

D. L. MOODY

I have no sympathy with the idea that our children have to grow up before they are converted. Once I saw a lady with three daughters at her side, and I stepped up to her and asked her if she was a Christian. "Yes, sir." Then I asked the oldest daughter if she was a Christian. Her chin began to quiver and tears came into her eyes and she said: "I wish I was." The mother looked very angrily at me and said, "I don't want you to speak to my children on that subject. They don't understand." And in great rage she took them away from me. One daughter was fourteen years old, one twelve, and the other ten, but they were not old enough to be talked to about religion! Let them drift into the world and plunge into worldly amusements and then see how hard it is to reach them. Many a mother is mourning today because her boy has gone beyond her reach. In those early days when his mind was tender and young, she might have led him to Christ.

ERWIN LUTZER

Yes, young children can understand enough of the gospel message to be saved. Yet we should never presume a child has savingly believed on Jesus just because they prayed a prayer. Let the Holy Spirit and the Word of God grant them assurance. We have the responsibility of sharing the gospel with them, but God has to do the saving.

As children grow older, they may doubt their salvation. If so, ask them to make their salvation a present reality. Let them affirm their faith in Christ by understanding repentance and sincerely accepting the gift of salvation.

Let us trust God for the miracle of our children's salvation, bringing them up in the "discipline and instruction of the Lord" (Ephesians 6:4).

PRAYER

Jesus, thank You for welcoming little children.
Give me the faith of a little child.

THE CURE WE NEED

"Behold, all souls are mine; the soul of the father as well as the soul of the son is mine: the soul who sins shall die."
EZEKIEL 18:4

D. L. MOODY

Suppose there was a law that man should not steal, but no penalty was attached to stealing; some man would have my pocketbook before the day was over. If I threatened to have him arrested, he would snap his fingers in my face. He would not fear the law if there was no penalty. It is not the law that people are afraid of, it is the penalty for transgression.

Do not suppose God has made a law without a penalty. What an absurd thing it would be! The penalty for sin is death: "The soul that sinneth, it shall die" (Ezekiel 18:20). If I have sinned, I must die or get somebody to die for me. If the Bible doesn't teach that, it doesn't teach anything. And that is where the atonement of Jesus Christ comes in.

ERWIN LUTZER

The Black Death killed many millions of people in the 1300s. But there is another epidemic in the human race. Everyone has caught it and, in every instance, it leads to death. I am referring to the poison of sin, which has infected the human race with a plague.

Interestingly, if you read a biography of D. L. Moody, you would discover he feared death as a young man but, as he grew older, he feared it no more. He learned that physical death is the natural consequence of our sin, but spiritually, we go on living. For believers, our eternal life will be in the presence of God. Just as we are punished for Adam's sin, we get credited with the righteousness of Jesus Christ—if we trust in Him. And, because He lives, we shall also live (John 14:19).

Let us honestly confront our own mortality; let us live for the reality of eternity, not just for the moment. We are not promised that the path to our death will be smooth, but thanks to Christ, we are promised a safe landing.

PRAYER

Father, thank You for Jesus, and that in Him, death has lost its sting.
Wean me from earthly values and may I seek that which is above.

AUGUST 23

PERSECUTION IS COMING

"I have said all these things to you to keep you from falling away. They will put you out of the synagogues. Indeed, the hour is coming when whoever kills you will think he is offering service to God."

JOHN 16:1–2

D. L. MOODY

A man said to me some time ago: "Mr. Moody, now that I am converted, have I to give up the world?"

"No," said I, "you haven't to give up the world. If you give a good ringing testimony for the Son of God, the world will give you up pretty quick; they won't want you."

ERWIN LUTZER

When Moody used the word world he was talking about the world of people, not the world system John warned about (1 John 2:15–17). But yes, all who live for Christ will be despised by at least some people in the world, and perhaps even suffer for our faith. There is suffering that comes to us because of the fallenness of this world: sickness, heartache, broken relationships, or poverty. But there's another kind of suffering that comes because we bear the name of Jesus.

Some Christians have decided to blend into the culture so that they experience no pushback because of their faith. Such Christians almost always are silent about their conversion; no one knows they are a Christ follower. But Christians are called to suffer. Jesus told His disciples that, since the world hated Him, the world will also hate them (see John 15:18). A servant is not above the master.

Philippians 1:29 says, "It has been granted to you that for the sake of Christ you should not only believe in him but also suffer for his sake." Suffering is part of our responsibility as believers. We who believe on Him should gladly suffer because of Him. Let us expect it. Anticipate it. That is our calling.

PRAYER

Father, help me to suffer well. Help me to lovingly share the gospel and receive any pushback with gratitude that I have been found worthy to suffer, even if but a little for You.

HOPEFUL, NOT HOPELESS

If in Christ we have hope in this life only, we are of all people most to be pitied.
1 CORINTHIANS 15:19

D. L. MOODY

To deny the resurrection is to say that we will never see more of the loved ones whose bodies have been committed to the clay. If Christ has not risen, this life is the only one.

How cruel it is to have anyone love you if this be true! How horrible that they should let the tendrils of your heart twine around them if, when they are torn away in death, that is to be the end! I would rather *hate* than *love* if I thought there would be no resurrection, because then I would feel no pangs at losing the hated thing. Oh, the cruelty of unbelief! It takes away our brightest hopes.

ERWIN LUTZER

I have never thought of putting it the way Moody did: If death were the end of it all, it would be best not to love the departed one, for it is love that makes the separation so difficult. Imagine, wrote Moody, if this life were the end, then hate would be better than love!

But loving those who have died is proper because we know we shall see them again. On our death bed, we need not say "goodbye." but rather, "See you later." Our love can continue and will be rekindled on the other side. And our love for Christ will be complete.

Jesus came to deliver us from hopelessness. If you are reading this and you feel hopeless, you are in the right place to receive comfort. As a believer, remember that eternity is coming and with it, the restoration of all relationships. And yes, "Our citizenship is in heaven, and from it we await a Savior, the Lord Jesus Christ, who will transform our lowly body to be like his glorious body" (Philippians 3:20–21).

For the Christian, this life is as bad as things will ever get. The best is yet to come.

PRAYER

Lord Jesus, grant me the ability to look beyond this world to the next.
May I know that my love will continue and my joy will be full.

AUGUST 25

SINCERE OBEDIENCE

And Samuel said, "Has the Lord as great delight in burnt offerings and sacrifices, as in obeying the voice of the Lord? Behold, to obey is better than sacrifice, and to listen than the fat of rams."

1 SAMUEL 15:22

D. L. MOODY

Did you ever notice all but the heart of man obeys God? If you look through history, you will find that this is true. In the beginning God said, "Let there be light," and there was light. "Let the waters bring forth," and the water brought forth abundantly. And one of the proofs that Jesus Christ is God is that He spoke to nature, and nature obeyed Him. At one time He spoke to the sea, and the sea recognized and obeyed. He spoke to the fig tree, and instantly it withered and died, it obeyed literally and at once. He spoke to devils, and the devils fled. He spoke to the grave, and the grave obeyed Him and gave back its dead. But when He speaks to man, man will not obey Him. That is why man is out of harmony with God, and it will never be different until men learn to obey God. God wants obedience, and He will have it, else there can be no harmony.

ERWIN LUTZER

Yes, we all disobey God. It's like the little boy whose mother told him to sit in the corner because he was being naughty. And he said, "Okay, I'm sitting down, but in my heart, I'm still standing up." You can educate somebody's mind, but that does not change their heart.

What does the New Testament say? By nature, we are dead in our sins, but God intervenes and gives us the desire and ability to come to Christ, and when we do, we become partakers of the divine nature. "If anyone is in Christ, he is a new creation" (2 Corinthians 5:17). Figuratively speaking, God takes our heart of stone and replaces it with a heart of flesh.

Today, look to Christ as the One whose obedience gives us the right to call God, *Father*.

PRAYER

Father, help me love Your law, which led me to Christ.
Help me live in sincere obedience.

RENOUNCE FEAR

In God I trust; I shall not be afraid. What can man do to me?
PSALM 56:11

D. L. MOODY

If God has hid me in the secret pavilion, let men slander me and abuse me if they like! If I can say that God is my Father, Jesus is my Saviour, and heaven is my home, let the world rail, let the flesh do what it pleases, I will not be afraid of evil tidings, for my trust is in God! Is not that a good footing for eternity? "Heaven and earth shall pass away, but my words shall not pass away" (Matthew 24:35).

ERWIN LUTZER

The following is an excerpt of a prayer I have sometimes invited others to join me in praying to banish fear. When our lives are threatened, when our future is ominous and tragedy strikes, fear can grip our hearts. Read these words as an expression of your own heart and mind as we approach God based on His promises.

I reject the fear of the future, for I believe that the future is in God's hands. I reject the fear of evildoers, for God's Word says, "Though an army encamp against me, my heart shall not fear" (Psalm 27:3). I renounce the fear of Satan, for God's Word says he has already been conquered "by the blood of the Lamb and the word of their testimony" (Revelation 12:11). I renounce the fear of death, for I affirm with the apostle Paul, "For to me to live is Christ, and to die is gain" (Philippians 1:21). Therefore, I choose to fear you more than I do any human being. I affirm, "The Lord is on my side; I will not fear. What can man do to me?" (Psalm 118:6–8).

Fear comes into our lives uninvited and at unexpected times. When it returns, refresh your mind by rereading the above words and adding other promises of Scripture.

PRAYER

Father, as I dwell on Your promises, give me the gift of peace
Jesus promised His disciples.

IDOL FACTORY

"That they should seek God, and perhaps feel their way toward him and find him. Yet he is actually not far from each one of us."
ACTS 17:27

D. L. MOODY

Philosophers are agreed that even the most primitive races of mankind reach out beyond the world of matter to a superior being. It is as natural for man to feel after God as it is for the ivy to feel after support. Hunger and thirst drive him to seek for food, and there is a hunger of the soul that needs satisfying, too. Man does not need to be commanded to worship, as there is not a race so high or so low in the scale of civilization but has some kind of a god. What man needs is to be directed aright in his worship.

ERWIN LUTZER

Most people don't abandon God, they refashion Him according to their liking. Every time we want to disobey, every time we want to manipulate, every time we want our own way, we reconstruct God to fit our desires. You're an idol lover, I'm an idol lover, and our default response is to fashion a god according to our liking.

Any god that we construct, any god that we want, wants us to bow down and it will, eventually, own us. Our self-made god wants complete total ownership of our lives. We have the illusion that we are free, but we are owned by whatever god we choose, and we worship at its shrine. Knowing who we should crown number One is really the most basic issue of life.

Let us bow to worship the one and only true God, "And this is eternal life, that they know you, the only true God, and Jesus Christ whom you have sent" (John 17:3). It is Jesus we proclaim to the nations (Acts 17:16–31).

PRAYER

Father, thank You for drawing me to Yourself to worship in spirit and truth.

AUGUST 28

GOD LOOKS AT ME AND SEES JESUS

When he calls to me, I will answer him.

PSALM 91:15

D. L. MOODY

Listen to the prodigal, "Father, I have sinned" (Luke 15:21). That was enough; the father took him right to his bosom. The past was blotted out at once.

Look at the men on the day of Pentecost. Their hands were dripping with the blood of the Son of God; they had murdered Jesus Christ. And what did Peter say to them? "It shall come to pass, that whosoever shall call on the name of the Lord shall be saved" (Acts 2:21).

Look at the penitent thief. Perhaps, as a boy, his mother taught him that passage in Joel, "It shall come to pass, that whosoever shall call on the name of the LORD shall be delivered" (Joel 2:32). As he hung there on the cross, it flashed into his mind that this was the Lord of glory, and though he was on the very borders of hell, he cried out, "Lord, remember me," and the answer came right then and there, "Today shalt thou be with me in paradise" (Luke 23:42–43). In the morning, as black as hell could make him; in the evening, not a spot or wrinkle. Why? Because he took God at His word. Why will men doubt Him?

ERWIN LUTZER

There is one prayer in which you'll receive an instant answer, without waiting: Moody quoted it, "Whosoever shall call on the name of the LORD shall be saved."

Twenty-four hours a day, God demands perfection from me if I'm going to be His child and fellowship with Him. Twenty-four hours a day, Jesus Christ supplies what God demands. Are we perfect in experience? No. There are days when I don't feel very spiritual. We face illnesses, migraines, depression, and temptations. God knows when we fall into sin. Yet because of Christ's substitution, God has declared us to be as perfect as Christ and is making us complete in Him.

PRAYER

Father, thank You for Your invitation to trust Christ.
May many take advantage of that gift today.

STEP OUT IN FAITH

Then he touched their eyes, saying, "According to your faith let it be done to you."
MATTHEW 9:29

D. L. MOODY

I remember a man telling me he preached for a number of years without any result. He used to say to his wife as they went to church, that he knew the people would not believe anything he said; and there was no blessing. At last, he saw his error; he asked God to help him and took courage, and then the blessing came.

"According to your faith be it unto you." This man had expected nothing, and he got just what he expected. Let us expect that God is going to use us. Let us have courage and go forward, looking to God to do great things.

ERWIN LUTZER

Sometimes we are puzzled by the promises of the New Testament. We might think God has over-promised, after all we read, "And this is the confidence that we have toward him, that if we ask anything according to his will he hears us. And if we know that he hears us in whatever we ask, we know that we have the requests that we have asked of him" (1 John 5: 14–15). We are tempted to become cynical because we often don't see our requests answered.

But are these and similar passages a *carte blanche* promise to ask for anything and get it? No. Even here we see a limitation: We are heard because we ask according to His will. We know God's sovereign will reigns supreme. Think of Jesus in Gethsemane, asking to be delivered and yet willingly praying "not my will, but yours, be done" (Luke 22:42). My point: Let us not become cynical about prayer. There are plenty of promises we can insist upon in all circumstances and at all times. And let us heed the words of Moody who said that if we expect nothing, we get nothing.

PRAYER

Father, I trust You to carry Your good work to completion.

JESUS FULFILLS THE LAW

"Do not think that I have come to abolish the Law or the Prophets; I have not come to abolish them but to fulfill them. For truly, I say to you, until heaven and earth pass away, not an iota, not a dot, will pass from the Law until all is accomplished."

MATTHEW 5:17–18

D. L. MOODY

Jesus never condemned the law and the prophets, but He did condemn those who did not obey them. Because He gave new commandments it does not follow that He abolished the old. Christ's explanation of them made them all the more searching. In His Sermon on the Mount, He carried the principles of the commandments beyond the mere letter. He unfolded them and showed that they embraced more, that they are positive as well as prohibitive.

"Remember ye the law of Moses my servant, which I commanded unto him in Horeb for all Israel, with the statutes and judgments" (Malachi 4:4). Does that look as if the law of Moses was becoming obsolete?

ERWIN LUTZER

The clearest statement we have about the purpose of the law is found in the book of Galatians where it says the law was "our guardian until Christ came" (Galatians 3:24). The law is like a plumb line, showing that a wall is crooked but is unable to straighten it out. There's nothing wrong with the plumb line, it simply can't do anything more than point out how crooked the wall is.

Today, we are not under the law, we are under grace. But this doesn't give us the liberty to be lawless. We have warnings in the New Testament about using grace to justify lawlessness (Jude 1:4).

Jesus fulfilled the demands of the law for us, but we must see the law as holy, just, and good. Let us learn to walk in the Spirit and fulfill not just the letter of the law, but also the spirit of the law as Jesus emphasized on the Sermon on the Mount.

PRAYER

Jesus, thank You for fulfilling the law in perfect obedience
and for paying my debt on the cross.

PROMISED THROUGHOUT TIME

These all died in faith, not having received the things promised, but having seen them and greeted them from afar, and having acknowledged that they were strangers and exiles on the earth.

HEBREWS 11:13

D. L. MOODY

We ought in these days to have far more faith than Abel or Enoch or Abraham had. They lived before the cross. We talk about the faith of Elijah and the patriarchs and prophets, but they lived in the dim light of the past, while we are in the full blaze of Calvary and the resurrection. When we look back and think of what Christ did, how He poured out His blood that men might be saved, we ought to go forth in His strength and conquer the world. Our God is able to do great and mighty things.

ERWIN LUTZER

Adam and Eve were given the first glimpse of the gospel in Genesis 3. Eve's eventual descendant, the Lord Jesus Christ, would crush the head of the serpent, and the serpent would strike back but with a minor wound. But for the time being, when Adam and Eve found themselves feeling the sting of shame, God gave them animal skins to cover their nakedness. Right from the beginning, God wanted them to know that there was no cheap covering for sin.

From the standpoint of eternity, all of Satan's victories are illusionary; he is out on bond doing all the damage he can, but his sentence has already been pronounced. As Moody pointed out, we see this much more clearly today than did the saints in the Old Testament. They looked forward to the coming of a redeemer, but the picture was unclear. Today, "with unveiled face, we behold the glory of the Lord" (see 2 Corinthians 3:18).

The resurrection of Jesus is proof that His work on the cross was completed. If you have doubts, bring your doubts to God—He will welcome and sustain you.

PRAYER

Father, thank You for all the promises You fulfilled at the cross.
Today, I walk in Christ's victory.

BADGE OF HONOR

"For whoever is ashamed of me and of my words in this adulterous and sinful generation, of him will the Son of Man also be ashamed when he comes in the glory of his Father with the holy angels."

MARK 8:38

D. L. MOODY

I do not believe there is any false religion in the world that men are not proud of. The only religion of which I have ever heard that men were ashamed of is the religion of Jesus Christ. I preached two weeks in Salt Lake City, and I did not find a Mormon that was not proud of his religion. When, within forty miles of Salt Lake City, the engineer came into the car and wanted to know if I wouldn't like to ride on the engine. I went with him, and in that forty-mile ride he talked Mormonism to me the whole time, and tried to convert me so that I would not preach against the Mormons. But how many, many times I have found men ashamed of the gospel of Jesus Christ, the only religion that gives men the power over their affections and lusts and sins!

ERWIN LUTZER

Why would any believer be ashamed of the gospel? The answer is that other religions appeal to what we can *do*—they tell us of the blessings that come to us. Christianity teaches that God can only help those who know they *cannot* help themselves! We must see ourselves as helpless and dependent solely on the death of the God-man on a cross two thousand years ago, who was raised from the dead and later taken to heaven. We must trust Him alone to take away our sins.

Furthermore, Christians are often seen as joyless, judgmental, and in opposition to what the world loves; and so, because of these and other caricatures, we are often ashamed of the gospel. I pray this brief devotional will be used of the Lord to motivate us to be willing to be identified with Christ, seeing it a badge of honor. Let us say with Paul, "I am not ashamed of the gospel, for it is the power of God for salvation to everyone who believes" (Romans 1:16).

PRAYER

Father, free me from fear of testifying to the gospel.

THE HEALING THAT MATTERS MOST

"Take heart, my son; your sins are forgiven."
MATTHEW 9:2

D. L. MOODY

That was more than his friends expected; they only thought of his body being made whole. So let us bring our friends to Christ, and we shall get more than we expect.

The Lord met this man's deepest need first. It may be his sins had brought on the palsy, so the Lord forgave the man's sin first of all.

ERWIN LUTZER

Jesus crossed the Sea of Galilee and upon His arrival in Nazareth, He was met by people carrying a paralytic. They expected only physical healing, but the hapless man also, unexpectedly, received the forgiveness of sins. Should it surprise us that the first words of Jesus were, "Your sins are forgiven"? In Jewish culture, there was a tight relationship between sin and sickness. For example, when Job's life came unraveled, his three "friends" kept saying, "Job, what sin have you committed? Admit to it!" (see Job 4–37). There are times when physical sickness is brought on because of sin, but this is not always the case (John 9:1–3). But let's not miss the point Jesus was making: Physical healing is proof that He can do spiritual healing as well.

But—and this is very important—it is possible to have a physical healing without a spiritual one. Modern medicine, surgeries, and a host of other things can often prolong a life, but only God can forgive sins. We must distinguish between the healing of the body and the healing of the soul. Commercials extol some new remedy for the body: drugs, special foods or vitamins, exercise equipment, and so on. But the conversion of the soul is a miracle only God can do.

What is this generation's need? They need to hear from Christ, "Your sins are forgiven." Let's share the gospel so more people might believe and be saved.

PRAYER

Father, thank You for forgiving my sins and meeting my deepest need: a relationship with You.

TAKE COURAGE

Joseph of Arimathea, a respected member of the council, who was also himself looking for the kingdom of God, took courage and went to Pilate and asked for the body of Jesus.

MARK 15:43

D. L. MOODY

I consider this one of the sublimest, grandest acts any man ever did. In the darkness and gloom, His disciples having all forsaken Him, Judas having sold Him for thirty pieces of silver, the chief apostle Peter having denied Him, the chief priests having found Him guilty of blasphemy, the council having condemned Him to death, and when there was a hiss going up to heaven from over all Jerusalem, Joseph went right against the current, right against the influence of all his friends, and begged for the body of Jesus.

Blessed act! Doubtless he chastened himself for not having been more bold in his defense of Christ when He was tried and before He was condemned to be crucified. The Scripture says he was an honorable man, an honorable councilor, a rich man, and yet we have only the record of that one thing—the one act of begging for the body of Jesus. What he did for the Son of God, out of pure love for Him, will live forever. That one act rises up above everything else that Joseph of Arimathea ever did.

ERWIN LUTZER

Do we understand the power of one courageous act—one courageous person? David's killing of Goliath plunged the Philistine army into fear while transforming Israel's army into one of triumph, victory, courage, and faith. Joseph of Arimathea, in requesting the body of Jesus, showed love and dignity to his Savior when no one else did—fulfilling a Messianic prophecy (Isaiah 53:9).

One person can make a huge difference by one heroic act of service, one opportunity to identify with Christ. Ask God, "What can I do today to inspire others to remain faithful to Christ?" Let us take these words to heart, "Be strong and courageous" (Joshua 1:6).

PRAYER

Lord, grant me the courage to identify with You.

SUPER GRACE

And he said, "Jesus, remember me when you come into your kingdom." And he said to him, "Truly, I say to you, today you will be with me in paradise."
LUKE 23:42–43

D. L. MOODY

When a prominent man dies, we are anxious to get his last words and acts. The last act of the Son of God was to save a sinner. That was a part of the glory of His death. He commenced His ministry by saving sinners, and ended it by saving this poor thief.

ERWIN LUTZER

Jesus was saving sinners up to and including His final breath. This thief heard the crowd mock Christ and in derision call Him, "The King of the Jews." But this thief thought if He is a king, He must have a kingdom. "Remember me" is all he could hope for. But he received something beyond his expectations. He was promised meeting Christ that very day in Paradise!

What will our last words be? Will we leave hope and encouragement for those left behind? Will we urge others to believe on Christ, no matter the greatness of their sin? John Newton, the author of "Amazing Grace," wrote his epitaph that speaks to us: "John Newton, once an infidel and libertine, a servant of slaves in Africa, was, by the rich mercy of our Lord and Saviour Jesus Christ, preserved, restored, pardoned, and appointed to preach the faith he had long labored to destroy."[22]

The apostle Paul, who preached the faith he once sought to destroy, said, "The grace of our Lord *overflowed* for me . . . that in me, as the foremost [of sinners], Jesus Christ might display his perfect patience" (1 Timothy 1:14–16). The Greek word for *overflowed* is where we get the word *hyper*. When God saves us, He gives us "hyper" or "super" grace. That's how God changes our legacy—and our eternal destiny.

PRAYER

Father, thank You for Jesus who changes our eternal destiny by His promises and His Word.

THE WORKS OF CHRIST DONE BY US TODAY

"Truly, truly, I say to you, whoever believes in me will also do the works that I do; and greater works than these will he do, because I am going to the Father."

JOHN 14:12

D. L. MOODY

I used to stumble over that verse, but the longer I live, the more I am convinced it is a greater thing to influence a man whose will is set against God, to have that will broken and brought into subjection to God's will—or, in other words, it is a greater thing to have power over a living, sinning, God-hating man, than to quicken the dead. He who could create a world could speak a dead man into life; but I think the greatest miracle this world has ever seen was the miracle at Pentecost. The men who surrounded the apostles were full of prejudice, full of malice, full of bitterness, their hands, as it were, dripping with the blood of the Son of God; and yet an unlettered man, a man whom they detested and hated, stood up and preached the gospel. And three thousand of them were immediately convicted and converted and became disciples of the Lord Jesus Christ.

ERWIN LUTZER

The greatest miracle God ever performed was for your salvation. The same God who created physical light by a single word is the One who created the moral and spiritual light within us. Salvation is more than a miracle of power, it's a miracle of cleansing, new birth, love, and grace. God overcame the moral and spiritual barrier between Him and us in order to save us.

Today, the church is doing greater miracles by the Holy Spirit being poured into believers around the world. Jesus' miracles were confined to Israel, but now the saving gospel is spreading around the world.

Let us personally claim this verse even as we witness to the power of Christ in our lives.

PRAYER

Father, thank You for the Holy Spirit who enables us to continue Christ's work on earth. Help me to see how I am a part of a worldwide movement spreading the miracle of the gospel each day.

SEPTEPMBER 6

THE OLD IS GONE, THE NEW HAS COME

Therefore, if anyone is in Christ, he is a new creation.
The old has passed away; behold, the new has come.
2 CORINTHIANS 5:17

D. L. MOODY

I saw an advertisement which read like this: "If you want people to respect you, wear good clothes." This is the world's idea of getting the world's respect. Why! A leper may put on good clothes, but he is a leper still. Mere profession of faith doesn't transform a man. It is the new nature spoken of in Corinthians, "Therefore if any man be in Christ, he is a new creature; old things are passed away; behold, all things are become new."

ERWIN LUTZER

The Pharisees had many outer rules, which they couldn't live up to themselves, and yet they imposed those rules on others. Rules are parameters to keep us from doing wrong, but they cannot give us life. We must come to Christ for life and for strength to live for Him, to say no to sin and yes to walking in the Spirit. When you do come to Him, He'll not leave you the way you came because He is the One who, despite our guilt, our confusion, and our wondering, gives us rest. This change goes beyond outer appearances.

Compare the religions of the world. Only Jesus Christ promises a transformation of your heart and desires. That's why we do not simply promote rules; there is an inner transformation of the heart, a miracle of God called "being born again." To be clear, there is something within you that wasn't there before you were born again. There is a new nature with new desires. It certainly doesn't make us perfect, but it does give us hope on our journey so we can stay on the path. That's the offer Jesus makes. The old is gone, the new has come.

PRAYER

Father, thank You for not leaving me as I was by transforming me into a new creation in and through Your Son.

HOLY WORK

Therefore, my beloved, as you have always obeyed, so now, not only as in my presence but much more in my absence, work out your own salvation with fear and trembling, for it is God who works in you, both to will and to work for his good pleasure.

PHILIPPIANS 2:12–13

D. L. MOODY

I have very little sympathy with any man who has been redeemed by the precious blood of the Son of God and who has not got the "spirit" of work. If we are children of God, we ought not to have a lazy drop of blood in our veins. If a man tells me he has been saved and does not desire to work for the honor of God, I doubt his salvation.

Laziness belongs to the old creation, not to the new. In all my experience, I never knew a lazy man to be converted—never. I have more hope for the salvation of drunkards and thieves and harlots than of a lazy man.

ERWIN LUTZER

Of course, a lazy man can be converted but, as Moody pointed out, if you are lazy after you claim conversion, others are right to question your conversion. Simply put, conversion results in both a new nature and a new motivation. God will test our works by fire to reveal whether they are gold, silver, precious stones—or wood, hay, and straw (1 Corinthians 3:12). Christians are no longer under condemnation, but we will give an account for our faithfulness, or lack of it (2 Corinthians 5:10). So Paul said, "Work out your own salvation with fear and with trembling."

"Fear and trembling," you ask? Yes, but not a soul-destroying fear, like a servant has of an unpredictable master. It's the kind of fear between a son and a father. I'm grateful my father would have never neglected or disowned me. But a look from my father compelled me to obey!

The bottom line: No true Christian wants to hear Jesus say, "You wicked and slothful servant!" (Matthew 25:26).

PRAYER

Father, show me the doors You have opened for me, and may I have the initiative to walk through them, wholly committed to work with You and for You.

TWICE BORN

Jesus answered him, "Truly, truly, I say to you, unless one is born again he cannot see the kingdom of God."

JOHN 3:3

D. L. MOODY

The only way to get into the kingdom of God is to be "born" into it. The law of this country requires that the president should be born in the country. When foreigners come to our shores, they have no right to complain against such a law, which forbids them from ever becoming president. Now, has not God a right to make a law that all those who become heirs of eternal life must be "born" into His kingdom?

An unregenerated man would rather be in hell than in heaven. Take a man whose heart is full of corruption and wickedness, and place him in heaven among the pure, the holy, and the redeemed, and he would not want to stay there. Certainly, if we are to be happy in heaven, we must begin to make a heaven here on earth. Heaven is a prepared place for a prepared people. If men were taken to heaven just as they are by nature, without having their hearts regenerated, there would be another rebellion in heaven. Heaven is filled with a company of those who have been twice born.

ERWIN LUTZER

We are being readied on earth to be citizens of heaven. The older we get, the more we anticipate heaven and wonder what it will be like. So yes, among God's people, we should begin to see a bit of heaven on earth.

As for those who are in hell, they have taken their stand against God and will maintain it with anger, curses, and with "weeping and gnashing of teeth" (Matthew 13:42). In that state, they would not be happy in heaven among those who are praising and blessing God.

The bottom line: Our new nature will find its full expression in heaven. Loving God now, we will love Him better forever; reject Him now, and we will reject Him forever.

PRAYER

Father, thank You for giving me a new nature. Thank You for bringing me into Your family and calling me to love what You love.

GOSPEL COMFORT AT DEATH

Jesus said to her, "I am the resurrection and the life. Whoever believes in me, though he die, yet shall he live."
JOHN 11:25

D. L. MOODY

At the Battle of Inkerman during the Crimean War, a soldier was just able to crawl to his tent after he was struck down. When found, he was lying upon his face, his open Bible before him, his hand glued fast to the page by his life-blood which covered it. When his hand was lifted, the letters of the printed page were clearly traced upon it, and with the ever-living promise in and on his hand, they laid him in a soldier's grave. The words were: "I am the resurrection, and the life: he that believeth in me, though he were dead, yet shall he live."

I want a religion that can comfort even in death, that can unite me with my loved ones. Oh, what gloom and darkness would settle upon this world if it were not for the glorious doctrine of the resurrection! Thank God, the glorious morning will soon break. For a little while, God asks us to be on the watchtower, faithful to Him and waiting for the summons. Soon our Lord will come to receive His own, whether they be living or dead.

ERWIN LUTZER

No matter how many victories death wins, they are only temporary. Thanks to Jesus, our final victory has been won; death will be abolished. It's been said that, for Christians, this life is the worst there will ever be; the future is eternally bright.

Let me repeat the good news: If you believe Jesus' death and resurrection was so sufficient and you trust only Him, you will be saved. Through repentance and faith, we receive the gift of eternal life and, like the soldier Moody referred to, we are assured of the words of Jesus, "I am the resurrection and the life. Whoever believes in me, though he die, yet shall he live and everyone who lives and believes in me shall never die" (John 11:25).

Is your faith in Christ alone?

PRAYER

Father, I thank You my hope is eternal, final, and secure.

SEPTEMBER 10

TRUTH, HALF-TRUTHS, AND LIES

Therefore, having put away falsehood, let each one of you speak the truth with his neighbor, for we are members one of another.
EPHESIANS 4:25

D. L. MOODY

We have got nowadays so that we divide lies into white lies and black lies, society lies, business lies, and so on. The Word of God knows no such letting down of the standard. A lie is a lie, no matter what are the circumstances under which it is uttered, or by whom. I have heard that in Siam, they sew up the mouth of a confirmed liar. I am afraid if that was the custom in this land, a good many would suffer.

Parents should begin with their children while they are young and teach them to be strictly truthful at all times. There is a proverb: "A lie has no legs." It requires other lies to support it. Tell one lie and you are forced to tell others to back it up.

ERWIN LUTZER

Many years ago I read the book *The Day America Told the Truth*, and I was surprised at how often people confessed they had lied, even several times a day. Jesus taught that the devil was the author of lies (John 8:44). It's frightening to think of how the human hearts sides with Satan, choosing to skew the truth rather than face reality. We must each ask ourselves: Are we truth-tellers, even at our own personal expense?

Let me repeat our verse, "Therefore, having put away falsehood, let each one of you speak the truth." If you find yourself telling a lie, confess it immediately to God and to the one whom you have wronged. Let it never be said that we can tolerate deceit. As the saying goes, "Truth hurts, but lies hurt even more."

Let's take this a step further. David wrote that a person in fellowship with God "swears to his own hurt and does not change" (Psalm 15:4). In other words, that person not only tells the truth, but lives by what they say, even at their personal expense.

PRAYER

Father, I desire the truth and to honor You wih the truth.
Help me to keep falsehood away from my tongue.

TWO PATHS, TWO ETERNAL DESTINATIONS

"Enter by the narrow gate. For the gate is wide and the way is easy that leads to destruction, and those who enter by it are many. For the gate is narrow and the way is hard that leads to life, and those who find it are few."

MATTHEW 7:13–14

D. L. MOODY

Many a man would be willing to enter into the kingdom of God if he could do it without giving up sin. A man may become a disciple of Muḥammad and continue to live in the foulest, blackest, deepest sin; but a man cannot be a disciple of Christ without giving up sin.

ERWIN LUTZER

What Moody said about Islam is true and also applies to other religions. How? All religions, except Christianity, are based on self-effort. Even religions claiming to seek God's help teach that we must make ourselves worthy of such grace and forgiveness. In other words: All other religions insist we must wash our hearts with the dirty, sin-infested water already existing within the human heart. But the sins remain.

One reason that the message of the cross is offensive is that it teaches our complete inability to save ourselves. All we can do is to receive what has already been provided for us in Christ. As I like to remind people, the issue is never the wickedness of our hearts, but the wonder of the gospel that changes our desires and gives us the righteousness of Christ. This might explain why Jesus said that the way to hell is broad but the way to heaven is narrow. The gospel is a free gift, but it's a difficult gift to receive because it requires us to admit to our inability to save or cleanse ourselves; it is the final admission that self-salvation cannot actually save. And, yes, in turning to Christ, we are turning our backs on sin. Islam requires its followers to be slaves to Muhammad's teaching; Christianity teaches we must become slaves of Christ, a joyful slavery, no longer dominated by our sinful, evil hearts.

PRAYER

Father, keep me from the temptation to envy those
on the broad way with their acceptance of sin and worldly pleasures.
I choose the narrow way of Your kingdom.

FAIR-MINDEDNESS AND COMPASSION

Do not withhold good from those to whom it is due, when it is in your power to do it.
PROVERBS 3:27

D. L. MOODY

After the Chicago fire, I came to New York for money, and I heard there was a rich man in Fall River who was very charitable. So I went to Massachusetts. He gave me a check for a large amount, and then got into his carriage and drove with me to the houses of other rich men in the city, and they all gave me checks. When he left me at the train, I grasped his hand and said: "If you ever come to Chicago, call on me, and I will return your favor."

He said: "Mr. Moody, don't wait for me; do it to the first man that comes along."

I never forget that remark; it had the ring of the true good Samaritan.

ERWIN LUTZER

The money Moody raised was for his ministry; in fact, he wanted to die a poor man, having given everything for the gospel. He was an astute businessman who directed his efforts in only one way: winning people to Christ. He was, perhaps, the most selfless person we've ever known about. If Moody had not been converted, Chicago might have a "D. L. Moody Hotel" or "D. L. Moody Jewelry Store." Instead, we have The Moody Church and the Moody Bible Institute. The ongoing impact of his life is enormous. But, as all who knew him realized, he was humble, approachable, and willing to help even "the least of these." He began his ministry with children in the slums, who were homeless and often fatherless.

Moody's world was as big as his heart. He stands as a rebuke to the rich and the famous who have only their own narcissistic interests at heart. The rich never have enough, and the famous are never famous enough. Meanwhile, the Bible reminds us, "God opposes the proud but gives grace to the humble" (James 4:6).

PRAYER

Lord, may I be quick to show Your generosity, love,
and goodness to those in need.

SEPTEMBER 13

NOURISHED BY THE WORD

Great peace have those who love your law; nothing can make them stumble.

PSALM 119:165

D. L. MOODY

The study of God's Word will secure peace.

Take those Christians who are rooted and grounded in the Word of God and you will find they have great peace. But it is these who don't study their Bible, who are easily offended when some little trouble comes, or some little persecution. Just a little breath of opposition, and their peace is all gone.

ERWIN LUTZER

How can we make sure we are rooted in God and not in something that cannot support us, especially when times are difficult? This trust in God can only come about by the Word of God itself. "Faith comes from hearing, and hearing through the word of Christ" (Romans 10:17). The person who meditates day and night on God's law shall be "like a tree planted by streams of water that yields its fruit in its season, and its leaf does not wither" (Psalm 1:3).

But I've discovered that even if I am nourished by the Word on Wednesday, I'm dry on Thursday. Like manna in the desert, you can only gather a day's supply in the morning, but it doesn't carry over until the next day. If you're simply coming to church but not meditating in God's Word, I can tell you that when hardship comes, and when the pressure is on, you aren't going to have the resources to enjoy peace when those struggles begin.

A final warning: Some study the Bible in order to take pride in how much they know, not to humbly seek the Lord and His promise. Your attitude when you approach the Bible matters. Are you teachable, humble, and obedient?

PRAYER

Father, may I faithfully study Your Word and meditate on it
so that I might be a tree rooted and planted by water, bearing fruit
and able to endure trials that surely will come.

ALL I CAN GIVE

My son, give me your heart, and let your eyes observe my ways.
PROVERBS 23:26

D. L. MOODY

I remember hearing a story about a Native American Indian who wanted to come to the Lord. He brought his blanket, but the Lord wouldn't have it. He brought his gun, his dog, his bow and arrow, but the Lord wouldn't have them. At last he brought himself, and the Lord took him. The Lord wanted himself.

What the Lord wants is not what you have got, but yourself, and you cannot do a thing to please God until you surrender yourself to Him.

ERWIN LUTZER

Before salvation, we are dead in our sins. Our fallenness permeates our entire being: Our minds are tainted with sin, our souls are stained, and our wills are paralyzed. Good people or not, we are in deep trouble. And even the best we bring to God will not be received.

If God's rescue program had included our efforts, grace would be diminished and salvation would not be wholly the work of God. Some things can exist together, but the grace that brings salvation and human works, like oil and water, do not mix. Our self-effort will be put on a shelf labeled "Unsuitable for Use." God acts alone when He saves us because He neither needs nor accepts our cooperation. He invites us only to believe.

When you come to Christ, you do not come to give, but to receive. You do not come to be helped, but to be rescued. You do not come just to be made better, though thankfully, that does happen, but you come to be made alive! Salvation is not based on our promise but on His promise. It is His work, not ours, that gives us the gift of grace. We bring nothing but ourselves and our need.

PRAYER

Father, You have saved me apart from anything I could ever do or offer.
Thank You for making me see my need for You and for saving me
by grace through faith alone.

DYING TO LIVE

"Truly, truly, I say to you, unless a grain of wheat falls into the earth and dies, it remains alone; but if it dies, it bears much fruit."

JOHN 12:24

D. L. MOODY

Take a little black flower seed and sow it; after it has been planted some time, dig it up. If it is whole, you know that it has no life; but if it has begun to decay, you know that life and fruitfulness will follow. There will be a resurrected life; and out of that little black seed will come a beautiful, fragrant flower.

Here is a disgusting grub, crawling along the ground. By and by old age overtakes it, and it begins to spin its own shroud, to make its own sepulchre, and it lies as if in death. Look again and it has shuffled off its shroud, it has burst its sepulchre open, and it comes forth a beautiful butterfly, with different form and habits.

So with our bodies. They die, but God will give us glorified bodies in their stead. This is law of the new creation as well as the old: light after darkness; life after death; fruitfulness and glory after corruption and decay.

ERWIN LUTZER

Moody's illustration is biblical: When we die, we are like a seed that has fallen into the ground, but shall be raised with an incorruptible body. We are sown in weakness, but raised with strength. There will be both continuity with our present body, but also discontinuity (see 1 Corinthians 15:35–49). For we shall have a body "like his glorious body" (Philippians 3:21). The point Jesus was making in John 12:24 not only applies to our physical death and resurrection, but to our present life. We must die to ourselves. As someone has said, we cannot pray, "thy kingdom come" until we have prayed, "let my kingdom die." Dying to self-will is the most challenging struggle we will ever have. In our sinfulness, we cling to self-will until our knuckles turn white. There is truth in the statement that we must "let go and let God."

PRAYER

Father, teach me to die that I might live only unto thee.

EVERY TALENT ACCOUNTED FOR

Above the Horse Gate the priests repaired, each one opposite his own house.
NEHEMIAH 3:28

D. L. MOODY

If this world is going to be reached, I am convinced it must be done by men and women of average talent. After all, there are comparatively few people in the world who have great talents. Here is a man with one talent; there is another with three; perhaps I may have only half a talent. But if we all go to work and trade with the gifts we have, the Lord will prosper us, and we may double or triple our talents. What we need is to be up and about our Master's work, every man building against his own house. The more we use the means and opportunities we have, the more will our ability and our opportunities be increased.

ERWIN LUTZER

Nehemiah was a gifted organizer who motivated the whole assembly to rebuild the walls of Jerusalem. Each family was given the assignment of securing its part of the wall; he knew they would work hard to ensure their part of the wall was insurmountable. People of both great and ordinary talent were enlisted to rebuild the wall.

In God's eyes, there are no ordinary people or extraordinary people—only faithful and unfaithful people. Each is given a talent and should have a mind to work. Our money is God's. Our talents are God's. Our home belongs to God. So, with a sense of praise and gratitude, we should always be asking, "Lord, what will you have me to do with what you have given to me?"

We are all managers of what God has given us. And since God is the one who gave us all we have, He has the right to take it away. He gives different gifts, different abilities, and different amounts. God created so many ordinary people with differing talents, but together we can do an extraordinary work.

PRAYER

Father, You call me to manage everything I have for Your glory.
Keep me from comparing my talents with another, and instead,
faithfully use what You've given me.

NO NEUTRALITY WITH CHRIST

And Simeon blessed them and said to Mary his mother, "Behold, this child is appointed for the fall and rising of many in Israel, and for a sign that is opposed."

LUKE 2:34

D. L. MOODY

Do you know that the gospel of Jesus Christ proves either a fragrance of life unto life or of death unto death? You sometimes hear people say: "We will go and hear this man preach. If it does us no good, it will do us no harm." Don't you believe it! Every time one hears the gospel and rejects it, the hardening process goes on. The same sun that melts the ice hardens the clay. The sermon that would have moved to action a few years ago makes no impression now.

There is not a true minister of the gospel who will not say that the hardest people to reach are those who have been impressed and whose impressions have worn away. It is a good deal easier to commit a sin the second time than it was to commit it the first time, but it is a good deal harder to repent the second time than the first.

ERWIN LUTZER

Have you ever wondered why a person can listen to hundreds of sermons and not believe on Jesus for the forgiveness of their sins? In the Parable of the Sower, some seed fell on the path and did not penetrate the soil. Perhaps this path had been trampled by people (see Mark 4:1–9). And there is no heart as hard as those who are rebelling against other Christians who have trampled on them. Also, many others feel very comfortable with their sins and with themselves, and so, in the midst of this comfort, they don't want to change; they don't want to have God break into their lives. And every time they reject the Word, the harder their heart becomes.

We are responsible for carefully sowing the seed; how people respond is out of our control. Let us trust God to determine the results (1 Corinthians 3:6).

PRAYER

Father, soften the hearts of those who hear Your gospel
and make me Your messenger.

RECONCILIATION: WORTH EVERY PENNY

And Zacchaeus stood and said to the Lord, "Behold, Lord, the half of my goods I give to the poor. And if I have defrauded anyone of anything, I restore it fourfold."
LUKE 19:8

D. L. MOODY

A short speech, but how the words have come ringing down through the ages! By making that remark, Zacchaeus confessed his sin—that he had been dishonest. Besides that, he showed that he knew the requirements of the law of Moses. If a man had taken what did not belong to him, he was not only to return it, but to multiply it by four. I think that men in this dispensation ought to be fully as honest as men under the Law. I am getting so tired and sick of your mere sentimentalism that does not straighten out a man's life. We may sing our hymns and psalms, and offer prayers, but they will be an abomination to God unless we are willing to be thoroughly straightforward in our daily life. Nothing will give Christianity such a hold upon the world as to have God's believing people begin to act in this way. Zacchaeus had probably more influence in Jericho after he made restitution than any other man in it.

ERWIN LUTZER

Restitution is always a product of revival. The restoration of stolen goods and the mending of broken relationships have been used by God to soften the hearts of those indifferent or even hardened to the gospel. It's not enough for us to claim a wonderful relationship with God unless we have done all we can to be reconciled to those we have wronged.

Because God seeks reconciliation, we should seek it also on behalf of others (2 Corinthians 5:18–19). Sin divides, grace unites. As Paul said in Acts 24:16, "I always take pains to have a clear conscience toward both God and man."

No doubt Zacchaeus had a positive impact in Jericho. He was willing to be reconciled to those he had wronged, even at a great personal cost.

PRAYER

Father, reveal to me the names of those I have wronged,
giving me the grace to make it right.

DOES GOD HELP THOSE WHO HELP THEMSELVES?

And to the one who does not work but believes in him who justifies the ungodly, his faith is counted as righteousness.

ROMANS 4:5

D. L. MOODY

I freely admit salvation is worth working for. It is worth a man's going round the world on his hands and knees, climbing its mountains, crossing its valleys, swimming its rivers, going through all manner of hardship in order to attain it. But we do not get it in that way. It is to him that *believeth*.

ERWIN LUTZER

Trying to make ourselves worthy of grace and earn salvation is the default position of the human heart. Somewhere I read that eighty percent of Americans believe the statement "God helps those who help themselves" is in the Bible! Well, it's not in the Bible and with good reason: God helps those who realize they *cannot* help themselves. The good news of the gospel is not based on our abilities or our motivation to do better.

I helped disciple a man who grew up in a home with the formalities of Christianity and a mother who kept telling him, "God helps those who help themselves." But that didn't help him get out of a life of drugs and immorality. Finally, at the end of himself, crying out in desperation to God, he found a path out of a wasted life. To the glory of God, he is in the ministry today.

While we work at our vocations, our relationships, and the ordinary events of life, as far as our eternal salvation is concerned, it cannot be bought, earned, or supported by religious rituals.

Let me quote Paul again, "Now to the one who works, his wages are not counted as a gift but as his due [In other words, you earn it]. And to the one who does not work but believes in him who justifies the ungodly, his faith is counted as righteousness" (Romans 4:4–5).

PRAYER

Nothing in my hand I bring, Simply to Thy cross I cling;
Naked, come to Thee for dress; Helpless, look to Thee for grace;
Foul, I to the fountain fly; Wash me, Savior, or I die.[23]

THE COMING WEDDING DAY

And the angel said to me, "Write this: Blessed are those who are invited to the marriage supper of the Lamb." And he said to me, "These are the true words of God."

REVELATION 19:9

D. L. MOODY

I would rather die tonight and be sure of sharing the bliss of the purified in yon world of light than live for centuries with the wealth of this world at my feet, and miss the marriage supper of the Lamb. I have missed many appointments in my life, but by the grace of God, I mean to make sure of that one. Why, the blessed privilege of sitting down at the marriage supper of the Lamb, to see the King in His beauty, to be forever with the Lord—who would miss it?

ERWIN LUTZER

Let me emphasize this: In most weddings today, the bride is the center of the attention. The groom shows up and stands at the front of the altar, but for the most part, nobody looks at him particularly. But at the marriage supper of the Lamb, the focus is going to be on the Groom, the Lord Jesus Christ, the Lamb of God.

Many years ago, when the Reverend Paul Gibson retired as principal of Cambridge, a portrait of him was commissioned and unveiled. And when Rev. Gibson looked at it, he actually paid a well-deserved compliment to the artist and said, "When people look at this, they aren't going to say, 'Who's that man?' They're going to say 'Who painted the portrait?'"[24] I believe throughout all of eternity, the question is not going to be so much, "Who are the redeemed?" but rather, "Who was their Redeemer?" It's all going to be about Jesus. And what a time that's going to be.

No wonder the multitude cries, "Let us rejoice and exult!" (Revelation 19:7). All of that is coming in our future. And like Moody, we might miss weddings here on earth, but let us not miss the marriage supper of the Lamb. All who have trusted Christ will be invited.

PRAYER

Father, thank You for uniting me to Your Son, and for making me a member of the church, His bride. May I be pure and faithful to You.

WAIT, THEN KEEP GOING

"Your bars shall be iron and bronze, and as your days, so shall your strength be."
DEUTERONOMY 33:25

D. L. MOODY

Many look forth at the Christian life and fear that they will not have sufficient strength to hold out to the end. They forget the promise, "As thy days, thy strength." It reminds me of the pendulum in the clock which grew disheartened at the thought of having to travel so many thousands of miles; but when it reflected that the distance was to be accomplished by "tick, tick, tick," it took fresh courage to go its daily journey.

So it is the special privilege of the Christian to commit himself to the keeping of his heavenly Father, and to trust Him day by day. It is a comforting thing to know that the Lord will not begin the good work without also finishing it.

ERWIN LUTZER

To build on Moody's illustration, when I have been busy with projects and interruptions, I've reminded myself that the pendulum has to only be concerned about the next second and then the second after that. In other words, if the clock thought about the millions of seconds it must count, it would become filled with anxiety. Just so, I really only have to be concerned about this moment, not about the next. God has strength, patience, wisdom, and if we are humble enough to receive it, He will give us what we need, but only when we need it.

"They who wait for the LORD shall renew their strength" (Isaiah 40:31). The life of the believer is a moment by moment reliance upon God. We depend on God consciously, hour by hour, as He sustains us until He calls us home to be with Him eternally. Waiting on God means physical and spiritual dependence; it is acknowledging our bankruptcy apart from His sustaining grace.

PRAYER

Father, I'm waiting on You for the strength I need for all my days.

LIVING IN BABYLON, YET NOT OF BABYLON

Therefore go out from their midst, and be separate from them, says the Lord, and touch no unclean thing; then I will welcome you.

2 CORINTHIANS 6:17

D. L. MOODY

I believe that a Christian should lead a separated life. The line between the church and the world is almost obliterated today. I have no sympathy with the idea that you must hunt up an old musty church record in order to find out whether a man is a member of the church or not. A man ought to live so that everybody will know he is a Christian. The Bible tells us to lead a separate life. You may lose influence, but you will gain it at the same time. I suppose Daniel was the most unpopular man in Babylon at a certain time, but, thank God, he has outlived all the other men of his day.

ERWIN LUTZER

Technology has made separation from the world more difficult than in any other period of history, past or present. The culture of Babylon is at our fingertips. With a smartphone in the hands of nearly every teenager (often in the hands of children), sensuality and every evil vice known to man is instantly and secretly available. The line between the church and world has been obliterated—a statement more true today than it was in Moody's day.

Our lifelong struggle with the culture of the world should follow three commands: We should *flee* from evil; each Christian should consider what that means for them. We should run from the temptations of the world, not seeking to get as close to temptation as we can. Cut yourself off from any temptation that leads you into evil. Second, we must *fight*, for we cannot win this battle unless we are blood earnest in warfare, praying, and standing together against the hosts of evil. Then we must also *follow*, that is, we must pursue godliness. The command still stands: "Go out from their midst, and be separate from them."

PRAYER

Father, teach me not to love the world nor the things of the world.

SEPTEMBER 23

THE BATTLE IS FIERCE

"Moses my servant is dead. Now therefore arise, go over this Jordan, you and all this people, into the land that I am giving to them, to the people of Israel."
JOSHUA 1:2

D. L. MOODY

We need the courage that will compel us to move forward.

We may have to go against the advice of lukewarm Christians; there are some who never seem to do anything but object because the work is not carried on exactly according to their ideas. They are very fruitful in raising objections to any plans that can be suggested. If any onward step is taken, they are ready to throw cold water on it and suggest all kinds of difficulties. We want to have such faith and courage as shall enable us to move forward without waiting for these timid unbelievers.

ERWIN LUTZER

God's command to Joshua can apply to us. The events of the entire book of Joshua took about thirteen or fourteen years. Israel didn't just walk casually though the land and suddenly it was theirs. Seven different warring nations were ready to fight against them; for Israel to inherit the land would be costly both in lives lost (consider Israel's failure at Ai) and in time spent. Families were displaced, men were taken from homes to fight in fierce battles. There were times of doubt, times of victory, and times of discouragement. And times of loss.

We have all been there, have we not?

I believe God has all kinds of blessings with our names on the title deed. But we need to fight; we need to be focused and willing to attack that which stands between us and victory. That one sin needs to be defeated; that one conflict needs resolution. That demands both faith and action!

PRAYER

Father, increase my faith. Let my faith bring forth holy living in all areas of my life. Help me to fight for Your kingdom.

MOTIVATED BY LOVE

If I speak in the tongues of men and of angels, but have not love, I am a noisy gong or a clanging cymbal.
1 CORINTHIANS 13:1

D. L. MOODY

If we want to be wise in winning souls and to be vessels for the Master's use, we must get rid of the accursed spirit of self-seeking. That is the meaning of this chapter in Paul's letter. He told the Corinthians that a man might be full of faith and zeal, he might be very benevolent, but if he had not love he was like sounding brass and a tinkling cymbal. I believe many men might as well go into the pulpit and blow a tin horn Sabbath after Sabbath as go on preaching without love. A man may preach the truth, he may be perfectly sound in doctrine, but if there is no love in his heart going out to those whom he addresses, and if he is doing it professionally, the apostle says he is only a sounding brass.

ERWIN LUTZER

Communicating the gospel is not just a matter of words; it is not just a matter of telling the truth. People don't just listen with their minds, they listen with their hearts. And if we show judgmentalism rather than love, if there is a spirit of superiority rather than humility, we are "a noisy gong and a clanging symbol."

Let's read the preceding verse, "Do all possess gifts of healing? Do all speak with tongues? Do all interpret? But earnestly desire the higher gifts. And I will show you a still more excellent way" (1 Corinthians 12:30). Then in 13:3, Paul says even if you were martyred yet have no love, it amounts to zero. What is it that should distinguish us from the world? Love.

Paul says love is more excellent than being a good prophet, a good teacher, or even having the supernatural gift of tongues. It is the way of love. One fruit of the Spirit is love (Galatians 5:22–23). It's supernatural! It comes to us from God and that's why we can love.

PRAYER

Father, teach me to love as You do, and that it might motivate all that I do.

SEPTEMBER 25

FOCUS ON THE LIFE TO COME

"Truly, truly, I say to you, whoever hears my word and believes him who sent me has eternal life. He does not come into judgment, but has passed from death to life."

JOHN 5:24

D. L. MOODY

Note that the difference between a believer and unbeliever is right here. An unbeliever is living in his day, and he has nothing but a long dark eternal night to look forward to; a Christian is now living in his night, and he has a grand morning that he is looking forward to. The day is ahead, the glory is ahead, the best of life is ahead, it is not behind. That is the teaching of Scripture. For a man whose life is hid with Christ in God, judgment is already passed; he will not come into judgment. Christ was judged for me, and judgment is behind me, not before me.

ERWIN LUTZER

If you have come under the shelter of Christ's death and what He did on the cross for sinners, then there is no eternal condemnation for you (Romans 8:1). We will die physically, but we will really not "see" death. God uses many ways to bring a believer into glory, but they will not see an eternal death. To be absent from the body is to be present with the Lord (2 Corinthians 5:8).

As believers, we are looking forward to the morning, an eternal morning that leads to noonday, forever. "The path of the righteous is like the light of dawn, which shines brighter and brighter until full day" (Proverbs 4:18). The older we get, the more physical challenges we may have, but spiritually, we are being renewed. Our eternal destiny in God's presence is assured. Visualize a string that goes from earth to the farthest star; in comparison, our lifespan would be, at best, a hairline.

Trials are momentary; death will be momentary. He who does the will of God abides forever (1 John 2:17).

PRAYER

Father, thank You that judgment is past and Your glory awaits me!

SUFFERING NEEDN'T STOP US

For the sake of Christ, then, I am content with weaknesses, insults, hardships, persecutions, and calamities. For when I am weak, then I am strong.
2 CORINTHIANS 12:10

D. L. MOODY

The devil thought he had done a very wise thing when he got Paul into prison, but he was very mistaken; he overdid it for once. I have no doubt Paul has thanked God ever since for that Philippian jail and for his stripes and imprisonment there. The world has made more by it than we shall ever know till we get to heaven.

ERWIN LUTZER

When Paul had a thorn in the flesh, he pleaded with God three times to take it away. The first two times, God was silent. God answered the third time, but it was not the answer Paul had been hoping for. God said, "Paul, the answer is *no*." The thorn would not be removed, but that was not the end of the story. God would not leave Paul stranded, suffering without hope. God promised Paul the grace to endure the thorn—to see it as a plus not a minus. Paul heard Jesus say, "My power is made perfect in weakness" (2 Corinthians 12:9). *God never leaves us without the strength needed to endure a trial.*

Paul said in effect, "If, through my weakness, the power of Christ is seen, and through my weakness, grace is given, then I can be content with my thorn. I was asking for a kernel, but God gave me a harvest. I was asking for a trinket, but God gave me true wealth."

With thorns comes grace; with burdens there are blessings.

PRAYER

Father, I thank You for using my suffering to bring me deeper into Your love.

SEPTEMBER 27

CALCULATE THE COST OF HIDDEN SIN

Good sense wins favor, but the way of the treacherous is their ruin.

PROVERBS 13:15

D. L. MOODY

Do you mean to say that God is a hard master? That it is a hard thing to serve God, that Satan is an easy master, and that it is easier to serve him than God? If I read my Bible right, I read *that the way of transgressors is hard*. It is the devil who is the hard master. If you doubt it, young man, look at the convict in the prison, right in the bloom of manhood, right in the prime of life. He has been there for ten years and must remain for ten years more—twenty years taken out of his life; and when he comes out of that miserable cell, he comes out a branded felon! Do you think *that* man will tell you that the way of the transgressor has been easy?

Go ask the poor drunkard, the man who is bound hand and foot, the slave of the infernal cup, who is hastening onward to a drunkard's hell. Ask him if he has found the way of the transgressor easy. "Easy?" he will cry, "The way of the transgressor is hard and gets harder every day!" Go ask the libertine and the worldling. Go ask the gambler and the blasphemer; take the most faithful follower of the devil and put the questions to him; with one voice they will all tell you their service has been hard.

ERWIN LUTZER

A flat tire is often the result of a long-term microscopic failure. Just so, sin is never static; so-called "small compromises and sins" soon grow in our lives until we are overwhelmed and enslaved. If the conviction of sin does not lead us to repentance, the hiding of sin continues. Achan, you might remember, disobeyed God and hid some spoils from the battle in his tent for himself. Joshua said to him, "Give glory to the Lord. . . . do not hide [what you have done] from me" (Joshua 7:19). Achan's sin was found out and the consequences were severe.

What sin are you hiding in your tent that smells foul? Sin always demands more, and it costs us dearly.

PRAYER

Father, grant me the grace to be convicted of my sin, even the hidden, cuddled, rationalized, seemingly satisfying sin. Have Your way in me.

DAILY GOD-ENCOUNTERS

They said to him, "Sir, give us this bread always."
JOHN 6:34

D. L. MOODY

I cannot but believe that the reason for the standard of Christian life being so low, is that we are living on stale manna. You know what I mean by that. So many people are living on their past experience—thinking of the grand times they had twenty years ago, perhaps when they were converted. It is a sure sign that we are out of communion with God if we are talking more of the joy and peace and power we had in the past than of what we have today. We are told to "grow in grace"; but a great many are growing the wrong way. The Israelites used to gather the manna fresh every day; they were not allowed to store it up. There is a lesson here for us. If we would be strong and vigorous, we must go to God daily. A man can no more take in a supply of grace for the future than he can eat enough today to last him for the next six months, or take sufficient air into his lungs at once to sustain life for a week to come. We must draw upon God's boundless stores of grace from day to day, as we need it.

ERWIN LUTZER

Robert G. Lee said, "You cannot live on skim milk during the days of the week and preach cream on Sunday!"[25] Well, those words apply to all of us. We can't neglect God daily and expect to receive His favor during the week. Many people say, "I've tried to meet with God every morning, but I gave up."

But imagine reading the Bible, anticipating a word from God; imagine praying for yourself and those you love every day from the Scriptures! I have a habit of praying soon after I awaken, "Today Lord, glorify yourself at my expense." Then I pray affirming that I intend to "walk in the Spirit" throughout the day, in total dependence on Him. Jesus, who had all power, would rise up before daybreak to commune with His heavenly Father. Can we do any less?

PRAYER

Father, increase my desire for You that I will never stop seeking You.

THE JOURNEY TO A THOUSAND SINS

"Not many days later, the younger son gathered all he had and took a journey into a far country, and there he squandered his property in reckless living."
LUKE 15:13

D. L. MOODY

He started off holding his head very high that morning. He was full of pride and conceit, and he had very lofty ideas. If anyone had told him what he was coming to, he would have laughed in scorn. But mind you, once a man starts on the downward track, he will sink lower and lower unless, by the grace of God, he turns from sin to righteousness. The first lie, the first drink, the first petty theft, is often a crisis in a man's life.

ERWIN LUTZER

Yes, the journey of a thousand miles begins with a single step. And if that first step is a compromise with sin, we might think we can turn back whenever we wish, but Jesus taught otherwise, "Everyone who practices sin is a slave to sin" (John 8:34). No one wakes up in the morning thinking they are going to become an addict, a slave to some practice and sinful lifestyle. But millions will testify, if they are honest, that a single wrong choice led them down to the path of destruction. Having boarded the train, they become a passenger all the way to the station. They are slaves to what has been called "the blinding self-absorption of sin."

Looking into the first step that leads us astray, Paul says it begins when we exchange God's truth and God's glory for lies and idolatry (Romans 1:18–25). Eve believed a lie and, thanks to her and Adam, the pattern is now followed with each sinful choice we make. To add to the confusion, many who are walking in darkness think it is light (Isaiah 59:9). The result of continual unrepentant sin is that God removes His hand and lets sin take over. What bondage!

We must warn one another to return to God (James 5:19–20). But only God can direct us back from the terrible danger we might be in. Only He can say, "Return, O backslider" (see Jeremiah 3:14).

PRAYER

Father, keep me from those first steps leading to the bankruptcy of sin.
Preserve me, O God!

JOIN THE WORK

"And the master said to the servant, 'Go out to the highways and hedges and compel people to come in, that my house may be filled.'"

LUKE 14:23

D. L. MOODY

Is it not time for us to launch out into the deep? I have never seen people go out into the lanes and alleys, into the hedges and highways, and try to bring the people in, but the Lord gave His blessing. If a man has the courage to go right to his neighbor and speak to him about his soul, God is sure to smile upon the effort. The person who is spoken to may wake up cross, but that is not always a bad sign, he may write a letter the next day and apologize. At any rate, it is better to wake him up in this way than that he should continue to slumber on to death and ruin.

ERWIN LUTZER

What we *are* determines what we *see*. When a farmer visited The Moody Church's large, beautiful sanctuary, he remarked, "You could put a lot of hay in here." And you could! He saw through the eyes of a farmer. We, as believers, should see the world through the eyes of Christ.

When Jesus saw the crowds, He said to the disciples, "The harvest is plentiful, but the laborers are few; therefore pray earnestly to the Lord of the harvest to send out laborers into his harvest" (Matthew 9:37–38). Let us ask God to be able to see the world as Jesus did.

Jesus didn't just see an immoral Samaritan woman or a self-righteous Pharisee; He saw people who needed the hope of eternal life. He had compassion for the multitude. We must see with His eyes and feel with His heart. When He asked us to "pray that the Lord of the harvest will send forth laborers into His harvest field," He was saying we should go and, figuratively speaking, be His feet. Finally, we must speak with our mouths. Who are you praying for to know the love, forgiveness, and redemption of God through Jesus Christ? Will you go to the highways and hedges urging them to come into God's kingdom?

PRAYER

Father, please soften my heart for the lost,
giving me opportunities to join in the harvest.

NO LONGER AN ENEMY

But God shows his love for us in that while we were still sinners, Christ died for us.
ROMANS 5:8

D. L. MOODY

I know of no truth in the whole Bible that ought to come home to us with such power and tenderness as that of the Love of God. There is no truth in the Bible that Satan would so much like to blot out. For more than six thousand years he has been trying to persuade men that God does not love them. He succeeded in making our first parents believe this lie; and too often he succeeds with their children.

The idea that God does not love us often comes from false teaching. Mothers make a mistake in teaching children that God does not love them when they do wrong, but only when they do right. That is not taught in Scripture. *You* do not teach your children that when they do wrong you hate them. Their wrongdoing does not change your love to hate, if it did, you would change your love a great many times. Because your child is fretful or has committed some act of disobedience, you do not cast him out as though he did not belong to you! No! He is still your child, and you love him. And if men have gone astray from God, it does not follow that He hates *them*. It is the sin that He hates.

ERWIN LUTZER

God loves the world at large, but His love is particularly focused on those who are His. We believers find it difficult to believe God loves us as much as He loves Jesus. Deeply ingrained within us is the false belief we must earn God's love. Yet we, as God's chosen, can confidently say, "Father, you love me as if I am Jesus" (John 17:23–26). Read Romans 8 and Paul's assurances that believers cannot ever be separated from the love of Christ. When we or our circumstances are out of control, let us remember that God still loves us.

PRAYER

Father, thank You that I am loved because I am joined to Christ,
Your beloved Son.

STANDING FIRM IN SUFFERING

Trust in him at all times, O people.

PSALM 62:8

D. L. MOODY

There are a good many who trust God when they see all is light and clear before them, but not in the dark. They will trust when everything is fair and bright—no opposition, no persecution or bitterness, but all smooth sailing. Well, that is walking by sight, and not by faith. We are to trust in the Lord at all times. The Lord will not have one who cannot be tried. If you are starting out in the Lord's work, you are going to be tempted. St. Augustine said that God has had one Son without sin, but no son without trials.

ERWIN LUTZER

Suffering of any kind seems to count against God's love for us. Whether an unexpected health crisis, injustice, abuse, or opposition because of our stand for Christ—we are easily deceived into thinking that God cannot be trusted. But it was Jesus who gave us a promise we don't particularly like, "In the world you will have tribulation. But take heart; I have overcome the world" (John 16:33). That tribulation can take many different forms, but if we suffer for His name, Jesus also said, "Blessed are you when others revile you and persecute you and utter all kinds of evil against you falsely on my account. Rejoice and be glad, for your reward is great in heaven, for so they persecuted the prophets who were before you" (Matthew 5:11–12).

Suffering has a purpose; it forces us to look beyond the present world to the future world; it reminds us that life here is temporary and eternity is forever. Suffering fuels anticipation; it tests our faith, so that it will be found to be "more precious than gold" (1 Peter 1:7). Paul put it clearly, "We rejoice in our sufferings, knowing that suffering produces endurance" (Romans 5:3).

PRAYER

Father, help me to trust, even when I do not understand.

OCTOBER 3

SIMPLE OBEDIENCE

"And all these blessings shall come upon you and overtake you, if you obey the voice of the Lord your God."
DEUTERONOMY 28:2

D. L. MOODY

Do you know *every man who was blessed while Christ was on earth, was blessed in the act of obedience?*

Ten lepers came to Him, and He said, "Go shew [show] yourselves unto the priests" (Luke 17:14). They might have said, "What good is that going to do us? It was the priest that sent us away from our families." But they said nothing. And it came to pass, that as they went, they were healed. Do you want to get rid of the leprosy of sin? Obey God. You say you don't feel like it. Did you always feel like going to school when you were a boy or a girl? Supposing a man only went to business when he felt like it, he would fail in a few weeks.

Jesus said to another man, "Go, wash in the pool of Siloam," and as he washed, he received his sight (John 9:7). He was blessed in the act of obedience.

The prophet said to Naaman, "Go and dip seven times in Jordan," and while he was dipping, he was healed (2 Kings 5:1–14). Simple obedience.

ERWIN LUTZER

Sometimes obedience doesn't make sense. When Christ's disciples had toiled all night on Galilee and yet caught no fish, Jesus said, "Put out into the deep and let down your nets for a catch." Peter objected because this was the wrong time of day (fishing at night was more profitable), and because it was in the wrong place (in the daytime, fish were more plentiful near the shore). But then Peter said, "But at your word I will let down the nets" (see Luke 5:4–5). The result was nets so full of fish they needed help to bring them in.

We must obey and leave the oft unexpected consequences to God.

PRAYER

Father, help me to obey You and seek Your face—not just for the blessings but to grow in love for You.

WHEN APPEARING CRAZY FITS

For if we are beside ourselves, it is for God; if we are in our right mind, it is for you.
2 CORINTHIANS 5:13

D. L. MOODY

In my opinion, no one is fit for God's service until he is willing to be considered mad by the world. They said Paul was mad. I wish we had many more who were bitten with the same kind of madness.

ERWIN LUTZER

There are times when Christians might appear mad to the people of the world. In response to Paul's teaching, the Roman officer Festus said, "Paul you are out of your mind, your great learning is driving you out of your mind" (Acts 26:24).

When Mary, in Mark 14:3–9, took that flask and broke it, pouring the perfume over the body of Jesus, some in the room thought this was foolish and asked, "Why was the ointment wasted like that? For this ointment could have been sold for more than three hundred denarii and given to the poor." Remember a denarius was a day's wage; three hundred would probably mean her life's savings. Jesus felt differently and said tenderly, "She has done a beautiful thing to me." What seems mad to the world might be very precious to God.

I've known young people who have gone to the mission field, and critics have said, "You could have had a good career here at home . . . what a waste!" The cost of surrender to God may appear as insanity to the people of the world. A life wasted in the eyes of men might be a life lived for eternal glory in the eyes of God.

Martin Luther's father was angry when his son enrolled in the monastery in Erfurt, Germany. He wanted Martin to become a successful lawyer and help with the family finances. But Martin's quest for salvation was more important; and eventually his Reformation changed the map of Europe and ushered in a spiritual revolution.

Are we seeking to please others or to please God?

PRAYER

Father, may I care more about what You think than what others think.

HEADED FOR GLORY

And as they were coming down the mountain, he charged them to tell no one what they had seen, until the Son of Man had risen from the dead.

MARK 9:9

D. L. MOODY

It is a singular fact that John, the only gospel writer who was with Christ on the Mount of Transfiguration, does not give an account of it. Perhaps the scene was so solemn, so impressive, and so holy that he could not bring himself to write of it. Peter, who was also present, barely mentioned it in his writings that have come down to us. His only reference to the scene is in his second letter, written many years afterward, when he was an old man: "We were eyewitnesses of his majesty. For he received from God the Father honour and glory, when there came such a voice to him from the excellent glory, This is my beloved Son, in whom I am well pleased. And this voice which came from heaven we heard, when we were with him in the holy mount" (2 Peter 1:16–18).

ERWIN LUTZER

What did Jesus' transfiguration mean to Peter, James, and John? Well, they were discussing His exodus, that is, Jesus' coming death in Jerusalem. And second, the transfiguration showed them the glory that would be waiting for them at death. James was the first disciple to be martyred, and I can imagine him thinking, "I have seen the glory waiting for me on the other side." Tradition says Peter was crucified for his faith, and John lived with persecution and was eventually exiled on the island of Patmos.

The three of them would never view death the same again for they had "seen the glory." For us, with the eye of faith, we see glory, and when we join Jesus in glory, "we shall be like him, because we shall see him as he is" (1 John 3:2).

If only we were to remember the glory that awaits us, we would face death without fear.

PRAYER

Father, may my coming glory motivate me to live on earth for Your glory alone.

OCTOBER 6

OBEDIENCE IS EASY WHEN IT'S EASY

"Yet you refuse to come to me that you may have life."
JOHN 5:40

D. L. MOODY

The battle is fought on that one word of the will; the door hangs on that one hinge of the will. Will you obey? That is the question! Will you obey the voice of God and do as He commands you? No man can obey for you any more than he can eat and drink for you. You must eat and drink for yourself, and you must obey God for yourself.

ERWIN LUTZER

No one can obey God in your stead, especially when the pressure is on. Where you turn to when the bottom falls out of life and tragedy strikes says much about who you are and what you really believe. Our hearts are revealed when we face a choice of obedience to God or going our own way. King Saul is an interesting study in psychological analysis; he was a peculiar mixture of good and bad. He was able to win battles, but when his personal desires clashed with God's will, he took the easy and most attractive route. His reputation and personal fortune meant more to him than hard obedience.

In brief, Saul was asked to slay the Amalekites, and though he was partially obedient, he spared the life of their king and claimed that he kept the best of their flocks to offer as a sacrifice to the Lord. But the prophet Samuel, speaking on behalf of God said, "Has the LORD as great delight in burnt offerings and sacrifices, as in obeying the voice of the LORD? Behold, to obey is better than sacrifice." Saul admitted that the reason for his disobedience was to please the people (see 1 Samuel 15:22–24).

Obedience is never easy. But it is always the best path. God commands all people to come to Him and repent, but very few obey.

The question is: Will we obey the voice of God or the voice of man?

PRAYER

Father, help me to keep my eyes and heart focused on You regardless of the trials.

SIN'S CHAINS ARE GONE

Because he holds fast to me in love, I will deliver him.

PSALM 91:14

D. L. MOODY

We all have some weak point in our character. When we would go forward, it drags us back, and when we would rise up into higher spheres of usefulness and the atmosphere of heaven, something drags us down. Now, I have no sympathy with the idea that God puts us behind the blood and saves us, and then leaves us in Egypt to be under the old taskmaster. I believe God brings us out of Egypt into the promised land, and that it is the privilege of every child of God to be delivered from every foe, from every besetting sin.

If there is some sin that is getting the mastery over you, you certainly cannot be useful. You certainly cannot bring forth fruit to the honor and glory of God until you get self-control.

ERWIN LUTZER

Did you have some wins in your battle against sin this past week? Did you have some losses? Why did you have those losses? Have you taken time to analyze? We are creatures of habit who develop habits of sin, telling ourselves all kinds of lies about how we aren't addicted, or that we don't have a serious problem. Our desire to believe something is more important than the facts.

Jesus Christ died for believers, setting us free from the penalty of sin; we died with Jesus Christ and that sets us free from the power of sin. But—and we agree—Paul does not say that sin is dead, but rather that we have no more obligation to obey its desires (Romans 6:11). Sin is no longer our taskmaster (Romans 6:6). This is the basis for us seeking God for deliverance.

PRAYER

Father, Your Word says I need not serve sin.
I say no to that terrible master. Help me to say yes to serving You.

GROUNDED AND SECURE

"Behold, God is my salvation; I will trust, and will not be afraid; for the Lord God is my strength and my song, and he has become my salvation."

ISAIAH 12:2

D. L. MOODY

Don't be watching your feelings. There is not one verse from Genesis to Revelation about being saved by feeling. When the devil sees a poor soul in agony in the waves of sin and getting close to the Rock of Ages, he just holds out the plank of "feeling" to him and says, "There, get on that; you feel more comfortable now, don't you?"

And while the man is getting his breath again, out goes the plank from under him, and he is worse off than ever. Accept no refuge but the Rock—the Everlasting Strength.

ERWIN LUTZER

Have you ever been in a pit? I'm not talking about the sand dunes, but an emotional pit of your own experience, the mire and the muck. This was David's experience in Psalm 40:1–2, "I waited patiently for the Lord; he inclined to me and heard my cry. He drew me up from the pit of destruction, out of the miry bog." This kind of pit is too deep to get out of alone; as the saying goes: If you want to get out of a pit, quit digging.

Verse 2 ends with David saying that God "set my feet upon a rock, making my steps secure." The solid rock is, basically, confidence in God. In the midst of circumstances over which we have no control, even there, God gives us the deep settled confidence that He will walk with us and can stand again.

You have heard this before: *Feelings are not facts.* Depression is a terrible experience, but it does not change God's love for us or the trustworthiness of His promises.

PRAYER

Father, root me in Your promises and keep me from rooting myself in my feelings.

HEAVENLY POSSESSIONS

"The one who conquers will have this heritage, and I will be his God and he will be my son."
REVELATION 21:7

D. L. MOODY

After the Chicago fire, I met a man who said, "Moody, I hear you lost everything in the Chicago fire." "Well," I said, "you understood it wrong; I didn't." He said, "How much do you have left?"

"I can't tell you; I have got a good deal more left than I lost." "You can't tell how much you have?"

"No."

"I didn't know that you were ever that rich. What do you mean?"

"I mean just what I say. I got my old Bible out of the fire; that was about the only thing. One promise came to me that illuminated the city a great deal more than the fire did. 'He that overcometh shall inherit all things; and I will be his God, and he shall be my son'" (Revelation 21:7).

You ask me how much I am worth. I don't know. You can't find out how much a child of God is worth. Why? Because he is a joint-heir with Jesus Christ. The weakest, poorest child of God is richer than a Vanderbilt because he has eternal riches. The stuff that burned in Chicago was like the dust in the balance. Joint-heir with Jesus Christ! That is what the eighth chapter of Romans teaches us.

ERWIN LUTZER

I love this story. D. L. Moody could have taken out his pen and added Romans 8:32: "He who did not spare his own Son but gave him up for us all, how will he not also with him graciously give us all things?" Jesus was raised again and seated in heaven that He might redeem and bring many sons into glory. In this life, we begin to receive some of the benefits of Sonship. In this life we receive the drop, and in the life to come we're going to receive the ocean. In this life we receive the flower, and in the life to come we are going to receive the whole garden.

PRAYER

Father, thank You for making me a joint heir with Christ.
Keep my focus on heavenly riches.

CHOOSE HUMILITY

"He must increase, but I must decrease."
JOHN 3:30

D. L. MOODY

If we preached down ourselves and exalted Christ, the world would soon be reached. The world is perishing today for the want of Christ. The church could do without our theories and pet views, but not without Christ; and when her ministers get behind the cross so that Christ is held up, the people will come flocking to hear the gospel.

Selfishness is one of the greatest hindrances to the cause of Christ. Everyone wants the chief seat in the synagogue (Matthew 23:6). One prides himself that he is pastor of this church, and another of that. Would to God we could get all this out of the way and say, "He must increase, but I must decrease." We cannot do it, however, except we get down at the foot of the cross. Human nature likes to be lifted up; the grace of God alone can humble us.

ERWIN LUTZER

Think of all of the divisions—arguments that would be avoided if only we were convinced that we do not need to be exalted; we do not need positions or power or control. If only we kept focusing on Christ, our humility would overcome our needless arguments.

Interestingly, humility is not a fruit of the Spirit. Why? Because it is a choice; we choose the path of humility. "Therefore it says, 'God opposes the proud but gives grace to the humble.' Submit yourselves therefore to God. Resist the devil, and he will flee from you" (James 4:6–7). And Peter echoes the same thought, "Humble yourselves, therefore, under the mighty hand of God so that at the proper time he may exalt you" (1 Peter 5:6).

If we don't humble ourselves, God may do it for us. I've seen proud leaders brought low when their secret sin was exposed; I have seen gifted people fail at their endeavors. Let us all say with John the Baptist, "He must increase, but I must decrease."

PRAYER

Father, help me choose humility and to see myself as You do.

CONSTANT GARDENING

"Bear fruit in keeping with repentance."
MATTHEW 3:8

D. L. MOODY

A friend had come to Christ and wished to consecrate himself and his wealth to God. He formerly had transactions with the government and had taken advantage of them. This thing came up when he was converted, and his conscience troubled him. He said, "I want to consecrate my wealth, but it seems as if God will not take it."

He had a terrible struggle; his conscience kept rising up and smiting him. At last, he drew a check for fifteen hundred dollars and sent it to the United States Treasury. He told me he received such a blessing when he had done it!

That was bringing forth "fruits meet for repentance" (Matthew 3:8). I believe a great many men are crying to God for light, and they are not getting it because they are not honest with themselves.

ERWIN LUTZER

I've emphasized this before, but one of the great roadblocks to spiritual progress is a troubled conscience due to past wrongs that have not been made right. Restoration is a component of revival. Sometimes we cannot rectify the past because circumstances have changed, but then we should ask the Lord for wisdom as to what steps we should take to set matters aright. That is a fruit of repentance.

And, there is only one way we can bear the fruit of repentance, "As the branch cannot bear fruit by itself, unless it abides in the vine, neither can you, unless you abide in me" (John 15:4). We cannot fully experience the fruit of the Spirit—the qualities of the inner life that bring glory to God, unless we have done all we can to make the past right. When that is accomplished, we repeatedly affirm our dependence on Christ each and every day.

PRAYER

Father, enable me to rest in Your provision and love
so that I might bear much fruit for Your glory.

OCTOBER 12

JUST A PREVIEW

Show him my salvation.
PSALM 91:16

D. L. MOODY

I believe we don't learn the fringe of the subject of salvation down here. When our Master was on earth, He said He had many more things to say, but He could not reveal them to His disciples because they were not ready to receive them. But when we go yonder, when these mortal bodies have put on immorality, when our spiritual faculties are loosed from the servitude of the flesh, I believe we shall be able to take more in. God will lead us from glory to glory, and show us the fullness of our salvation. Don't you think Moses knew more at the Mount of Transfiguration than he did at Pisgah (where Moses saw the promised land)? Didn't Christ talk with him then about the death He was to accomplish at Jerusalem? He couldn't have received this truth before, but when he had received his glorified body, Christ could show him everything.

ERWIN LUTZER

John Bunyan, in *The Pilgrim's Progress*, said that when pilgrims Hopeful and Christian could see the holy city in the distance, it was too beautiful for human eyes. So, they needed a special instrument by which they could see it because they could not look at it directly.

We have this marvelous account in God's Word (see Revelation 19:1–6; Revelation 21; 22) of what eternity with Christ will be like. We know the meaning of the words written on the page, but when we try to grasp the concept, it always eludes us. It is never what we really think it is—it is so much better. So much better! Though we see, thank God, we see dimly (1 Corinthians 13:12). We don't get it all, but we try to because it is so much better than we could imagine it to be.

PRAYER

Father, inspire me to live in light of eternity
and to eagerly desire the revealing of Your glory.

LIFELONG COMMAND

"Honor your father and mother" (this is the first commandment with a promise), "that it may go well with you and that you may live long in the land."
EPHESIANS 6:2–3

D. L. MOODY

Disobedience and disrespect for parents are often the first steps in the downward track. Many a criminal has testified that these are the points where he first went astray. I have lived over sixty years and I have learned one thing if I have learned nothing else—that no man or woman who dishonors father or mother ever prospers in the long run.

ERWIN LUTZER

The commandment, "Honor your father and your mother" (Deuteronomy 5:16) is the one that is centrally located within the heart of God's social program for the world because the family must be strong. God invests in parents an awesome responsibility; and in some respects, parents represent Him to their children.

When do we obey our parents? We obey even when it hurts, even when the will of our parents seems to be contrary to our own desires and our own inclinations. If your parents are commanding you to sin, then you should not obey them but seek wisdom for a different course of action. But the Bible simply says, "Children, obey your parents" (Ephesians 6:1). Why? It is so "that it may go well with you."

How this commandment should be applied in difficult family circumstances should be discussed with people who can provide wise, biblical, counsel. But as a general rule, we must honor our parents with our actions, attitude, and also with the attention that we should give them. This command does not have a timeframe. When God gave the Ten Commandments, He probably had in mind the responsibility of young people taking care of their older parents as they approach old age.

Blessed are those who keep this commandment.

PRAYER

Father, help me to honor my parents at every stage in life.
Continue to heal my family by Your grace.

TEMPTATION WILL COME

"Simon, Simon, behold, Satan demanded to have you, that he might sift you like wheat, but I have prayed for you that your faith may not fail. And when you have turned again, strengthen your brothers."

LUKE 22:31–32

D. L. MOODY

There is no one beyond the reach of the tempter. Keep that in mind. Life may run smoothly for a while, but the testing time is coming.

ERWIN LUTZER

Yes, testing is coming.

Even Christ was tempted of the devil. In fact, we read that Jesus was "led up by the Spirit" into the wilderness (Matthew 4:1). You might say, "Well, God doesn't tempt anybody." That is true. He does not solicit anyone to do evil, but God does test us (Deuteronomy 13:3–4; James 1:13). Furthermore, it wasn't God soliciting Jesus to evil—it was Satan. But it was God who brought Jesus to the place of temptation, the place of testing. Satan's agenda is to tempt us to do evil; God's intention is to test us to prove our character and commitment to Him.

How do we overcome the devil when temptations come our way? Through the Word of God! When we are under the authority of the Word, we can exercise the power of the Word. Then we can say, "Be gone, Satan" (Matthew 4:10) and quote a relevant verse of Scripture. Temptation is resistible. But let's not think we can face the tempter with will power; we need the intervention of God's Spirit though the Word.

Through our tough obedience, character is built, God is glorified, Jesus receives honor, and the cause of Christ is advanced (see Romans 5:3–4; James 1:3–4). That's God's intention. God's purpose in testing is to bring out the best in us and to give us an opportunity to love God more than our passions.

PRAYER

Father, in the name of Jesus, help me to resist temptation
through the power of Your Word.

BREAKING THE TEMPTATION OF DISHONESTY

Peter said, "Ananias, why has Satan filled your heart to lie to the Holy Spirit and to keep back for yourself part of the proceeds of the land?"
ACTS 5:3

D. L. MOODY

"Mr. Moody," you say, "How can I check myself? How can I overcome the habit of lying and gossip?" A lady once said to me that she had got so into the habit of exaggerating, her friends said they could never trust her.

The cure is simple, but not very pleasant. Treat it as a sin and confess it to God and the person whom you have wronged. As soon as you catch yourself lying, go straight to that person and confess you have lied. Let your confession be as wide as your transgression. If you have slandered or lied about anyone in public, let your confession be public. Many a person says some mean, false thing about another in the presence of others, and then tries to patch it up by going to that person alone. This is not making adequate confession. I need not go to God with confession until I have made it right with that person and the others who heard my remarks if it is in my power to do so; If not, God will not hear me.

ERWIN LUTZER

"Let God be true, but every man a liar" (Romans 3:4 KJV).

Remember Jesus said of Satan, "When he lies, he speaks out of his own character, for he is a liar and the father of lies" (John 8:44). When we lie, we are doing the devil's work. Interestingly, Ananias and Sapphira did not know that their decision to lie was inserted into their minds by Satan (read Acts 5:1–6). This gives us insight as to how the deceiver works: The devil puts lies into our minds that we think are our own.

Moody's advice is excellent: Let us confess the lie to the person to whom we told it. And, if necessary, to a wider audience if they were included in our deception.

PRAYER

Father, help my heart and lips and to speak only truth,
no matter the consequences.

SHELTERED BY GOD

He who dwells in the shelter of the Most High will abide in the shadow of the Almighty.
PSALM 91:1

D. L. MOODY

The psalm might have been written by Moses after some terrible calamity had come upon the children of Israel. It might have been after that terrible night of death in Egypt, when the firstborn from the palace to the hovel were slain; or after that terrible plague of fiery serpents in the wilderness, when the people were full of fear and in a nervous state. Perhaps Moses called Aaron and Miriam, along with Joshua and Caleb, and a few others into his tent and read this psalm to them first. How sweet it must have sounded, and how strange!

I can imagine Moses asking, "Do you think that will help them? Will that quiet them?" And they all thought it would. And then (it may be), on one of those hilltops of Sinai at twilight, this psalm was read. How it must have soothed them, how it must have helped them, how it must have strengthened them!

ERWIN LUTZER

What do we need when troubles mount? At a time of war and loss? When we face our own death? We need a *shelter*. We need someone who is stronger than whatever befalls us. Let me share a song that strengthened and soothed me as a child, and it still helps me to this day.

The Lord's our Rock; in Him we hide,
A Shelter in the time of storm;
Secure whatever ill betide,
A Shelter in the time of storm.
A Shade by day, Defense by night,
A Shelter in the time of storm;
No fears alarm, no foes affright
A Shelter in the time of storm.[26]

PRAYER

Father, thank You for trouble which reveals whom I really trust.
Help me to trust You.

GROWING, NOT LEAPING

Grow in the grace and knowledge of our Lord and Savior Jesus Christ.

2 PETER 3:18

D. L. MOODY

Although you must be born again, it will require time to become a full-grown Christian. Justification is instantaneous, but sanctification is a lifework. We are to grow in wisdom. We are to add grace to grace. A tree may be perfect in its first year of growth, but it has not attained its maturity. So with the Christian: He may be a true child of God, but not a matured Christian.

ERWIN LUTZER

Wouldn't it be wonderful if we could grow spiritually by osmosis? Imagine going to bed at night and while sleeping, God works in your heart and develops your spirituality, and when you wake up, suddenly you have "a heart hot for God."

That's not the way it happens.

Yes, we must rest in the Lord, but discipline is necessary! Recently, I have been reading through the book of Joshua, being reminded that the Lord gave them the promised land, but they had to possess it—and in the process, they had both victories and defeats.

Both the meat and the milk of the Word must enter our souls (Hebrews 5:12; 1 Peter 2:2). When we read the Word of God, it should not pass through our minds as water passes through a pipe; we need to ponder it and be changed by it, soaking in its moisture like the roots of a tree. Is there a promise to be claimed? Is there a command I should keep? What thought can I take with me for the day? Praying the Word of God has such transforming power that when we are exposed to it, it brings transformation.

We don't leap into growing in grace, but yes, we do *grow* into it.

PRAYER

Father, grow and nourish me day by day as I pray Your Word.

REPENTANCE AND BAPTISM

Then Jerusalem and all Judea and all the region about the Jordan were going out to him, and they were baptized by him in the river Jordan, confessing their sins.
MATTHEW 3:5–6

D. L. MOODY

Think of the whole population going out into the wilderness to hear this wonderful open-air preacher, to be "baptized of him in Jordan, confessing their sins!" John was a preacher of *repentance.* Perhaps no one ever rang out the word "Repent!" like John the Baptist. Day after day, as he came out of the desert and stood on the banks of that famous river, you could hear his voice, "Repent ye: for the kingdom of heaven is at hand" (Matthew 3:2). We can almost now hear the echoes of his voice as they floated up and down the Jordan.

Many wonderful scenes had been witnessed at that stream. Naaman had washed away his leprosy there. Elijah and Elisha had crossed it dry-shod. Joshua had led through its channel the mighty host of the redeemed on their journey into the promised land. But it had never seen anything like this: men, women, and children, mothers with babes in their arms, scribes, Pharisees, Sadducees, publicans, and soldiers flocked from Judea, Samaria, and Galilee, to hear this lonely wilderness prophet.

ERWIN LUTZER

We seldom hear the word *repentance.* It's not merely changing our minds, it's changing the direction of our lives, turning away from sin. If properly understood, to *savingly believe in Jesus* means to repent; it's an act of trust. Prayer alone doesn't save us. Without a heart that acknowledges its sin and its need for the gift of forgiveness and grace, there is no salvation.

Baptism should follow our conversion as an expression of our identification with Jesus' death, burial, and resurrection (Romans 6:4). Because we're identified with Christ, let's "Bear fruit in keeping with repentance" (Matthew 3:8).

PRAYER

Father, thank You for the gift of repentance;
I trust that divine work will be evident in my life.

OCTOBER 19

ALL WE NEED

And my God will supply every need of yours according to his riches in glory in Christ Jesus.
PHILIPPIANS 4:19

D. L. MOODY

Look at these words carefully. It does not say He will supply our wants. There are many things we want that God has not promised to give. It is our need, and all our need.

My children often want many things they do not get; but I supply all they need if it is in my power to do it. I do not supply all their wants by any means. And so, though God may withhold from us many things we desire, He will supply all our need. There can come upon us no trouble or trial in this life, but God has grace enough to carry us right through it, if we will only go to Him and get it. But we must ask for it day by day. "As thy days, so shall thy strength be" (Deuteronomy 33:25).

ERWIN LUTZER

God will give us what we need when we need it, and often not before. The apostle Paul was given a thorn in the flesh to keep him humble; it could have been any kind of weakness, insult, hardship, persecution, or calamity (2 Corinthians 12:7–10). Paul specifically prayed three times "that it should leave" him.

God said no to what Paul wanted, but God gave him what he needed, "My grace is sufficient for you, for my power is made perfect in weakness" (2 Corinthians 12:9). In effect, God said, "I'm not giving you what you want, but I am giving you what you need." You will have grace to bear your burden.

As Moody said, there is often a vast difference between what we want and what we need. Grace is a wonderful pillow upon which many a weary traveler has laid his head. Sufficient grace comes with sufficient faith.

PRAYER

Father, may I rest in Your sufficient grace with my wants and my needs.

DRINKING FREELY FROM THE WATER OF LIFE

"Come, everyone who thirsts, come to the waters; and he who has no money, come, buy and eat! Come, buy wine and milk without money and without price."
ISAIAH 55:1

D. L. MOODY

I pity those people who are all the time looking to see what they will have to give up. God wants to bestow His marvelous grace on His people, and there is not a soul who has believed on Jesus for whom God has not an abundance of grace in store.

What would you say of a man dying of thirst on the banks of a beautiful river with the stream flowing past his feet? You would think he was mad! The river of God's grace flows on without ceasing; why should we not partake of it, and go on our way rejoicing?

ERWIN LUTZER

Centuries ago, Blaise Pascal, a French theologian, wrote about our inborn desire to find hope and meaning, and concluded, "the infinite abyss can only be filled by an infinite and immutable object, that is to say, only by God Himself."[27]

When Jesus was at the Feast of Tabernacles, He watched the people bringing jugs of water as a part of their prescribed ritual, yet, they were missing the deeper meaning of their worship. Hear Him, "If anyone thirsts, let him come to me and drink. Whoever believes in me, as the Scripture has said, 'Out of his heart will flow rivers of living water'" (John 7:37–38).

Just as water is needed for physical life, so living water is needed for spiritual life. We may come for an initial drink, but then we come again and again to partake of God's grace and the power of the Holy Spirit.

PRAYER

Father, teach me to drink from the fountain of living water
so my soul can be refreshed.

THE SOUND OF HYMNS

And suddenly there was with the angel a multitude of the heavenly host praising God and saying, "Glory to God in the highest, and on earth peace among those with whom he is pleased!"

LUKE 2:13–14

D. L. MOODY

I have read that on the shores of the Adriatic Sea, the wives of fishermen whose husbands have gone far out upon the deep are in the habit of going down to the seashore at night and singing the first verse of some beautiful hymn. After they have sung it, they listen until they hear, brought on the wind across the sea, the second verse sung by their brave husbands—and both are happy. Perhaps, if we would listen, we too might hear on this storm-tossed world of ours some sound, some whisper, born from afar to tell us there is a heaven which is our home; and when we sing our hymns upon the shores of the earth, perhaps we may hear their sweet echoes breaking in music upon the sands of time and cheering the hearts of those who are pilgrims and strangers along the way.

ERWIN LUTZER

Interestingly, Moody saw the need for singing in the midst of the storms of life. This is excellent advice because singing hymns does lift our souls to God, and there is no time when we need such faith as when we are in a storm. Storms come in many different forms, and almost always in the most inopportune of times.

I've noticed this: As older believers struggle with dementia, they are often still able to quietly sing hymns they learned earlier in life. If we want to prepare for eternity, today would be an excellent time to either review the lyrics of hymns we know or learn those classic hymns so often neglected today.

Let us learn to sing amid the storms of life.

PRAYER

Father, may the song of my heart be focused on You on this daily pilgrimage. May I find peace in the incarnate Christ, bringing You much glory.

PERFECTION REALIZED

For whoever keeps the whole law but fails in one point has become guilty of all of it.
JAMES 2:10

D. L. MOODY

The Ten Commandments are not ten different laws; they are one law. If I am being held up in the air by a chain with ten links and I break one of them, down I come just as surely as if I broke the whole ten. If I am forbidden to go out of an enclosure, it makes no difference at what point I break through the fence. "For whosoever shall keep the whole law, and yet offend in one point, he is guilty of all." The golden chain of obedience is broken if one link is missing.

ERWIN LUTZER

This statement from James indicts all of us. It shatters every deception of self-righteousness and humbles all of us who think we are better than others. True, it is better to be a decent citizen than a criminal, but we all stand in need of abundant grace. We are all guilty of breaking all of the commandments.

Our problem? Nobody can get to heaven unless he is as perfect as God. No one understood this better than Martin Luther who spent hours in confession, trying to make sure that each sin he had committed was forgiven. But then he saw the answer to his quest: we receive the righteousness of Christ by faith.

As we sing:

Dressed in His righteousness alone, Faultless to stand before the throne.[28]

To break one commandment is to break them all; but Christ fulfilled the law perfectly, and we receive His righteous obedience and sacrifice.

PRAYER

Father, thank You for Jesus, who took my sin on the cross and gave me His righteousness, so that You now see me as perfect in Him.

LEADING PEOPLE TO CHRIST

The fruit of the righteous is a tree of life, and whoever captures souls is wise.
PROVERBS 11:30

D. L. MOODY

If we have known Jesus Christ for years, and have not been able to introduce an anxious soul to Him, there has been something wrong somewhere. If we were full of grace, we should be ready for any call that comes to us. Paul said, when he had that famous interview with Christ on the way to Damascus, "Lord, what wilt thou have me to do?" (Acts 9:6). Isaiah said, "Here am I; send me" (Isaiah 6:8). No man can tell what he can do until he moves forward. If we do that in the name of God, instead of there being a few scores or hundreds converted, there will be thousands flocking into the kingdom of God. Remember that we honor God when we ask for great things. It is a humiliating thing to think we are satisfied with very small results.

ERWIN LUTZER

As an evangelist speaking to tens of thousands, Moody led multitudes to faith in Christ. Clearly, that is not what you and I are gifted to do. But we can share the gospel individually, seeking opportunities to lead people to faith in Christ.

Here are some questions I've often shared to begin a spiritual conversation. Ask, "Where are you on your spiritual journey?" Then follow up with other questions on why they hold the beliefs they do. Or you might want to ask, "What is your idea of God?" Again let them tell you where they stand, spiritually speaking. Don't feel you must be quick to rebuke them, rather ask clarifying questions and how their beliefs have helped them. Then tell them about your belief in Christ and the promises of eternal life He offers.

Sow the seed. Trust God for the harvest.

PRAYER

Father, open opportunities for me to be used by You
to influence others for the gospel and for eternity.

OCTOBER 24

WEARING HUMILITY

Likewise, you who are younger, be subject to the elders. Clothe yourselves, all of you, with humility toward one another, for "God opposes the proud but gives grace to the humble."

1 PETER 5:5

D. L. MOODY

Some years ago, I saw what is called a sensitive plant. I happened to breathe on it, and suddenly it drooped its head; I touched it, and it withered away. Humility is as sensitive as that; it cannot safely be brought out on exhibition. A man who is flattering himself that he is humble and is walking close to the Master, is self-deceived. Humility consists not in thinking meanly of ourselves, but in not thinking of ourselves at all. Moses did not know that his face shone. If humility speaks of itself, it is gone.

ERWIN LUTZER

The idea of a proud, arrogant Christian is an oxymoron, or at least it should be. Yet, I have met Christians who ooze a sense of superiority, a need for attention and constant praise. But the root of all other sins is pride. We might do well to practice the discipline of fasting, both to show how desperately we need God and to also search our souls for unacknowledged pride. David wrote, "I humbled my soul with fasting" (Psalm 35:13 KJV). To fast is to fall on our knees with prayer, asking God to search us first before we make our petitions for others. We come to God with our great need; but we should leave our prayer time focused on our great God.

A judgmental, self-righteous attitude has created great harm within the church and to the unbelieving world. We must engage the world with humility, giving a reason for the hope within us (1 Peter 3:15). We do it with meekness and fear rather than judgmentalism and superiority.

I read that when pride walks onto the platform, God walks off.

PRAYER

Father, by Your grace, I choose the path of humility, not self-promotion.

PRAYING WITH PURPOSE

"O Lord, let your ear be attentive to the prayer of your servant, and to the prayer of your servants who delight to fear your name, and give success to your servant today, and grant him mercy in the sight of this man."
NEHEMIAH 1:11

D. L. MOODY

When Nehemiah began to pray, I have no idea whether he thought he himself was to be the instrument in God's hand of the rebuilding the walls of Jerusalem. But when a man gets into sympathy and harmony with God, then God prepares him for the work He has for him. No doubt he thought the Persian king might send one of his great warriors and accomplish the work with a great army of men; but after he had been praying for months, it may be, the thought flashed into his mind: "Why shouldn't I go to Jerusalem myself and build those walls?"

Prayer for the work will soon arouse your own sympathy and effort.

ERWIN LUTZER

People ask, "Why pray for missionaries? Can't God bless them without our prayers?" The answer is, of course, absolutely! Thankfully, He often blesses them even when we neglect to pray for them. But the purpose of prayer is not just to ask God to change circumstances; the purpose is to have our prayers change us. Even more important, prayer is intended to help us reenter into a time of fellowship with God.

As Moody pointed out in the case of Nehemiah, God used his prayer to recruit him to be a part of the answer. Prayer is asking God, "What will you have *me* to do?" And, as I like to emphasize, never interpret the silence of God as the indifference of God. God's work may be invisible to us, but behind the scenes, He is putting events in place to accomplish His purpose.

"The prayer of a righteous person has great power as it is working" (James 5:16).

PRAYER

Father, my heart longs to be prepared for all You want me to do.

OCTOBER 26

DYING GRACE

But he said to me, "My grace is sufficient for you, for my power is made perfect in weakness." Therefore I will boast all the more gladly of my weaknesses, so that the power of Christ may rest upon me.

2 CORINTHIANS 12:9

D. L. MOODY

I find many Christians worry about the future; they think they will not have grace enough to die by. It is much more important that we should have grace enough to live by. It seems to me that death is of very little importance in the meantime. When the dying hour comes, there will be dying grace; but you do not require dying grace to live by. If I am going to live for fifteen or twenty years, what do I want with dying grace? I am far more anxious about having grace enough for my present work.

I have sometimes been asked if I had grace enough to enable me to go to the stake and die as a martyr. No; what do I want with a martyr's grace? I do not like suffering, but if God should call on me to die a martyr's death, He would give me martyrs' grace. If I have to pass through some great affliction, I know God will give me grace when the time comes; but I do not want it till it comes.

ERWIN LUTZER

Corrie Ten Boom, who survived Nazi concentration camps, was about six years old when she told her father she was afraid of death. He responded, "Corrie, when you and I go to Amsterdam—when do I give you your ticket?" She replied, "Why, just before we get on the train."[29] He was making the point that we don't need dying grace until our time comes to die. As Moody said, we would even have martyr's grace if we were led to the stake to be killed for our faith. We have sufficient grace for today; fresh grace will be given to us tomorrow.

PRAYER

Father, teach us to receive grace for each moment.
Let the burdens of tomorrow be borne with tomorrow's grace.

OCTOBER 27

WATER THAT SATISFIES

On the last day of the feast, the great day, Jesus stood up and cried out, "If anyone thirsts, let him come to me and drink."
JOHN 7:37

D. L. MOODY

How this world is thirsting for something that will satisfy! What fills the places of amusement, the dance houses, the music halls, and the theatres, night after night? Men and women are thirsting for something they have not got. The moment a man turns his back upon God, he begins to thirst, and that thirst will never be quenched until he returns to "the fountain of living waters." As the prophet Jeremiah tells us in 2:13, we have forsaken the fountain of living waters, and hewn out for ourselves cisterns, broken cisterns, that can hold no water. There is a thirst this world can never quench: the more we drink of its pleasures, the thirstier we become. We cry out for more and more, and we are, all the while, being dragged down lower and lower. But there is a fountain opened to the House of David for sin and for uncleanness. Let us press up to it and drink and live.

ERWIN LUTZER

Israel had exchanged the living God for gods that don't really exist. In the process, they became slaves to themselves, their insatiable lusts, desires, and attitudes. The sooner we learn that the wells of the world are dry, the better we will get on with turning to God again and again for our sense of satisfaction and identity.

> Jesus, Thou joy of loving hearts, Thou fount of life, Thou light of men,
> From the best bliss that earth imparts, we turn unfilled to Thee again.[30]

PRAYER

Father, forgive me for seeking satisfaction in empty cisterns;
quench my thirst with Your true fulfillment.

THE GREATEST MIRACLE

Jesus answered him, "Truly, truly, I say to you, unless one is born again he cannot see the kingdom of God."

JOHN 3:3

D. L. MOODY

If the words of this text are true, they embody one of the most solemn questions. We can afford to be deceived about many things rather than about this one thing. Christ makes it very plain. He says, "Except a man be born again, he cannot see the kingdom of God"—much less inherit it. This doctrine of the new birth is therefore the foundation of all our hopes for the world to come. It is really the A B C of the Christian religion. My experience has been this—that if a man is unsound on this doctrine he will be unsound on almost every other fundamental doctrine in the Bible. A true understanding of this subject will help a man to solve a thousand difficulties he may meet with the Word of God. Things that before seemed very dark and mysterious will become very plain.

ERWIN LUTZER

We did not choose to be born physically, and this birth is described as being from "corruptible seed" (1 Peter 1:23 KJV), meaning we were born with a sin nature. Jesus taught we must be born again by God. Speaking of this new birth we read, "who were born, not of blood [not by our parents] nor of the will of the flesh [it was not because of your will power] nor of the will of man [it was not because of the will of others], but of God" (John 1:13). Our decision to receive Christ as Savior was the result of our heavenly Father's work in our hearts. A miracle indeed.

To summarize: The Word of God combined with the Spirit of God, creates within us the life of God. As Moody said, this divine work is foundational to all the hopes we have for the world to come.

PRAYER

Father, thank You for making me alive in Christ.
Thank You that I have been born again by faith in Christ!

REST FROM YOUR LABORS

And I heard a voice from heaven saying, "Write this: Blessed are the dead who die in the Lord from now on." "Blessed indeed," says the Spirit, "that they may rest from their labors, for their deeds follow them!"

REVELATION 14:13

D. L. MOODY

Think of Paul up yonder. People are going up every day and hour, men and women who have been brought to Christ through Paul's writings. He set streams in motion that have flowed on for more than a thousand years. I can imagine men going up to him and saying, "Paul, I thank you for writing that letter to the Ephesians; I found Christ in that." "Paul, I thank you for writing that epistle to the Corinthians." "Paul, I found Christ in that epistle to the Philippians." "I thank you, Paul, for that epistle to the Galatians; I found Christ in that."

When Paul was put in prison, he did not fold his hands and sit down in idleness! No, he began to write. His epistles have come down through the ages and brought thousands on thousands to knowledge of Christ crucified.

ERWIN LUTZER

Like a pebble thrown into the water, the ripple goes all the way to shore, just so, the deeds we do have eternal repercussions. We might not all be writers as was the apostle Paul but, nevertheless, our impact never ends. Everything we do for God is eternally preserved.

God never allows us to see all the good we do. We just have the bits and pieces of our own experience, but we are influencing those around us in ways that are unknown to us. No good deed is lost, and what we consider to be a meager though positive influence, might be much greater than we can ever imagine.

PRAYER

Father, I thank You for any good deeds I have done that have impacted others. And thank You for those whose works have followed them to glory.

BITTERNESS AND FAITH

And they heard the sound of the LORD God walking in the garden in the cool of the day, and the man and his wife hid themselves from the presence of the LORD God among the trees of the garden.

GENESIS 3:8

D. L. MOODY

A rule I have had for years is to treat the Lord Jesus Christ as a personal friend. It is not a creed, a mere empty doctrine, but it is Christ Himself we have. The moment we receive Christ, we should receive Him as a friend. When I go away from home, I bid my wife and children goodbye, I bid my friends and acquaintances goodbye; but I never heard of a poor backslider going down on his knees and saying: "I have been near you for ten years. Your service has become tedious and monotonous. I have come to bid you farewell. Goodbye, Lord Jesus Christ!"

I never heard of one doing this. I will tell you how they go away; they just run away.

ERWIN LUTZER

The word *deconstruction* we hear about today can refer to people who leave the Christian faith. I know children who were raised in the church, they memorized all the verses, they may have even professed some kind of faith in Christ. And yet, they have walked away from the faith—often they are bitter. Believe it or not, this is not a new phenomenon.

But even so, I think Moody was right to say that backsliders do not say goodbye to Christ even if they might say goodbye to the church. Here is a challenge for us, "And have mercy on those who doubt; save others by snatching them out of the fire; to others show mercy with fear" (Jude 1:22–23). We need God's wisdom as to how to respond to those who have left the faith. Each situation is different; and yes, our response should best reflect their situation and needs.

PRAYER

Father, help me to have mercy on those who have walked away from the faith and help them to return.

OCTOBER 31

THE POWER OF EDIFICATION

And the brothers there, when they heard about us, came as far as the Forum of Appius and Three Taverns to meet us. On seeing them, Paul thanked God and took courage.

ACTS 28:15

D. L. MOODY

If you are not able to go and invite the people to hear the gospel, you can give a word of cheer to others, and wish them "Godspeed." Many a time when I have come down from the pulpit, some old man, trembling on the very verge of another world, living perhaps on borrowed time, has caught hold of my hand, and in a quavering voice said, "God bless you!" How the words have cheered and helped me! You can speak a word of encouragement to younger friends if you are too feeble to work yourselves.

ERWIN LUTZER

Words, either good or bad, have tremendous power. "Death and life are in the power of the tongue, and those who love it will eat its fruits" (Proverbs 18:21). We can use words to either build or destroy, to bless or to curse. One negative comment can undo a thousand positive words.

Paul says, "Let no corrupting talk come out of your mouths, but only such as is good for building up" (Ephesians 4:29). If you want to effect change in someone's life, positive speech is better than negative speech. Even criticism can be couched in the language of helpfulness rather than the language of condemnation.

Like Barnabas, may we also be known as sons and daughters of "encouragement" and speak words of hope, of appreciation, and use our tongues to motivate people toward achievement and blessing (Acts 4:36). As Moody said, let us bless the younger generation.

PRAYER

Father, today, let the words of my mouth bring hope
and encouragement to all I meet.

ALWAYS RIGHTEOUS

The very commandment that promised life proved to be death to me. For sin, seizing an opportunity through the commandment, deceived me and through it killed me.

ROMANS 7:10–11

D. L. MOODY

A friend in England was telling me that an acquaintance of his, a minister, was once called upon to officiate at a funeral in the place of a chaplain of one of Her Majesty's prisons who was absent. He noticed that only one solitary man followed the body of the criminal to the grave. When the grave had been covered, this man told the minister that he was an officer of the law whose duty it was to watch the body of the culprit until it was buried out of sight; that was "the end" of the British law.

And that is what the law of God does to the sinner; it brings him right to death, and leaves him there. I pity deep down in my heart those who are trying to save themselves by the law. It never has, it never will, and it never can save the soul.

ERWIN LUTZER

As I've mentioned before, God's law is like a plumb line, showing that a wall is crooked, but it can do nothing to straighten it out. God's standards have not changed; all the demands of the law are continuously upon us (Romans 8:2; 10:4; Galatians 3:10–14). Living under grace does not mean we can flaunt the law; it means that Christ meets all of the demands of the law for us. And as believers with a new nature, we are to strive to keep the inner meaning of the law. To paraphrase Martin Luther, "O God, I am thy sin, and thou art my righteousness."[31] But that righteousness must now be wrought within our hearts.

PRAYER

Father, thank You for using the law to show me I need a Savior;
now, Lord, work Your righteousness in me.

SAME LORD

Christ is all, and in all.
COLOSSIANS 3:11

D. L. MOODY

Christ is all to us that we make Him to be. I want to emphasize that word all. Some men make Him to be "a root out of a dry ground," who "hath no form nor comeliness" (Isaiah 53:2). He is nothing to them; they do not want Him. Some Christians have a very small Saviour, for they are not willing to receive Him fully and let Him do great and mighty things for them. Others have a mighty Saviour because they make Him to be great and mighty.

ERWIN LUTZER

I'm sure you have heard it said, "If you are a great sinner, let me recommend a great Savior!" Yes, Christ must be all in all. As believers, our unity in Christ as Savior and Lord must always transcend politics, race, and geography. Division within the church is not new, that's why Paul had to remind believers that, in Christ, "there is not Greek and Jew, circumcised and uncircumcised, barbarian, Scythian, slave, free; but Christ is all, and in all" (Colossians 3:11). We must hear those words anew today.

One pastor put it this way, "When we gather at the Lord's table, there are no white spaces, black spaces, or brown spaces." And I might add, "There are no Democratic spaces, Republican spaces, or politically independent spaces." We have been bought with the same blood, and we worship the same Lord. And we will share in the same joy in a united heaven for all eternity.

PRAYER

Father, teach me what it means to believe Jesus is all, and in all.
Let that be true in my life and in the lives of all who gather in Your name.

SALVATION CITY

His divine power has granted to us all things that pertain to life and godliness, through the knowledge of him who called us to his own glory and excellence.

2 PETER 1:3

D. L. MOODY

There is glory for the time to come. A great many people seem to forget that the best is before us. Dr. Andrew Bonar once said that everything before the true believer is "glorious." This thought took hold on my soul, and I began to look the matter up and see what I could find in Scripture that was glorious hereafter. I found that the kingdom we are going to inherit is glorious; our crown is to be a "crown of glory"; the city we are going to inhabit is the city of the glorified; the songs we are to sing are the songs of the glorified; we are to wear garments of "glory and beauty"; our society will be the society of the glorified; our rest is to be "glorious"; the country to which we are going is to be full of "the glory of God and the Lamb" (see Revelation 21:23).

There are many who are always looking on the backward path and mourning over the troubles through which they have passed; they keep lugging up the cares and anxieties they have been called on to bear, and are forever looking at them. Why should we go reeling and staggering under the burdens and cares of life when we have such glorious prospects before us?

ERWIN LUTZER

The story of the Bible begins in the garden, but it ends in a city, New Jerusalem, in which God will display His eternal glory (Revelation 21:1–2).

Why a city? Because a city is where there are many common places with people doing life together in the presence of God. His name shall be on our foreheads and we shall reign with Him forever. Imagine that! The future is coming and, for believers, it is glorious: No sin, no death, no goodbyes. Let's look forward, not backward! The glories of tomorrow give us strength for the sorrows of today.

PRAYER

Father, may I live for the day when You will wipe away every tear and we will glorify You forever.

THE SUN WILL SHINE AGAIN

"Do not disbelieve, but believe."
JOHN 20:27

D. L. MOODY

People say, "If I could only get rid of these doubts and fears, I think I would be ready to work."

Go to work and these doubts will disappear. There is work to be done. Life is short at the longest, so let us be about our Master's business. While you are engaged in His work, these doubts will not assail you so much. I believe any Christian would have doubts in less than six months if he did nothing.

ERWIN LUTZER

When fears and doubts assail us, we are tempted to isolate ourselves from the resources God has given us, and try to go it alone. Spiritually speaking, this is not healthy. God has given us at least three resources to help us during dark times.

First, there are the members of the body of Jesus Christ. If you are struggling with doubt or fear, it's not enough to hear Christian friends say, "We'll pray for you." No. Get down on your knees with them. Let them bear your burdens, let them go to God on your behalf (Galatians 6:2). God gives us the body of Christ when we can't get through on our own.

Second, cleave to God's Word. We need to return to God's promises which assure us of His presence by His Spirit. Meditate upon Romans 8:31–39, one of many examples of His promises.

Finally, give your doubts to God; bring them to Him in all honesty. God welcomes honest doubters. He met Thomas who doubted the resurrection (John 20:24–29). He praised John the Baptist's greatness, even though John doubted whether Jesus was the Messiah (Luke 7:19–23). He gives honest doubters acceptance and the reality of His presence.

So go to work to serve God!

PRAYER

Father, may I never doubt in the darkness what I have learned in the light.
Give me the assurance of Your presence and the truth of Your promises.

DIFFICULT PEACE

Have nothing to do with foolish, ignorant controversies; you know that they breed quarrels.

2 TIMOTHY 2:23

D. L. MOODY

There are two kinds of skeptics—one class with honest difficulties, and another class who delight only in discussion. I used to think that this latter class would always be a thorn in my flesh, but they do not prick me now. I expect to find them right along the journey. Men of this stamp used to hang around Christ to entangle Him in His talk.

Many young converts make a woeful mistake. They think they are to defend the whole Bible. I knew very little of the Bible when I was first converted, and I thought that I had to defend it from beginning to end against all corners. A Boston infidel got hold of me, floored all my arguments at once, and discouraged me. But I have got over that now. There are many things in the Word of God that I do not profess to understand.

ERWIN LUTZER

Imagine the relief Moody must have felt when he realized he was not called to defend the whole Bible! Rather, he preached it and saw the Holy Spirit change lives. If you speak to a hardened skeptic, there is little that can be said to change their minds. Perhaps if they saw the people of God live differently, it might help them to see reality of the Christian faith through the fruit of the Spirit (love, joy, etc.). Sometimes a changed life can do what a rational argument can't.

God is reproducing the fruit of the Spirit in our lives by developing faith both through our personal struggles and our response to others. "Be kind to one another, tenderhearted, forgiving one another, as God in Christ forgave you" (Ephesians 4:32). We should not breed division but rather strive to live at peace—even with angry skeptics who pick fights.

PRAYER

Father, I want to strive for both truth and love
and represent You to a skeptical world.

WHO WILL HEAR "WELL DONE . . ."?

For we must all appear before the judgment seat of Christ, so that each one may receive what is due for what he has done in the body, whether good or evil.
2 CORINTHIANS 5:10

D. L. MOODY

Some people say that you never can tell till you are before the throne of judgment whether you are saved or not. Why, if our life is hid with Christ in God, we are not coming into judgment for our sins. We may come into judgment for *reward*. This is clearly taught where the lord reckoned with the servant to whom five talents had been given, and who brought other five talents. His lord said unto him, "Well done, thou good and faithful servant: thou hast been faithful over a few things, I will make thee ruler over many things: enter thou into the joy of thy lord" (Matthew 25:21). We shall be judged for our stewardship—that is one thing; but salvation—eternal life—is quite another thing.

ERWIN LUTZER

We must distinguish between the judgment seat of Christ, where believers will appear, and the great white throne judgment before which all unbelievers will appear (Revelation 20:11–15). Although Jesus paid for our sins, believers will be judged on the basis of what we did with what we were given. We receive rewards for being faithful stewards.

This is sobering. Even though we are exempt from final judgment, Christians should recognize we are not exempt from a kind of judgment that is going to determine our rewards and level of responsibility in the coming kingdom of heaven. I personally take the point of view that not every Christian is going to hear, "Well done, good and faithful servant" (Matthew 25:23). May we live in light of the coming judgment seat of Jesus Christ.

PRAYER

Father, teach me to serve and glorify You with all I've been entrusted.
May I hear "Well done" from Your lips.

A UNIQUE HOPE

May the God of hope fill you with all joy and peace in believing, so that by the power of the Holy Spirit you may abound in hope.

ROMANS 15:13

D. L. MOODY

Wherever I have found a worker in God's vineyard who has lost hope, I have found a man or woman not very useful.

It is very important to have hope in the church; and it is the work of the Holy Ghost to impart hope. Let Him come into some of the churches where there have not been any conversions for a few years, and let Him convert a score of people and see how hopeful the church becomes at once. He imparts hope. A man filled with the Spirit of God will be very hopeful. He will be looking out into the future, and he knows that it is all bright, because the God of all grace is able to do great things.

ERWIN LUTZER

As you look around the world, you will agree that there are few reasons to hope. But *our* hope as believers is the assurance that, in eternity, the evils of this world are going to serve a larger and eternal purpose. And yes, all evil acts will be properly adjudicated.

For believers, the best is yet to come. Ponder one of my most treasured promises: "May the God of hope fill you with all joy and peace in believing, so that by the power of the Holy Spirit you may abound in hope."

And this hope is the motivation for faithfulness.

PRAYER

Lord, my hope is in You—and You alone. Holy Spirit, fill me.

A GOD-CENTERED CONSCIENCE

Pray for us, for we are sure that we have a clear conscience, desiring to act honorably in all things.
HEBREWS 13:18

D. L. MOODY

Is not conscience a safe guide?

No, it is not. Some people don't seem to have any conscience and don't know what it means. Their education has a good deal to do with conscience. There are persons who will say that their conscience did not tell them they had done wrong until after the wrong was done. What we want is something to tell us a thing is wrong before we do it.

ERWIN LUTZER

Ogden Nash said, "There is only one way to achieve happiness on this terrestrial ball, and that is to have either a clear conscience, or none at all."[32] If you do not have a clear conscience, you are not currently filled with the Spirit nor will you know enduring joy in your relationships. The apostle Paul said, "The aim of our charge is love that issues from a pure heart and a good conscience and a sincere faith" (1 Timothy 1:5). Because sin defiles our conscience, it enables Satan to tell us two lies. The first lie is that one sin really doesn't matter. Lie number two is: "Now that you've messed up, you might as well mess up your life good and proper." Once your conscience is defiled, you almost always continue to defile it. Christians walking in the Spirit discover that before we do wrong, the Holy Spirit gives an internal warning, reminding us that we are about to cross a line into sinful behavior. We must always listen to that voice; the conscience, informed by the Spirit, warns us how sin grieves the Holy Spirit and always has negative consequences.

Paul exemplified doing all within your power to live with a conscience that was clear before both God and men (Acts 24:16). It is not enough to clear our conscience before God, we must always strive to experience the horizontal issues of personal reconciliation as well.

PRAYER

Father, teach me to keep a conscience that is undefiled before God and others.

NOVEMBER 9

THE FEAR-KILLER

There is no fear in love, but perfect love casts out fear. For fear has to do with punishment, and whoever fears has not been perfected in love.

1 JOHN 4:18

D. L. MOODY

There cannot be true peace where there is fear. "Perfect love casteth out fear." How wretched a wife would be if she doubted her husband! And how miserable a mother would feel if after her boy had gone away from home she had reason, from his neglect, to question that son's devotion! True love never has a doubt.

ERWIN LUTZER

Fear is debilitating; it disrupts our sense of well-being and paralyzes our ability to think clearly. Thoughts of fear replace thoughts of God's love and faithfulness. As John, the disciple whom Jesus loved, wrote in the verse above, fear can only be cast out by insisting on the promises of God's love and trusting in His sovereignty. But this is more difficult than it seems; sometimes the love of God seems contrary to our own experience.

The best way to renew our confidence in God's love is to remember His love was displayed on the cross. In other words, because of the cross, we need not fear being cast aside or abandoned—we are His forever. That love of God casts out fear. And we cannot accept the love of God without also believing in the sovereignty of God for our future—and for our eternity.

Let's take a lesson from David, "The LORD is my light and my salvation; whom shall I fear? The LORD is the stronghold of my life; of whom shall I be afraid?" (Psalm 27:1). Perhaps the secret of overcoming fear is best exemplified in Psalm 27:4: "One thing have I asked of the LORD, that will I seek after: that I may dwell in the house of the LORD all the days of my life, to gaze upon the beauty of the LORD and to inquire in his temple." That "one thing" will cast out fear.

PRAYER

Father, expand my view of You so I may understand Your perfect love.

NOVEMBER 10

UNCHANGING FAITHFULNESS

What if some were unfaithful? Does their faithlessness nullify the faithfulness of God?
ROMANS 3:3

D. L. MOODY

I am so tired of the Christianity that is made up of negations: what people *don't* believe. I met a man some time ago, and he said, "I don't believe this." I talked with him a little and made another statement; he didn't believe that. Finally, I said, "Man, will you tell me what you do believe?" and I found he didn't believe anything except that he didn't believe.

ERWIN LUTZER

The man of whom Moody spoke was certainly not a believer. It is not possible to be saved without believing something, namely, the message of the gospel. We are comforted by Romans 3:3 because, even as believers, there are times we might not be faithful but, thankfully, that doesn't negate the faithfulness of God. God is faithful to us, even when we are not faithful to Him.

Here is a striking example: Think of the faithfulness of God toward Lot. When angels came to Sodom to rescue him from the coming judgment, you might think he would have welcomed them. Not so. He had to be, almost literally, dragged out of the city. God could have destroyed him, along with his wife and daughters. But at some point, Lot had believed in the God of his uncle Abraham. So, God was faithful to this man, sparing him the judgment that fell on the city (Genesis 19). Tragically, though Lot left Sodom geographically, Sodom remained in his heart. Yet we read, "If [God] rescued righteous Lot . . . then the Lord knows how to rescue the godly from trials and to keep the unrighteous under punishment until the day of judgment" (2 Peter 2:7, 9). God is faithful even when we are not; He cannot deny Himself (2 Timothy 2:13).

PRAYER

Father, forgive me for the times I have doubted Your promises
and have not been faithful to You. Thank You for standing beside me
even when I was faithless.

LIGHT BEYOND THE ECLIPSE

"You are the light of the world. A city set on a hill cannot be hidden."
MATTHEW 5:14

D. L. MOODY

God has left us down here to shine. We are not here to buy and sell and get gain, to accumulate wealth, to acquire worldly position. This earth, if we are Christians, is not our home; it is yonder. God has sent us into the world to shine for Him—to light up this dark world. Christ came to be the Light of the world, but men put out that light. They took it to Calvary and blew it out. Before Christ went up on high, He said to His disciples: "Ye are the light of the world. Ye are my witnesses. Go forth and carry the gospel to the perishing nations of the earth."

ERWIN LUTZER

Our hearts should be broken just thinking about the many people who are walking in the darkness of this world. As Jesus said, those who walk in darkness do not know where they are going (John 12:35). Furthermore, many stumble in the darkness; in fact, "the way of the wicked is like deep darkness; they do not know over what they stumble" (Proverbs 4:19). Light reveals reality; light is also needed for life.

We are called to *walk* in the light as He is in the light. We must *share* the light, *defend* the light, and *live* in the light (1 John 1:5–7; 2:9–10, 21–23). It has often been said, "You are the best witness someone in this world has."

If I am asked, "What is more important, the life we live or the words we speak?" I answer, "Which wing on an airplane is most important, the right or the left?" Let's live and speak for the glory of Jesus and shine a light in the darkness.

PRAYER

Father, empower me to walk in Your light, to defend the light,
and to shine forth with the light of Christ in this dark world. Bring to mind
one person for whom I can be a light today.

TRUSTING GOD TO DO WHAT WE CAN'T

"And when he comes, he will convict the world concerning sin . . .
because they do not believe in me."
JOHN 16:8–9

D. L. MOODY

Some men seem to think it is a great misfortune that they do not have faith. They seem to look upon it as a kind of infirmity, and they think they ought to be sympathized with and pitied. Bear in mind, it is not a misfortune, it is the most damning sin of the world.

The greatest enemy God and man have got is unbelief. Christ found it on both sides of the cross. It was the very thing that put Him to death. The Jews did not believe Him. They did not believe God had sent Him. They took Him to Calvary and murdered Him. And the first thing we find after He rose from the grave was unbelief again. Thomas, one of His own disciples, did not believe He had risen. He said, "Thomas, feel these wounds;" and Thomas believed and said, "My Lord and my God" (see John 20:24–29).

ERWIN LUTZER

There are two kinds of doubters: one is a hardened unbeliever; the other is an honest doubter, open to faith but, for intellectual or emotional reasons, cannot accept the gospel. Thomas was of the second sort. Yet, Jesus graciously met his request. Notice Christ's response, "Blessed are those who have not seen and yet have believed" (John 20:29).

I read about a ship that sent an SOS for drinking water, not realizing they were in the fresh waters of the St. Lawrence River. They could have simply lowered buckets to quench their thirst.

If you are an honest doubter, I encourage you to admit your doubts without shame or self-condemnation. Acknowledge that you can't believe, then come to God and tell Him about your doubts—He is not put off by honest doubts (see Psalm 77). Put down your bucket in faith and God will meet you.

PRAYER

Father, thank You for showing me, by Your Spirit, my need for a Savior.
I believe; help my unbelief (Mark 9:24).

THE EXCLUSIVE NAME

"And there is salvation in no one else, for there is no other name under heaven given among men by which we must be saved."

ACTS 4:12

D. L. MOODY

If there is one word above another that will swing open the eternal gates, it is the name of *Jesus*. There are a great many passwords and bywords down here, but that will be the countersign up above. Jesus Christ is the "Open Sesame" to heaven. Anyone who tries to climb up some other way, is a thief and a robber. And when we get in, what a joy, above every other joy we can think of, will it be to see Jesus Himself and to be with Him continually!

ERWIN LUTZER

The gospel of Jesus Christ must be constantly guarded. Christians are the keepers of the gospel, making sure the clear message of the cross continues to go forth with its transforming power. Throughout history, there have been many attacks against Christianity, many ways in which the gospel has been polluted and becomes unclear. We must defend the exclusivity of the gospel: Jesus—and Jesus alone—can bring us to the Father. God took the initiative to reconcile us to Himself (2 Corinthians 5:11–21). We can only come to God on His terms, not ours.

Jesus came to earth to die, and when He died, on Him was laid God's judgment for all the sins of those who would believe on Him. This gift is received by faith. This faith is not merely intellectual, it is a transfer of trust through repentance of sin and accepting Jesus as Savior. God declares believers to be righteous in Christ, then the Holy Spirit of God comes into our lives and changes us from within; this results in a new love for Christ.

Our world wants many options. While Jesus' love is *inclusive* (offered to everyone), His salvation is *exclusive*. There is no one else like Him. Jesus—there's no other name.

PRAYER

Father, thank You that there is power in the name of Jesus.
I look to Him alone for my acceptance and assurance of salvation.

DETERMINING DESTINY

"Truly, truly, I say to you, whoever hears my word and believes him who sent me has eternal life. He does not come into judgment, but has passed from death to life."

JOHN 5:24

D. L. MOODY

The cross of Christ divides all mankind. There are only two sides, those for Christ, and those against Him. Think of the two thieves; from the side of Christ one went down to death cursing God, and the other went to glory.

What a contrast! In the morning, he is led out, a condemned criminal; in the evening, he is saved from his sins. In the morning, he is cursing— Matthew and Mark both tell us that those two thieves came out cursing (Matthew 27:44; Mark 15:32); in the evening, he is singing hallelujahs with a choir of angels. In the morning, he is condemned by men as not fit to live on earth; in the evening, he is reckoned good enough for heaven. In the morning, nailed to the cross; in the evening in the Paradise of God, crowned with a crown he should wear through all the ages. In the morning, not an eye to pity; in the evening, washed and made clean in the blood of the Lamb. In the morning, in the society of thieves and outcasts; in the evening, Christ is not ashamed to walk arm-in-arm with him down the golden pavements of the eternal city.

ERWIN LUTZER

Take a moment to imagine it: That evening in Paradise, Jesus is dining with Abraham, Isaac, and Jacob, when the thief shows up, and they ask, "Who are you? What did you do to get here?" And he answers, "I don't know…how I got here except that the dying man next to me said He would remember me." And Jesus steps forward and says, "Yes, I remembered you!"

> The dying thief rejoiced to see, That fountain in his day,
> And there may I, though vile as he, Wash all my sins away.[33]

PRAYER

Father, thank You for redeeming rebels like me through the power of the gospel.

NO GRAVE DEEP ENOUGH

"God raised him up, loosing the pangs of death, because it was not possible for him to be held by it."
ACTS 2:24

D. L. MOODY

It has always been a mystery to me when every disciple of Jesus Christ who was anywhere near Jerusalem, was not at the sepulchre on the morning of the third day after the crucifixion. Over and over again, He told them that He would arise. One of the last things He said to them, as they were on their way to the Mount of Olives, was—"After I am risen again, I will go before you into Galilee" (Matthew 26:32). But there is not one solitary passage that tells us that they had any expectation of His resurrection. It seems as if His enemies had better memories than His friends. When His body was laid away in the tomb, the Jews went to Pilate, and wanted him to make it secure because, they said, "We remember that that deceiver said, while he was yet alive, After three days I will rise again" (Matthew 27:63).

ERWIN LUTZER

One day, a missionary was sharing the gospel with someone. The person responded, "Oh, I wouldn't follow Jesus because I would follow a loser." That person was evidently thinking of Jesus on the cross; they did not understand He was a mighty victor in His resurrection!

By His death and resurrection, Jesus proved that death, Satan, and sin do not get the last word. Jesus crushed the head of the serpent (Genesis 3:15). On the cross, we are told Jesus forgave our trespasses and "disarmed the rulers and authorities and put them to open shame, by triumphing over them in him" (Colossians 2:15). The resurrection sealed that victory.

There was not a tomb deep enough, there were not grave clothes strong enough, and there was not a stone heavy enough to keep Jesus in the tomb. He was raised to redeem us—He alone qualifies as a Savior.

PRAYER

Lord Jesus, deepen my faith in You as I navigate life's journey in Your resurrection power.

CREATED WITH A PURPOSE

For by grace you have been saved through faith. And this is not your own doing; it is the gift of God, not a result of works, so that no one may boast.

EPHESIANS 2:8–9

D. L. MOODY

Before my conversion, I worked toward the cross, but since then, I have worked from the cross. Then I worked to be saved; now I work because I am saved.

ERWIN LUTZER

This is so encouraging. Right after we read that we are saved by grace through faith, and that not of ourselves it is the gift of God, the next verse reads, "For we are his workmanship, created in Christ Jesus for good works, which God prepared beforehand, that we should walk in them" (Ephesians 2:10).

You and I are God's *workmanship*; the Greek word is *poiēma* from which we get the English word *poem*. We are like a poem written by God for His glory and to fulfill His purpose in our lives. Regardless of our parents, our upbringing, positive or negative, we as individuals can be redeemed by God's gracious power to serve Him effectively. Our gifts, talents, and even our appearance are freely given to us by God, and they are to be used according to His purpose.

The sin of envy charges God with unfairness and reveals our unwillingness to accept who we are by divine providence. You and I could have been born in a different era, a different country, to different parents, or in a radically different environment. But we are who we are at this time of history "for such a time as this" (Esther 4:14). We work, not to be saved, but because we are saved! We are a poem with a message to be read by all those around us (2 Corinthians 3:2).

PRAYER

Father, I thank You that I am special—a poem composed by You for Your glory.

NOVEMBER 17

A FRANK WARNING

John had been saying to Herod, "It is not lawful for you to have your brother's wife."
MARK 6:18

D. L. MOODY

If your minister comes to you frankly, tells you of your sin, and warns you faithfully, thank God for him. He is your best friend; he is a heaven-sent man. But if your minister speaks smooth, oily words to you, tells you it is all right when you know, and he knows, that it is all wrong and that you are living in sin, you may be sure that he is a devil-sent man. I want to say I have a contempt for a preacher that will tone his message down to suit someone in his audience: some senator, or big man who he sees present. If the devil can get possession of such a minister and speak through him, he will do the work better than the devil himself. All the priests and ministers of all the churches cannot save one soul that will not part with sin.

ERWIN LUTZER

If you go to restore someone who has fallen into sin, go with a spirit of meekness and take heed to yourself, because you also may be tempted (Galatians 6:1). I cannot tell you the number of times I have had to mourn over my own sin until God restored my joy and peace because of His forgiveness for my sin that grieved the blessed Holy Spirit.

Let us make sure that we have dealt with our own sin before we go restore others. And as Moody said, as necessary, we should restore the fallen. We should not be intimidated because the fear of man is a snare (Proverbs 29:25). Where sin is not taken seriously, it is not dealt with thoroughly. And that means speaking the truth. Somewhere I read it is better to be slapped with the truth than to be kissed by lies.

PRAYER

Father, soften my heart so that I might receive
and give a rebuke in truth and love.

FEED YOURSELVES

I fed you with milk, not solid food, for you were not ready for it.
And even now you are not yet ready.
1 CORINTHIANS 3:2

D. L. MOODY

You know it is always regarded a great event in the family when children can feed themselves. They are propped up at table and at first, perhaps, they use it all right, and mother, or perhaps sister, claps her hands and says: "Just see, baby's feeding himself!"

What we need as Christians is to be able to feed ourselves. How many there are who sit helpless and listless, with open mouths, hungry for spiritual things, and the minister has to try to feed them, while the Bible is a feast prepared, into which they never venture!

ERWIN LUTZER

When we are born again into the family of God, we begin as spiritual infants. If a child is born without an appetite, they would starve. But my wife and I soon discovered that an infant lets you know very loudly when they are hungry! If a baby were to be fed only once a week, it would starve to death. But, spiritually speaking, there are Christians who attend church once a week to get some food only to starve themselves during the week. Even on Sunday, they sing songs, pray, and hear the Word of God, but alas, only milk is available.

The Bible, however, is a feast; it is a full meal, it is milk, it is meat, it is bread, and it is "sweeter than honey to my mouth," which is a wonderful dessert (see 1 Peter 2:2; Hebrews 5:14; Matthew 4:4; Psalm 119:103). A newborn baby has everything necessary for growth as long as they are fed. Just so, newborns in God's kingdom have the capacity to grow, but they need to learn to feed themselves and also to be fed by the people of God (Colossians 3:16). Together, let us enjoy the feast!

PRAYER

Lord, I'm hungry for You.
Give me a more acute appetite for You and Your Word.

GOD IS TRUTH

"You shall not bear false witness against your neighbor."
EXODUS 20:16

D. L. MOODY

You don't like to have anyone bear false witness against you, or help to ruin your character or reputation; then why should you do it to others? How public men are slandered in this country! None escape, whether good or bad. Judgment is passed upon them, their family, their character, by the press, and by individuals who know little or nothing about them. If one-tenth that is said and written about our public men was true, half of them should be hung. Slander has been called "tongue murder." Slanderers are compared to flies that always settle on sores, but do not touch a man's healthy parts.

If the archangel Gabriel should come down to earth and mix in human affairs, I believe his character would be assailed inside of forty-eight hours. Slander called Christ a gluttonous man and a winebibber (see Matthew 11:19). He claimed to be the Truth, but instead of worshiping Him, men took Him and crucified Him.

ERWIN LUTZER

God's command, "Thou shalt not bear false witness," actually refers to a false witness in a court of law. But it does have a wider application. Proverbs 6:16–19 says God hates seven things: "Haughty eyes, a *lying tongue*, and hands that shed innocent blood, a heart that devises wicked plans, feet that make haste to run to evil, a *false witness* who breathes out lies, and one who sows discord among brothers." Notice *lying* is mentioned twice. Moody couldn't have predicted all the slander, gossip, and lies Christians say about each other. Too often, slander is called "transparency," and to "heap vengeance" is called a "quest for justice." Nothing pleases Satan more than to see Christians form a firing squad, self-righteously destroying each other under the guise of seeking the truth.

The truth in the Scriptures often hurts, but lies hurt even more.

PRAYER

Father, may I rejoice in Your truth, no matter how much it humbles me or what it costs me.

MIGHTY TO SAVE

Who shall bring any charge against God's elect? It is God who justifies.
ROMANS 8:33

D. L. MOODY

That word "justifieth" seems too good to be true. No wonder Martin Luther shook all of Germany when that truth dawned upon him, "the just shall live by faith" (Romans 1:17). Do you know what "justified" means? I will tell you. It is to stand before God without spot or wrinkle, without a sin. It is to be put back beyond Eden. God looks over His ledger, and says: "Moody, I have no account against you. Your debt has all been wiped out by another."

ERWIN LUTZER

Let's ask the question: Who can make a charge against God's elect? Well, your enemies can, a coworker, a family member, a friend can. If you're married, your spouse may be able to make a charge against you, and the charge may be true. Satan does this all the time. How shall we respond? Before his conversion, Martin Luther confessed his sins in the monastery in Erfurt, trying to do everything he could to gain the perfection he needed to enter heaven. Consider his dilemma: Sins, in order to be forgiven, have to be confessed; in order to be confessed, they have to be remembered. Even if he remembered them all and confessed them all, tomorrow was a new day with new sins. It was like mopping up the floor with the sink still running over. Then as he was studying the book of Romans, Luther discovered that the righteousness of God is a free gift given to those who believe. Thus, the true believer stands with the righteousness of Christ credited to their account. Yes, we still confess our sins to maintain fellowship, but our eternal destiny is assured. Nothing can separate us from the love of God (Romans 8:35).

God finds no lasting charge against us.

PRAYER

Father, when accusations come—whether from others, Satan, or my own heart—help me remember that You have declared me righteous. Free me from the exhausting cycle of trying to earn what You freely give.

SECURE IN THE SPIRIT

If the Spirit of him who raised Jesus from the dead dwells in you, he who raised Christ Jesus from the dead will also give life to your mortal bodies through his Spirit who dwells in you.

ROMANS 8:11

D. L. MOODY

I had rather be in the heart of the eighth chapter of Romans than Adam in the heart of Paradise. Adam might have stayed in Paradise ten thousand years, and the devil could have come in then and snatched his life away from him, but I challenge the devil himself to get my life away from me, because it is hid with Christ in God, and Christ conquered Satan. "The prince of this world cometh, and hath nothing in me" (John 14:30). Christ conquered him, and oh, how safe the believer is! When the sinner is hid in Christ, hid in God, how is Satan going to get at him? He must go by the Almighty and by Christ before he can get at that sinner.

It is a great thing to be an heir of glory. It is a great thing to have your life guarded by the Son of God, and to have the angels of God encamping round about you (Colossians 3:3; Psalm 34:7).

ERWIN LUTZER

Being "in Christ" means we are in a sphere of safety and security, with no condemnation from God (Romans 8:1). Because we have a new identity and focus, we can dwell on the things of the Spirit, and not just the flesh. To clarify: *Flesh* doesn't mean the *body* (Romans 8:5). The body is neutral, but the "flesh" refers to the old nature—the principle and propensity to satisfy our lusts and desires outside of God's purity, holiness, and will.

Believers fight against the flesh from the standpoint of victory, knowing that, eventually, even our bodies will be resurrected from the dead!

PRAYER

Father, thank You that my future is secure; Jesus, by means of the Holy Spirit, dwells within me, and because He lives, so shall I.

DECLARED WORTHY

And when they came to Jesus, they pleaded with him earnestly, saying, "He is worthy to have you do this for him, for he loves our nation, and he is the one who built us our synagogue."

LUKE 7:4–5

D. L. MOODY

The Jews could not understand grace, so they thought Christ would grant the request of this man, because he was worthy.

"Why," they said, "he hath built us a synagogue!"

It is the same old story we hear today. Let a man give a few thousand dollars to build a church and he must have the best pew; "he is worthy." Perhaps he made his money by selling or making strong drink; but he has put the church under an obligation by this gift of money, and he is considered "worthy." This same spirit was at work in the days of Christ.

ERWIN LUTZER

I agree with Moody. We are never made "worthy" because of our good works. I'm reminded of the words of Martin Luther, when his friend, George Spalatin came to him, thinking he had sinned too greatly to be forgiven, Luther responded, and I paraphrase, "You are a great sinner? Come over to us because we are hardboiled sinners. Jesus died for great sins . . . for damnable iniquities."[34]

Those who are unworthy are wonderful candidates for salvation. Indeed, God saves only unworthy people. Many people today are striving to make themselves worthy of grace; no wonder they have no assurance of salvation, there is no end to their striving to be "worthy."

Let us come to Jesus knowing we are unworthy. The minute you say, "I need to get my life straightened up so that I am worthy of grace," proves you don't understand grace. Grace accepts you as you are if you are willing to transfer all your trust to Jesus and accept what He did on the cross. Christ alone makes us worthy to be accepted by the Father.

PRAYER

Father, I rejoice today that I am made worthy by Your grace.

THE GOOD GARDENER

"Be sure your sin will find you out."
NUMBERS 32:23

D. L. MOODY

Do you want to know the reason why, every now and then, the church is scandalized by the exposure of some leading church member or Sabbath-school superintendent? It is not his Christianity, but his lack of it. Some secret sin has been eating at the heart of the tree, and in a critical moment, it is blown down and its rottenness revealed.

ERWIN LUTZER

Many Christians (including high-profile leaders) have succumbed to temptation, often with severe consequences. A pastor friend of mine fell into immorality, his reputation was ruined. After he resigned from his church, he found a warehouse job. Rejected and marginalized, he could have become bitter, but he served God where he was. He remained faithful, spending time being quiet before God. "God loves to hurt His people," he would say. "It's the branch that bears fruit that feels the pruning knife" (see John 15:1).

Jesus is the Vine and the Father is the Gardener. God prunes the fruitful branches that they may bear more fruit. A good gardener will go through the vineyard, cut off the leaves and the little twigs so that the real branches connected to the vine will do two things. First, the branches won't dissipate their energy by bearing too many leaves. Secondly, the branches are then able to further engraft their relationship to the vine, becoming more firmly rooted into the vine.

God frequently lets hidden sin be exposed so that we might be brought to deep repentance. When that happens, we might never be restored to the position we once had, but the work that God does in us, may be more important than the work God does through us. He keeps pruning the branches until we die.

PRAYER

Father, search my heart and convict me of my sin that I might repent.
Prune me that I might bear fruit for You.

NOVEMBER 24

WHEN THE DEAD HEAR

Give ear, O my people, to my teaching; incline your ears to the words of my mouth!
PSALM 78:1

D. L. MOODY

Man lost spiritual life and communion with his Maker by listening to the voice of the tempter instead of the voice of God. We get life again by listening to the voice of God. The Word of God gives life. "The words that I speak unto you," says Christ, "they are spirit, and they are life" (John 6:63). So, what people need is—to incline their ear, and *hear*.

It is a great thing when the preacher gets the ear of a congregation—I mean the inner ear, for a man has not only two ears in his head, he has what we may call the outer ear and the inner ear—the ear of the soul. You may speak to the outward ear, and not reach the ear of the soul at all. Many in these days are like the "foolish people" to whom the prophet Jeremiah spoke: "Which have eyes, and see not; which have ears, and hear not" (Jeremiah 5:21). "He that hath ears to hear, let him hear."

ERWIN LUTZER

When I taught a preaching class, I would take the students to a cemetery and ask them to preach to the dead. That sounds bizarre of course, but I wanted them to know that when we preach the gospel to the unconverted, we are preaching to those who are "dead in trespasses and sins" (Ephesians 2:1). We cannot raise the dead; only God can give a corpse life.

Jesus came to take *dead* men and women and make them *alive*. He comes to the cemetery, so to speak, and breathes spiritual life into our souls! Our part is to share the gospel; God's part is to do the miracle.

PRAYER

Father, thank You for intervening in my life and opening my spiritual eyes to see and unplugging my ears to hear Your voice. Thank You that my salvation is entirely dependent on Your sovereign power and grace.

COME AND SEE WHAT GOD HAS DONE

Nathanael said to him, "Can anything good come out of Nazareth?" Philip said to him, "Come and see."

JOHN 1:46

D. L. MOODY

So we say to you, "Come and see!" I thought, when I was converted, that my friends had been very unfaithful to me because they had not told me about Christ. I thought I would have all my friends converted inside of twenty-four hours, and I was quite disappointed when they did not at once see Christ to be the Lily of the Valley and the Rose of Sharon and the Bright and Morning Star (Song of Solomon 2:1; Revelation 22:16). I wondered why it was. But we need to learn that God alone can do that.

ERWIN LUTZER

Parents cannot convert their children; we cannot convert our friends or relatives. After Moody was converted, he didn't understand this right away, and was surprised his friends were not immediately converted by his testimony. Only God can draw people to Himself and convict them of their sins. However, we are not called to do God's work for Him, we only have to point people in the right direction.

And a large part of evangelism is giving our own testimony. As Philip said to Nathanael, "Come and see!" Just so, we share the transformation Christ has made in our lives. Jesus said we are to be lights in the world, both by what we say and the testimony we have (Matthew 5:14). Sometimes seminars on evangelism stress only the content of the gospel, but a true story of conversion often speaks to the heart.

We do our part by both speaking and living out the gospel; the miracle is up to God (Ezekiel 36:26; 1 Corinthians 3:6). And God will not hold us accountable if others do not believe the gospel; but He will hold us accountable if we do not share the gospel.

PRAYER

Father, thank You for opening my heart to Your gospel.
I'm ready to cooperate with You in bringing the good news to others.

THE CALLING TO PERSECUTION

"If you were of the world, the world would love you as its own; but because you are not of the world, but I chose you out of the world, therefore the world hates you. Remember the word that I said to you: 'A servant is not greater than his master.' If they persecuted me, they will also persecute you. If they kept my word, they will also keep yours."

JOHN 15:19–20

D. L. MOODY

Now mark you, no man can be true for God, and live for Him without, at some time or other, being unpopular in this world. Those men who are trying to live for both worlds make a wreck of it; for at some time or other, the collision is sure to come.

ERWIN LUTZER

Moody put his finger on a problem that has existed in every era of the church, and we see it very clearly today: Christians who are attempting to live in two worlds, or two spheres: the sphere of worldly values and the sphere of God's kingdom. Of course, they are in conflict.

The apostle James called this kind of doublemindedness adultery, "You adulterous people! Do you not know that friendship with the world is enmity with God? Therefore whoever wishes to be a friend of the world makes himself an enemy of God" (James 4:4). And, as a corollary to this, if we clearly live for Christ, we will be hated by some. As Jesus stated, "If they persecuted me, they will also persecute you" (John 15:20). In Nazi Germany, I'm told a pastor said, "The time has come in Germany when the gospel can no longer simply be proclaimed in words. It must be proclaimed in suffering." Often that is the price paid for following Christ fully. But any such suffering is worth it, both in this life and the life to come.

Let us be done with spiritual adultery. May we, like Joshua, *wholly* follow the Lord (Joshua 14:14). And if we suffer for Christ, let it be accepted as a badge of honor.

PRAYER

Purify my life, and if persecution comes,
let me gladly be identified with You, Lord Jesus.

UNKNOWN SERVANTS WANTED

And I said to the king, "If it pleases the king, and if your servant has found favor in your sight, that you send me to Judah, to the city of my fathers' graves, that I may rebuild it."

NEHEMIAH 2:5

D. L. MOODY

It meant a good deal for Nehemiah to give up the palace of Shushan and his high office and identify himself with the despised and captive Jews. He was among the highest in the whole realm. Not only that, but he was a man of wealth, lived in ease and luxury, and had great influence at court. For him to go to Jerusalem and lose caste was like Moses turning his back on the palace of Pharaoh and identifying himself with the Hebrew slaves. Yet we might never have heard of either of them if they had not done this. They stooped to conquer; and when you get ready to stoop, God will bless you. Plato, Socrates, and other Greek philosophers lived in the same century as Nehemiah. How few have heard of them and read their words compared with the hundreds of thousands who have heard and read of Nehemiah during the last two thousand years!

ERWIN LUTZER

Yes, millions of believers have read about Nehemiah, not known for his philosophical writings but for his willingness to give up a life of ease to choose a hard path—a path with eternal implications.

Moody himself is an example of this. He came from Massachusetts to Chicago to sell shoes and was well on his way to becoming very wealthy. But God laid on his heart the forgotten, hungry, and largely homeless children of Chicago, so he began a Sunday school in 1864. When he saw what the gospel could do in the life of these children—when he heard them pray—he said money could never tempt him again. He quit seeking money and went into the ministry of seeking souls. Hard choices made for the glory of God are the most pleasing to God.

PRAYER

Father, humble me—regardless of any fame or fortune. I desire to serve only You, using my talents, skills, and resources for Your glory.

NOVEMBER 28

A DISSATISFYING "GOD"

But those who desire to be rich fall into temptation, into a snare, into many senseless and harmful desires that plunge people into ruin and destruction.

1 TIMOTHY 6:9

D. L. MOODY

The Bible speaks of the deceitfulness of two things—"the deceitfulness of *sin*" and "the deceitfulness of *riches*" (Hebrews 3:13; Mark 4:19). Riches are like a mirage in the desert, which has all the appearance of satisfying and lures on the traveler with the promise of water and shade, but he only wastes his strength in the effort to reach it. So, riches never satisfy; the pursuit of them always turns out a snare.

ERWIN LUTZER

Money is deceitful because it makes all the same promises as God, saying in effect, "I will be with you when you are healthy and seeking pleasure; I will be with you when you are sick and need the best of care; I will take care of you when the economy collapses."

But money cannot take away our sin, cleanse our conscience, or give us eternal life. Furthermore, "He who loves money will not be satisfied with money" (Ecclesiastes 5:10). Those who pursue the god of wealth are left with a dissatisfied heart. And for all who are not wealthy, let them remember that covetousness is idolatry (Luke 12:15).

As Paul says, "We brought nothing into the world, and we cannot take anything out of the world" (1 Timothy 6:7). Imagine climbing the ladder of success only to learn it was leaning up against the wrong wall. The reason riches cannot satisfy is because God has created us for Himself and therefore, money cannot produce contentment. As Augustine said, "Thou madest us for Thyself, and our heart is restless, until it repose in Thee."[35] Money should never compete with God within our hearts.

PRAYER

Father, teach me to build up richness of faith in You
rather than the deceitfulness of riches.

A SCANDALOUS REVERSAL

A dispute also arose among them,
as to which of them was to be regarded as the greatest.
LUKE 22:24

D. L. MOODY

To me, one of the saddest things in all the life of Jesus Christ was the fact that just before His crucifixion, His disciples should have been striving to see who should be the greatest. It was His last night on earth, and they never saw Him so sorrowful before. He knew Judas was going to sell Him for thirty pieces of silver. He knew Peter would deny Him. And yet, in addition to this, when going into the very shadow of the cross, there arose this strife as to who should be the greatest.

He took a towel and girded Himself like a slave, and He took a basin of water and stooped and washed their feet. That was another object lesson of humility. He said, "Ye call me Master and Lord: and ye say well" (John 13:13). If you want to be great in my kingdom, be servant of all. If you serve, you shall be great.

ERWIN LUTZER

God on His hands and knees! Seems to be something strange about that: the Creator bowing low to wash the feet of His creation! This is the only instance in Jewish and Greco-Roman literature that I know of where you have a superior washing the feet of an inferior.

Let's visualize the scene: None of the disciples were willing to do what Jesus did. He "rose from supper. He laid aside his outer garments, and taking a towel, tied it around his waist" (John 13:4). He then washes the feet of His disciples. "Truly, truly, I say to you, a servant is not greater than his master, nor is a messenger greater than the one who sent him" (v. 16). That should have put an end to their questions as to who is the greatest in the kingdom!

Jesus changed the world, not as coming King, but *first* as a servant.

PRAYER

Father, remove my pride and humble me as a servant,
conforming me to Christ.

FOREVER JOY

"So also you have sorrow now, but I will see you again, and your hearts will rejoice, and no one will take your joy from you."

JOHN 16:22

D. L. MOODY

I am so thankful I have a joy that the world cannot rob me of; I have a treasure that the world cannot take from me; I have something that is not in the power of man or devil to deprive me of: the joy of the Lord. "No man taketh it from you."

ERWIN LUTZER

Imagine prisoners sequestered in a concentration camp where people die daily. Suddenly, whispers spread and some prisoners begin to sing, smiles breaking across their faces. Why rejoice amid such depressing circumstances? Someone had a hidden radio and heard the news: Germany had surrendered unconditionally. The war was over. Help was coming!

Joy comes not by looking around us, but by looking beyond us! Jesus said, "In the world you will have tribulation. But take heart; I have overcome the world" (John 16:33). The sorrows of today are temporary but lead to permanent joy. "So . . . you have sorrow now, but I will see you again, and your hearts will rejoice, and no one will take your joy from you" (John 16:22).

In fact, the greater the present sorrow, the greater the future joy. As you walk through a dark valley without an end in sight, this is what the apostle Paul would say to you: "This light momentary affliction is preparing for us an eternal weight of glory beyond all comparison" (2 Corinthians 4:17). Our troubles will end, but glory goes on forever. And, "No one will take your joy from you."

PRAYER

Father, thank You for the assurance of joy from the lips of Jesus.
Help me to look beyond today, to an eternal tomorrow,
when my joy will be complete!

LOT'S LOT IN LIFE

So Lot went out and said to his sons-in-law, who were to marry his daughters, "Up! Get out of this place, for the LORD is about to destroy the city." But he seemed to his sons-in-law to be jesting.

GENESIS 19:14

D. L. MOODY

The Saviour tells us they were eating and drinking, buying and selling, planting and building; all went on as usual. Sodom was never more prosperous than now. There is no sign of a coming judgment, no sign that Sodom is going to be burnt up.

The sun shone as brightly the day before its destruction as it had shone for years. The stars, perhaps, were glittering in the heavens as brightly as ever, and the moon threw her light down upon the city; but Lot's sons-in-law mocked him, he couldn't get them out. I see him going through the streets with his head bowed down and great tears trickling down his cheeks. Ask him now about his life, and he will tell you it has been a total failure. He goes back to his home; and early in the morning, the angels have to take him almost by force and hasten him out of the city. He could not bear the thought of leaving his loved ones there to perish, while God dealt in judgment with that city.

Is not that a fair picture of hundreds and thousands at the present time? Have you been trying to accumulate wealth even to the neglect of your children so that, today, they are lifting up their voices against your God and against your Bible and against you? What an example we have in the case of Lot, and how it ought to open the eyes of many a businessman, and cause him to see that his life is going to be a total wreck if he takes his children into Sodom's judgment when the judgment comes.

ERWIN LUTZER

Sin takes us further than we intended to go, keeps us longer than we intended to stay, and costs us more than we ever intended to pay! Lot's greed and self-promotion destroyed him and his family.

PRAYER

Lord, grant me a pure heart; may I turn from the world to You alone.

OF FIRST IMPORTANCE

For I delivered to you as of first importance what I also received: that Christ died for our sins in accordance with the Scriptures.

1 CORINTHIANS 15:3

D. L. MOODY

You ask me what my hope is. It is that Christ died for my sins, in my stead, in my place, and therefore, I can enter into life eternal. You ask Paul what his hope was. "Christ died for our sins according to the scriptures." This is the hope in which died all the glorious martyrs of old, in which all who have entered heaven's gate have found their only comfort. Take that doctrine of substitution out of the Bible, and my hope is lost. With the law, without Christ, we are all undone. The law we have broken, and it can only hang over our head the sharp sword of justice. Even if we could keep it from this moment, there remains the unforgiven past. "Without shedding of blood [there] is no remission" (Hebrews 9:22).

ERWIN LUTZER

How can we live with ourselves knowing what we have done can't be changed? We cannot go to bed at night with a troubled conscience and awake with hope in the morning. Hymn writer E. E. Hewitt said it well, "It is enough that Jesus died, and that He died for me."[36]

Even the good deeds we do are tainted with sin. Because of our corruption, God only accepts what Christ did. That's why the apostle Paul emphasized Jesus' death, burial, and resurrection as a perfect, complete act (1 Corinthians 15:3–4). The one requirement on our part is to trust in Christ's work as our Lord and Savior (John 6:29; Romans 4:5). God changes our heart and credits us with Christ's righteousness. This is the hope of all believers: Christ died for our sins, rose from the dead, and is coming again (1 Thessalonians 4:16–17).

PRAYER

Father, teach me to not look within but to look without to what You have done for me. Increase my faith in Christ who paid my debt.

FROM NUMB SOULS TO GRATEFUL HEARTS

Naaman, commander of the army of the king of Syria, was a great man with his master and in high favor, because by him the Lord had given victory to Syria. He was a mighty man of valor, but he was a leper.

2 KINGS 5:1

D. L. MOODY

Did you ever ask yourselves which is the worse—the leprosy of sin or the leprosy of the body? For my own part, I would a thousand times sooner have the leprosy of the body eating into my eyes and feet and arms! I would rather be loathsome in the sight of my fellow men than die with the leprosy of sin in my soul, and be banished from God forever! The leprosy of the body is bad, but the leprosy of sin is a thousand times worse. It has cast angels out of heaven. It has ruined the best and strongest men that ever lived in the world. Oh, how it has pulled men down!

ERWIN LUTZER

Sin does to the soul precisely what leprosy does to the body. Leprosy shuts down the nervous system, anesthetizing the body, and preventing the sensation of pain. When we're guilty of sin, we either seek forgiveness or harden our hearts, becoming numb to our own sinfulness. The hardened soul feels no pain, no guilt—it tries to angrily find contentment in just being the way it is.

Let's take the story of Naaman a step further. Elisha told him that if he dipped himself in the Jordan River seven times he would be healed from his leprosy. He objected, saying he expected the prophet to just wave his hand and the miracle would take place—and there had to be better rivers in his area. But a servant appealed to him, "Wash and be clean!" He obeyed and "his flesh was restored like the flesh of a little child, and he was clean" (2 Kings 5:13–14).

What a beautiful picture of a defiled soul cleansed by Christ. Repent, wash, and be clean!

PRAYER

Lord, make me sensitive to sin, deeply desiring Your daily cleansing.

THE FINAL INVITATION

The Spirit and the Bride say, "Come." And let the one who hears say, "Come." And let the one who is thirsty come; let the one who desires take the water of life without price.
REVELATION 22:17

D. L. MOODY

How many men fold their arms and say: "If I am one of the elect, I will be saved, and if I am not, I won't. No use bothering about it."

I have an idea that the Lord Jesus saw how men were going to stumble over this doctrine of election, so after He had been thirty or forty years in heaven, He came down and spoke to John. One Lord's Day in Patmos, He said to him: "Write these things to the churches" (see Revelation 1:11). John kept on writing. His pen flew very fast. And then the Lord, when it was nearly finished, said, "John, before you close the book, put in one more invitation. 'The Spirit and bride say, Come. And let him that heareth say, Come. And let him that is athirst, come. And *whosoever will*, let him take the water of life freely.'"

ERWIN LUTZER

We must humbly acknowledge, although this invitation is indeed open to everyone, the Bible also teaches that those who respond are the ones who "hear his voice" (John 10), and that the saved are those whose names are "written from the foundation of the world in the book of life of the Lamb who was slain" (Revelation 13:8). We must live with the tension of divine sovereignty and human responsibility since both are taught in the Scriptures.

D. L. Moody was once in a meeting where an old man stood up and said, "It took me forty years to learn these three things." And everybody listened intently. "Number one, I cannot earn my way to heaven. The second thing I learned is that God doesn't expect me to earn my way to heaven. God knows we can't." And then, "The third thing is that Jesus paid it all for those who believe in and trust Him." Amen!

PRAYER

Jesus, You are my Savior. I thirst. I receive.

THIS PRECIOUS GIFT OF GOD

For the wages of sin is death, but the free gift of God is eternal life in Christ Jesus our Lord.

ROMANS 6:23

D. L. MOODY

If an angel came straight from the throne of God, and proclaimed that God has sent him to offer us any one thing we might ask—that each one should have his own petition granted—what would be your cry? There would be but one response, and the cry would make heaven ring: "Eternal life! Eternal life!" Everything else would float away into nothingness.

It is life men want and value most. Let a man worth a million dollars be on a wrecked vessel, and if he could save his life for six months by giving that million, he would give it in an instant. But the "*gift of God is eternal life.*" And is it not one of the greatest marvels that men have to stand and plead and pray and beseech their fellow men to take this precious gift of God?

ERWIN LUTZER

To all who think they can manage their own sin, we are warned of its ultimate destination in today's verse: "The wages of sin is death." Not just physical death, which comes to us all, but spiritual and moral death. The invitation to sin is replete with false advertising headlines such as, "This way to happiness" or "This is the path to greatness," and what follows is a litany of ways to supposedly satisfy the desires of the flesh.

In contrast, "The gift of God is eternal life." Thank God that justification—to be declared righteous—happens in a point of time and extends to eternity. The free gift of God is eternal life through Jesus Christ!

PRAYER

Father, open my eyes to sin's false advertising and help me treasure Your free gift in Christ above all earthly pleasures.

THE HOLY SPIRIT'S FULLNESS

Or do you not know that your body is a temple of the Holy Spirit within you, whom you have from God? You are not your own, for you were bought with a price. So glorify God in your body.

1 CORINTHIANS 6:19–20

D. L. MOODY

I think it is clearly taught in the Scripture that every believer has the Holy Ghost dwelling in him, that there is a divine resident in every child of God. He may be quenching the Spirit of God, and he may not glorify God as he should, but if he is a believer on the Lord Jesus Christ, the Holy Ghost dwells in him. But I want to call to attention to another fact. I believe today that though Christian men and women have the Holy Spirit dwelling in them, He is not dwelling within them in power; in other words, God has a great many sons and daughters without power.

ERWIN LUTZER

Why are we so often powerless? Let me give you a clue: If you are living in perpetual sin, the Spirit is grieved. "Do not grieve the Holy Spirit of God, by whom you were sealed for the day of redemption" (Ephesians 4:30). What grieves the Spirit? *Sin*. But when we confess, God forgives and cleanses so that the heart and conscience are clear. Then the Holy Spirit says, "Now I can begin to do my work."

To be "filled with the Spirit" is to receive the Spirit's fullness through faith, trusting the Spirit to be in us all that we need. We can't walk in the fullness of the Spirit based on our emotions; we must choose to believe in the Spirit's work and companionship. "As you received Christ Jesus the Lord, so walk in him" (Colossians 2:6).

PRAYER

Father, I thank You for the Holy Spirit who dwells within me, baptized me into the body of Christ, and sealed me. Now, in faith, I receive the Spirit's filling for all that lies before me today.

INVEST NOW

"So I was afraid, and I went and hid your talent in the ground. Here, you have what is yours."
MATTHEW 25:25

D. L. MOODY

I read of a man who had a thousand dollars. He hid it away, thinking he would, in that way, take care of it, and that when he was an old man, he would have something to fall back upon. After keeping the deposit receipt for twenty years, he took it to a bank and got just one thousand dollars for it. If he had put the money at interest in the usual way, he might have had three times the amount.

He made the mistake a great many people are making today throughout Christendom of not trading with his talents. My experience has been, as I have gone about in the world and mingled with professing Christians, that those who find most fault with others are those who themselves do nothing. If a person is busy improving the talents God has given him, he will have too much to do to find fault and complain about others.

ERWIN LUTZER

Jesus' parable is sobering. Each of us will be judged for our faithfulness or unfaithfulness when we give an account to Him. "To one he gave five talents, to another two, to another one, to each according to his ability. Then he went away" (Matthew 25:15). Jesus is talking about money (a *talent* was currency in biblical times) but we can also apply it to our abilities as well.

Each servant received different amounts, yet all could earn the same reward. Both the five-talent and two-talent servants heard, "Well done" (Matthew 25:21, 23). The man who hid his talent and refused to invest did not hear those words and was severely judged.

Consider this: The only money we can keep is what we give away. Our talent is both our trust and our test, all from the Lord.

PRAYER

Father, by your grace, break me out of the cycle of insecurity and grant me the faith to trust You with all You have given me.

PERSUADED

I know whom I have believed, and I am convinced that he is able to guard until that day what has been entrusted to me.

2 TIMOTHY 1:12

D. L. MOODY

Notice the confidence that breathes through Paul's last words to Timothy. It is not a matter of doubt, but of knowledge: "I know," "I am persuaded." The word "Hope" is not used in the Scripture to express doubt. It is used in regard to the second coming of Christ, or to the resurrection of the body. We should not say we "hope" we are Christians. I do not say that I "hope" I am an American, or that I "hope" I am a married man. These are settled things. I may say that I "hope" to go back to my home, or that I "hope" to attend such a meeting. If we are born of God, we know it; He will not leave us in darkness if we search the Scriptures.

ERWIN LUTZER

As a ten-year-old, I prayed nightly, "Jesus, come into my heart." I had no sense of God's presence or assurance. I even read Revelation, fearing I might never be saved and would serve the antichrist. I was wrestling with deep spiritual questions. My parents, seeing my struggle, explained I needed to accept Christ by faith. So, on our farm, six miles from a tiny town in Canada, I knelt and received Christ in faith. Doubts vanished, and I knew—I was persuaded—Jesus was all I needed to stand before a holy God. Was I saved during those earlier prayers? I don't know. Perhaps I was saved but lacked assurance.

What is saving faith? It's a persuasion of the heart, based on the promises of God, confirmed by the Holy Spirit. Let's be as persuaded as Paul was, that the One in whom we have believed will keep us until the day of redemption.

PRAYER

Father, replace my anxious questioning with the soul-settling persuasion that Jesus is all I need—period.

GREATER LOVE

"Greater love has no one than this, that someone lay down his life for his friends."
JOHN 15:13

D. L. MOODY

When we wish to know the love of God, we should go to Calvary. Can we look upon that scene and say God did not love us? That cross speaks of the love of God. Greater love never has been taught than that which the cross teaches. What prompted God to give up Christ—what prompted Christ to die—if it were not love? "Greater love hath no man than this, that a man lay down his life for his friends." Christ laid down His life for His enemies; Christ laid down His life for His murderers; Christ laid down His life for them that hated Him; and the spirit of the cross, the spirit of Calvary, is love (Romans 5:8). When they were mocking Him and deriding Him, what did He say? "Father, forgive them; for they know not what they do" (Luke 23:34). That is love. He did not call down fire from heaven to consume them; there was nothing but love in His heart.

ERWIN LUTZER

In *A Tale of Two Cities* by Charles Dickens, a Frenchman sacrifices his life by switching places with a condemned Englishman who had a wife and family. A guard unknowingly escorts the disguised Englishman to freedom while the Frenchman was executed in his place.

This sacrificial act in Dickens' novel reflects the sacrificial love Jesus embodies. Most of those we love are people with whom we are compatible, people whose company we enjoy. But Jesus said, "If you love those who love you, what benefit is that to you? For even sinners love those who love them" (Luke 6:32). Jesus' kind of love is supernatural. It is so contrary to our natural inclinations, even including those who are unlovable or even our enemies. This is a love which is based on committed, deep, and generous sacrifice. We love as God loves us in Christ.

PRAYER

Father, because Christ died for the ungodly like me,
help me to love others as You love me.

WHAT IS TRUTH?

Jesus said to him, "I am the way, and the truth, and the life. No one comes to the Father except through me."

JOHN 14:6

D. L. MOODY

People say: "I want to know what is the truth."

Listen: "*I am the truth*," says Christ. If you want to know what the truth is, get acquainted with Christ.

People also complain that they have not life. Many are trying to give themselves spiritual life. You may galvanize yourselves and put electricity into yourselves, so to speak, but the effect will not last very long. Christ alone is the Author of life. If you would have real spiritual life, get to know Christ. Many try to stir up spiritual life by going to meetings. These may be well enough, but it will be of no use unless they get into contact with the living Christ. Then spiritual life will not be a spasmodic thing, but will be perpetual, flowing on and on, and bringing forth fruit to God.

ERWIN LUTZER

When Jesus was standing before Pilate, He said, "For this purpose I was born and for this purpose I have come into the world—to bear witness to the truth. Everyone who is of the truth listens to my voice" (John 18:37). Pilate then asked, "What is truth?" He didn't wait for an answer and went instead to speak to the mob. Pilate discovered something: *You can crucify a man, but you cannot crucify truth.* Jesus told us the truth about God, the truth about ourselves, and our need for His salvation. He speaks truth and embodies it.

In our age, truth has been redefined to include what we feel the truth is, but Jesus taught that truth was objective; it exists outside of us, and it is the truth whether we believe it or not. But we must remember, Jesus is to be believed.

PRAYER

Father, do a deep and lasting work in my life: Let Your truth sink deeply into my soul. Guide me according to truth.

DECEMBER 11

DUST YOU ARE

Just as we have borne the image of the man of dust,
we shall also bear the image of the man of heaven.
1 CORINTHIANS 15:49

D. L. MOODY

Thank God, we are to gain by death! We are to have something that death cannot touch. When this earthly body is raised, all the present imperfection will be gone. Jacob will leave his lameness (Genesis 32:25). Paul will have no thorn in the flesh (2 Corinthians 12:7). We shall enter a life that deserves the name of life, happy, glorious, everlasting—the body once more united to the soul, no longer mortal, subject to pain and disease and death, but glorified, incorruptible, "fashioned like unto his glorious body," everything that hinders the spiritual life left behind (Philippians 3:21). We are exiles now, but then, we who are faithful, shall stand before the throne of God, joint heirs with Christ, kings and priests, citizens of that heavenly country.

ERWIN LUTZER

Death certainly has many reasons to be proud. No matter how often you exercise, no matter how well you eat, no matter how many supplements you take, no matter how hard you fight against death, in the end, it will win. But as Moody said, death is a gift; we gain in death what we did not have in life. This is based on the apostle Paul's words: "All things are yours, whether . . . life or death . . . all are yours, and you are Christ's" (1 Corinthians 3:21–23).

How is death the possession of a Christian? The early martyrs said, in effect, "The pagans can rob us of everything. They can take away our health. They can persecute us. They can destroy our property, but there is one thing they cannot do, and that is rid us of the gift of death, because it ushers us into the presence of God."

"O death, where is your victory? O death, where is your sting?" (1 Corinthians 15:55). Let us remember that we gain much more in death than we ever had in life. Death be not proud.

PRAYER

I thank You Father, that death no longer has authority over me.

FUTURE SIGHT

And we know that for those who love God all things work together for good, for those who are called according to his purpose.
ROMANS 8:28

D. L. MOODY

I have an idea we will thank God in eternity for anything we face. I believe John Bunyan thanked God for the Bedford Jail more than for anything that happened to him down here. I believe Paul thanked God more for the rods and stripes than for anything else that happened to him.

Are you passing through the waters? Don't get discouraged! You are an heir of glory; He is with you. He was with Joseph when he was cast into prison (see Genesis 39–41). I had rather be in prison with the Almighty than outside without Him. You needn't be afraid of prison, and you needn't be afraid of the grave, you needn't be afraid of death. Cheer up, child of God, the time of our redemption draweth near! We may have to suffer a little while, but when you think of the eternal weight of glory, you can afford to suffer.

ERWIN LUTZER

Romans 8:28 is a promise, not an explanation. It doesn't tell us exactly how God causes all things to work together for good. The Greek word *sunergeō* ("with work") means God brings things together in ways we don't understand. With faith, we believe this promise encompasses everything in the lives of all those who love God and are "called according to his purpose."

And what is the good to which God is working? In verse 29, we read that His larger purpose is that we might "be conformed to the image of his Son." Christlikeness is God's great goal for us. Let us accept life as it comes, knowing that God is silently working for His glory and for our good as well.

PRAYER

Father, grant me the strength to glorify You in my suffering.
You're worth living for, in this life and the world to come.

GOD'S GARDEN

Oh, the depth of the riches and wisdom and knowledge of God! How unsearchable are his judgments and how inscrutable his ways!

ROMANS 11:33

D. L. MOODY

I thank God there is a height in the Bible I do not know anything about, a depth I have never been able to fathom, and it makes the Book all the more fascinating. If I could take that Book up and read it as I can any other book and understand it as one reading, I should have lost faith in it years ago. It is one of the strongest proofs that it must have come from God, that the sharpest men who have dug for fifty years have laid down their pens and said, "There is a depth we know nothing of." "No Scripture," said Spurgeon, "is exhausted by a single explanation. The flowers of God's garden bloom not only double, but sevenfold; they are continually pouring forth fresh fragrance."[37]

ERWIN LUTZER

How do we experience God's transforming power? How do we get changed from the inside out? We must meditate on God's Word. The attention that you pay to God can be directly measured by the attention that you pay to His Book.

Let's take Charles Spurgeon's imagery and think of the Bible as a garden. It is meant to be a source of beauty, a place of refuge, and a place of hope amid the weeds that are all around us. When I was in my teens, I heard a sermon by Franklin Logsdon, a previous pastor of The Moody Church, who began each message with this short poem.

> Think of it carefully, study it prayerfully
> Deep in thine heart let its oracles well
> Ponder its mystery, slight not its history,
> None e're can love it too fondly or well.[38]

Let us begin each day meditating in the garden of God.

PRAYER

Lord, I will not put Your Word down until You have given me a thought, an idea, an assurance, a promise for today.

GRACE AND LAW

Christ redeemed us from the curse of the law by becoming a curse for us—for it is written, "Cursed is everyone who is hanged on a tree."
GALATIANS 3:13

D. L. MOODY

Life never came through the law. As someone has observed: "When the law was given, three thousand men lost life; but when grace and truth came at Pentecost, three thousand obtained life." Under the law, if a man became a drunkard, the magistrates would take him out and stone him to death. When the prodigal came home, grace met him and embraced him. Law said, "Stone him!"—grace said, "Kiss him!" Law went after him and bound him; grace said, "Loose him and let him go!" Law tells me how crooked I am; grace comes and makes me straight.

ERWIN LUTZER

While the law displays God's holiness and exposes our sinfulness, it also reveals our need for grace. The grace of atonement was made for us when Jesus was crucified and died; He became a curse on our behalf when He was "hung on the tree" (see Deuteronomy 21:22–23). Having taken our punishment, He offers us grace.

We make one of two errors: We don't believe we need God's grace because we see ourselves as superior to others; or we conclude we are so bad that we cannot be saved. Both are errors. The best among us are still sinners in need God's grace, and even the worst among us can be redeemed. God, in His grace, does not simply give us a hand, He gives us a resurrection.

Marvelous grace of our loving Lord,
Grace that exceeds our sin and our guilt,
Yonder on Calvary's mount out-poured,
There where the blood of the Lamb was spilt.

Grace met the demands of the law in Christ Himself.

PRAYER

Father, thank You for Jesus who bore the curse of the law
and saved me by grace alone.

GOING IT ALONE

So the sisters sent to him, saying, "Lord, he whom you love is ill."
JOHN 11:3

D. L. MOODY

The communion those sisters had with Jesus brought them so near to His heart that when the time of trouble came, they knew where to go for comfort. A great many people do not learn that secret in prosperity, and so when the billows come rolling up against them, they don't know which way to turn. The darkest and most wretched place on the face of the earth, is a home where death has entered, and where Christ is unknown. No hope of resurrection, no hope of a brighter day coming.

ERWIN LUTZER

If we are not walking with God during the day, how will we fare when night comes? As Moody said, these sisters had welcomed Jesus into their home when they and their brother were well; now He comes to them in their desperation.

But there is another lesson. Although Jesus loved Lazarus, Lazarus died. God's love may not shield us from death, though He certainly has the power to do so. The love of God prepares us for death. No doubt these sisters depended on their brother for their livelihood; they missed him not just because of their love for him, but because they depended upon him. And now he was dead.

We know how this story ended: Jesus raised Lazarus from the grave. We don't know how long Lazarus lived after this, but Jesus had a specific purpose for this miracle: to prove to the sisters, to us, and to the entire world that He is "the resurrection and the life" (John 11:25). We can rejoice that the day is coming when we too shall be raised with an eternal, incorruptible, resurrection body (1 Corinthians 15:53).

So until then, let us walk closely with the Lord so that when our bodies decline or those around us die, we shall remember we are loved by the One who will raise us to new life.

PRAYER

Father, draw me near, believing in Your love and knowing
You are with me when my time comes to die.

INTIMACY WITH GOD

When Daniel knew that the document had been signed, he went to his house where he had windows in his upper chamber open toward Jerusalem. He got down on his knees three times a day and prayed and gave thanks before his God, as he had done previously.

DANIEL 6:10

D. L. MOODY

There is many a businessman today who will tell you he has no time to pray: his business is so pressing that he cannot call his family around him and ask God to bless them. He is so busy that he cannot ask God to keep him and them from the temptations of the present life—the temptations every day. "Business is so pressing." I am reminded of the words of an old Methodist minister: "If you have so much business to attend to that you have no time to pray, depend upon it, you have more business on hand than God ever intended you should have."

But look at this man. He has the whole, or nearly the whole, of the king's business to attend to. He was Prime Minister, Secretary of State, and Secretary of the Treasury, all in one. He had to attend all his own work, and to give an eye to the work of lots of other men. And yet he found time to pray, not just now and then, nor once in a day, not just when he happened to have a few moments to spare, but "three times a day."

ERWIN LUTZER

The real purpose of prayer is a stepping stone for us to develop intimacy with God. God gives us many trials because He knows that only desperate people pray. When we come to Him with our need, we leave His presence realizing that our greatest need is our need of Him. A fresh vision of God and His love for us is always our greatest need.

PRAYER

Father, thank You for the trials I face that assure me why Your presence is what I need most.

DECEMBER 17

WHEN THE PAST COMES BACK

For they sow the wind, and they shall reap the whirlwind.
HOSEA 8:7

D. L. MOODY

Whenever I hear a young man talking in a flippant way about sowing his wild oats, I don't laugh. I feel more like crying because I know he is going to make his grey-haired mother reap in tears; he is going to make his wife reap in shame; he is going to make his old father and his innocent children reap with him. Only ten or fifteen or twenty years will pass before he will have to reap his wild oats; no man has ever sowed them without having to reap them. Sow the wind, and you reap the whirlwind.

ERWIN LUTZER

We always reap more than we sow. Out on the farm, for every bushel of wheat my family sowed, we expected to reap twenty times more. That also applies to when we sow sinful choices and lifestyles. David's sin of murder and adultery is well known. God said to him, "The sword shall never depart from your house, because you have despised me and have taken the wife of Uriah the Hittite to be your wife" (2 Samuel 12:10). Although David repented in sorrow and returned to the Lord, his family did not—four of his sons ended badly. David reaped a terrible harvest for his sin.

Yet, God showed David grace. Despite killing her husband, David did marry Bathsheba, and Solomon was born. Solomon was blessed of God despite his own sinful lifestyle and doublemindedness. He built a great temple and left us much of the Bible's wisdom literature, including the book of Proverbs.

Committing sin reaps a harvest of more sin, and though the past cannot be relived, it can be redeemed. Grace in the midst of failure, hope in the midst of despair, and wheat in the midst of wild oats.

PRAYER

Lord, I believe with all my heart that You can take my painful circumstances and my open wounds to turn them into healed scars.

NO LIMIT TO HIS LOVE

So that Christ may dwell in your hearts through faith—that you, being rooted and grounded in love, may have strength to comprehend with all the saints what is the breadth and length and height and depth, and to know the love of Christ that surpasses knowledge, that you may be filled with all the fullness of God.

EPHESIANS 3:17–19

D. L. MOODY

Many of us think we know something of God's love, but centuries hence, we shall admit we have never found out much about it. Many of us have discovered something of the love of God, but there are heights, depths, and lengths of it we do not know. That Love is a great ocean, and we require to plunge into it before we really know anything of it.

Among the many victims of the Paris Commune was a Catholic bishop. He was a man who knew something of the love of God in his own experience. In the little cell where he was confined, awaiting execution, there was a small window in the shape of a cross. After his death, there was found written above the cross "height"; below it, "depth"; and at the end of each arm of the cross, "length" and "breadth." He had learned that God's love was unfailing in the hour of adversity and death.

ERWIN LUTZER

Paul prayed that Christ would dwell within our hearts by faith so that we might be "rooted and grounded in love." Of course, all believers have Christ in their hearts, but what he means is "that Christ might feel at home in your heart by faith." Only then can we grasp the magnitude of God's love for us. We sing:

> The love of God is greater far
> Than tongue or pen can ever tell;
> It goes beyond the highest star,
> And reaches to the lowest hell.[39]

PRAYER

Come be at home in my heart, Lord Jesus.
Thank You for Your unfathomable love.

FREE WISDOM

If any of you lacks wisdom, let him ask God, who gives generously to all without reproach, and it will be given him. But let him ask in faith, with no doubting, for the one who doubts is like a wave of the sea that is driven and tossed by the wind.

JAMES 1:5–6

D. L. MOODY

So faith is the golden key that unlocks the treasures of heaven. It was the shield David took when he met Goliath on the field; he believed that God was going to deliver the Philistine into his hands. Someone has said that faith could lead Christ about anywhere; wherever He found it, He honored it.

Unbelief sees something in God's hand and says, "I cannot get it." Faith sees it, and says, "I will have it."

ERWIN LUTZER

Clearly, God takes delight in giving us wisdom when we are confronted with difficult choices. To receive wisdom, we must meet these requirements. First, James says we are to *ask in faith*. We have to believe that God will actually give wisdom as generously as He has promised. Second, it's clear that we have to *be willing to obey* the wisdom God gives us. Third, we must *ask ourselves*: "How does God's wisdom come to us?" The wise path is always consistent with the Scriptures (Psalm 119:105; James 1:22–25).

Beyond that, wisdom comes through peace in our minds and hearts that we're doing the right thing (Isaiah 26:3; Philippians 4:7); or wisdom often comes to us through the counsel of another person whom God puts in our path (Psalm 1:1; Proverbs 12:15).

God can close or open doors as He leads those willing to be led.

PRAYER

Father, give me a heart of wisdom willing to obey You and respond in faith.

A NEW COMMANDMENT

Having loved his own who were in the world, he loved them to the end.

JOHN 13:1

D. L. MOODY

It is recorded of Jesus Christ, just when He was about to be departed from His disciples and led away to Calvary, that: "having loved his own which were in the world, he loved them unto the end." He knew that one of His disciples would betray Him, yet He loved Judas. He knew another disciple would deny Him and swear he never knew Him, and yet He loved Peter. It was the love which Christ had for Peter that broke his heart and brought him back in penitence to the feet of his Lord. For three years, Jesus had been with the disciples trying to teach them His love, not only by His life and words, but by His works. And on the night of His betrayal, He takes a basin of water, girds Himself with a towel, and taking the place of a servant, washes their feet; He wants to convince them of His unchanging love.

ERWIN LUTZER

When Jesus washed His disciples' feet, He did what they were too proud to do. He "laid aside his outer garments" the same way He laid aside His glory (John 13:4; Philippians 2:7). Then He gave a new commandment: "Love one another: just as I have loved you" (John 13:34). What made this new? The standard of this love was nothing less than "as I have loved you."

This "eleventh commandment" established Christ's own love as the measure for believers. He loved them to the end—to the "full extent." The full extent involved the cross. Because He loved us, we love Him and one another—sacrificially, even irrationally. Love doesn't confine itself to reason. It goes on loving. That is how Christ loved us.

How will others know you've been with Christ? Through God's work as we obey Christ's new command: Love one another.

PRAYER

Holy Spirit, empower me to love not by the world's standards,
but by Christ's—loving beyond reason or convenience.

EVERYTHING IS WORSHIP

I will . . . honor him.
PSALM 91:15

D. L. MOODY

God's honor is something worth seeking. Man's honor doesn't amount to much. Suppose Moses had stopped down there in Egypt. He would have been loaded down with Egyptian titles, but they would never have reached us. Suppose he had been Chief Marshal of the whole Egyptian army, "General" Moses, "Commander" Moses; suppose he had reached the throne and become one of these Pharaohs and his mummy had come down to our day. What is that compared with the honor God put upon him? How his name shines on the pages of history!

The honor of this world doesn't last, it is transient, it passes away; and I don't believe any man or woman is fit for God's service that is looking for worldly preferment, worldly honors, and worldly fame. Let us get it under our feet, let us rise above it and seek the honor that comes down from above.

ERWIN LUTZER

Seeking honor from men (or women) has led many a person to ruin. Christ asked, "How can you believe, when you receive glory from one another and do not seek the glory that comes from the only God?" (John 5:44). The curse of being well thought of by others leads to selfish pursuits; it leads to a wasted life seeking that which vanishes in the end. To pray that we live to the glory of God may seem relatively easy, but to have our motives purified by God, seeking His approval alone, is more difficult. That battle goes to the heart of our innate sinfulness and desires.

Only what God thinks of us really matters. I quote Paul, "So, whether you eat or drink, or whatever you do, do all to the glory of God" (1 Corinthians 10:31). Only what God thinks of us really matters. Today, may we live our lives only for His glory and not seek the glory of others.

PRAYER

Father, may all that I say, do, and think honor You.

CHRISTIANS DIE DIFFERENTLY

"Truly, truly, I say to you, if anyone keeps my word, he will never see death."
JOHN 8:51

D. L. MOODY

Someday you will read in the papers that D. L. Moody of East Northfield is dead. Don't you believe a word of it! At that moment I shall be more alive than I am now. I shall have gone up higher, that is all; gone out of this old clay tenement into a house that is immortal, a body that death cannot touch, that sin cannot taint, a body like unto His own glorious body. I was born of the flesh in 1837. I was born of the Spirit in 1856. That which is born of the flesh may die. That which is born of the Spirit will live forever.

ERWIN LUTZER

What a confident affirmation from Moody, a man who, in his youth, feared death! Christians should approach death—and die—differently. There is a verse we cannot repeat too often. Speaking of Jesus, we read that He came as God in the flesh so that "through death he might destroy the one who has the power of death, that is, the devil, and deliver all those who through fear of death were subject to lifelong slavery" (Hebrews 2:14–15). Even hardened atheists fear death; but for the Christian, it is the doorway to glory. Jesus said there are two resurrections: a resurrection to life and a resurrection to damnation (John 5:29).

Imagine that—a resurrection to damnation! But for those whose security is in Christ, death is eradicated. Its sting and power are gone (see 1 Corinthians 15:54–55). The day is coming when death will only be a memory. No matter how many victories death wins, those victories are only temporary.

Let's approach death with confidence in the promises of Christ.

PRAYER

Father, I thank You that death is the pathway.
It is the chariot You send to bring Your children home to glory.

SUDDENLY CONVERTED

"Truly, truly, I say to you, whoever hears my word and believes him who sent me has eternal life. He does not come into judgment, but has passed from death to life."
JOHN 5:24

D. L. MOODY

Salvation is instantaneous. I admit that a man may be converted so that he cannot tell when he crossed the line between death and life, but I also believe a man may be a thief one moment and a saint the next. I believe a man may be as vile as hell itself one moment and be saved the next.

Christian growth is gradual, just as physical growth is; but a man passes from death unto everlasting life quick as an act of the will—"He that believeth on the Son *hath* everlasting life."

ERWIN LUTZER

Paul was going along to Damascus when he was struck to the ground by light. Later, he explained how the risen Christ had appeared to him (1 Corinthians 15:8). His conversion was sudden and dramatic. At that moment, he passed from death unto life.

We don't always have such experiences today, but when we were converted we also crossed a line from darkness to light. Jesus said, "You must be born again" (John 3:3). There may be a period of gestation, but then the birth happens in a moment of time—followed by growth.

Perhaps you cannot remember the exact time you were converted, but you can have the assurance that you belong to God forever. I had heard it said that you don't have to know the exact time the sun arose to know it is shining. There are marks of conversion such as a change in our affections. There is a love for Jesus implanted in our hearts by God (1 Peter 1:8). And we have a new direction in life.

God's miracles happen quickly, and "all things become new."

PRAYER

Father, use my testimony—dramatic or quiet—to show others how genuine conversion to Christ can transform a heart from death to life.

THE TRUE BEAUTY OF HEAVEN'S PROMISE

He will wipe away every tear from their eyes, and death shall be no more, neither shall there be mourning, nor crying, nor pain anymore, for the former things have passed away.
REVELATION 21:4

D. L. MOODY

There are no tears in heaven, and there would be few on earth if the will of God was only done.

ERWIN LUTZER

And the reason there are no tears in heaven is because Jesus was born in Bethlehem to redeem us. Today, on this Christmas Eve, we remind ourselves, "the Word became flesh and dwelt among us" (John 1:14). Jesus left glory for earth, died, rose again, and returned to heaven—this same Jesus will guide us safely to eternity. And there will be no more tears.

Let's look more carefully at Jesus: "The Lamb in the midst of the throne will be their shepherd . . . and God will wipe away every tear from their eyes" (Revelation 7:17). The Greek word for *from* can actually mean *out of*. We could read it, "God shall wipe away all tears out of their eyes." It's as if God is going to get to the very heart of our sorrow, the very source of our regrets, failures, and deep disappointments. There will be no mourning, no crying, and no fear for the former things are passed away—gone forever.

As of this writing, Joni Eareckson Tada has been in a wheelchair for over fifty years, living in constant pain, but what she looks forward to most about eternity isn't just getting rid of her handicap or constant distress—it's being in God's presence without sin ever coming between. So, in this Christmas season, let's look beyond the manger to the destiny of all believers. The tears of Bethlehem will be wiped away forever in the streets of the New Jerusalem.

PRAYER

Lord, as I celebrate Your incarnation this Christmas, fill me with hope for that day when Your dwelling place will be with us forever.

WELCOMING THE CHRIST OF CHRISTMAS

And she gave birth to her firstborn son and wrapped him in swaddling cloths and laid him in a manger, because there was no place for them in the inn.
LUKE 2:7

D. L. MOODY

The natural human heart is like that inn at Bethlehem—no room for Christ! Every true saint of God for four thousand years had been gazing out into the future, looking and listening that they might hear the footfall of the Coming One. Bible students think that when Eve brought forth her firstborn and said: "I have gotten a man from the Lord" (Genesis 4:1), she thought he was the Promised One. And right on for four thousand years, the mothers in Israel had been looking for that Child. And now the time has arrived. He appears on earth, and the first thing we read is that there is no room for Him! He came on no secret mission; He tells us what He came for, "to seek and to save that which was lost" (Luke 19:10).

He came to get His arm under the vilest sinner and lift him up to God; to bind up the brokenhearted and to comfort those that mourn. And yet, from time to time, it was announced in Jerusalem that He had come, until He was put to death on the cross, the sword was not put back into its scabbard until it had pierced the very heart of the God-man.

ERWIN LUTZER

Bethlehem. Why not Jerusalem or Rome? That stable smelled like a pet shop—His humble crib borrowed from animals. This metaphorically represents Jesus' life: no room in the religious, political, or business worlds (Matthew 8:20; John 18:36). Today, He's often unwelcome at His own party.

But there was room on the cross. "Crucify Him!" (Luke 23:21). And some would keep Him there. Jesus begins in a borrowed manger and ends in a borrowed grave. Let us never forget He made this journey for us!

PRAYER

Lord Jesus, there's room in my heart for You.

DECEMBER 26

STARING AT DEATH WITH DEFIANCE

When the perishable puts on the imperishable, and the mortal puts on immortality, then shall come to pass the saying that is written: "Death is swallowed up in victory." "O death, where is your victory? O death, where is your sting?"

1 CORINTHIANS 15:54–55

D. L. MOODY

I turn my back on death and journey toward life from this time on, and away into the eternity beyond the grave I see *life*.

ERWIN LUTZER

Somewhere I read that death is just as near to the young as to the old; the difference is that for the young, death stands behind them; for the old, death stands in front of them, staring them in the face. And try as we might, we cannot evade death; exercise, vitamins, and a host of other anti-aging remedies can only postpone the inevitable.

But death has lost its sting. Think of it this way: A bee has only one stinger; once used, it cannot create another. To carry the analogy further, Jesus took our "sting," so to speak, and now there is nothing we must fear.

In the sacrificial life and death of Jesus, we see all of the attributes of God on full display: mercy, grace, wrath, love, justice. The fullness of God's perfections accomplished our redemption so that death could become the pathway to life.

The curse of death was in our cup:
The cup was full for Thee;
But Thou hast drained the last dark drop,
And emptied it for me.[40]

The question isn't, "Who are the redeemed?" The question is, "Who is this Redeemer?" Think of what He did to make us His forever! Nothing else matters.

PRAYER

Father, help me to bring You glory in the days You have allotted for me. Simplify my life by showing me that it's not about me. It's all about You.

FINAL MOMENTS

"Honor your father and your mother, that your days may be long in the land that the Lord your God is giving you."
EXODUS 20:12

D. L. MOODY

The one glimpse the Bible gives us of thirty out of the thirty-three years of Christ's life on earth shows that He did not come to destroy the Fifth Commandment. The secret of all those silent years is embodied in that verse in Luke's gospel—"And he went down with them, and came to Nazareth, and was subject unto them" (Luke 2:51). Did He not set an example of true filial love and care when, in the midst of the agonies of the cross, He made provision for His mother (Mark 10:35–45)?

ERWIN LUTZER

Yes, even on the cross Jesus was thinking about others. He said to Mary, "Woman, behold, your son!"—referring to John, not Himself. To John: "Behold, your mother!" (John 19:26–27). He prepared her for His death; apparently, her husband Joseph was dead by this time. As a firstborn, Jesus fulfilled His responsibility to care for His mother until the end. This is His last will and testament. Christ's cross is a place of responsibility.

The attitude of Jesus as He neared an excruciating death destroys any ladder-climbing or self-exaltation, teaching us how to care for others, particularly our parents. Before the cross, we tremble and ask: "In light of what Jesus has done, why is my own self-exaltation so important?" If one or both of your parents are still living, seek to honor them and you will be rewarded.

And then, let us also honor the wider body of Christ. Paul lamented how most people are selfish, "For they all seek their own interests, not those of Jesus Christ" (Philippians 2:21). Let the cross of Christ motivate us to live for God and others—not ourselves.

PRAYER

Lord Jesus, You who thought not of Yourself but thought of others throughout Your life to the cross, lead me. Keep me near the cross.

THE LAMB WHO IS WORTHY

Then I looked, and I heard around the throne and the living creatures and the elders the voice of many angels, numbering myriads of myriads and thousands of thousands, saying with a loud voice, "Worthy is the Lamb who was slain, to receive power and wealth and wisdom and might and honor and glory and blessing!"

REVELATION 5:11–12

D. L. MOODY

Yes, He is worthy of all this. Heaven cannot speak too well of Him. Oh that earth would take up the echo, and join with heaven in singing, "*Worthy* to receive power, and riches, and wisdom, and strength, and honour, and glory, and blessing!"

ERWIN LUTZER

Jesus made it clear to the woman at the well that the Father was seeking worshipers, and since He could not find them among the smug religious leaders of the day, He was looking for volunteers among the unsung and unknown people of the world. "The hour is coming, and is now here, when the true worshipers will worship the Father in spirit and truth, for the Father is seeking such people to worship him" (John 4:23). In other words, the best way to prepare for heaven is to become a worshiper on earth.

Interestingly, in heaven, we will sing remembering not the birth of Jesus, nor the miracles of Jesus, but rather "the Lamb who was slain." Throughout all of eternity, we will remember Jesus as Redeemer, as the One who died a death He didn't deserve to give us what we didn't deserve. In heaven, Jesus is described as a Lamb "as though it had been slain" (Revelation 5:6). The nail prints He had on earth will be scars in heaven; healing will have occurred but the remembrance of His death will remain. It may be the only reminder of sin in heaven.

Let us prepare for heaven and sing, "Worthy is the lamb who was slain!"

PRAYER

Father, I can only repeat from my heart,
"Worthy is the Lamb who was slain."

SHIELDED BY PROMISES

As far as the east is from the west, so far does he remove our transgressions from us.
PSALM 103:12

D. L. MOODY

Not *some* of them; He takes them *all* away. You may pile up your sins till they rise like a dark mountain and then multiply them by ten thousand for those you cannot think of; and after you have tried to enumerate all the sins you have ever committed, just let me bring one verse in, and that mountain will melt away: "The blood of Jesus Christ his Son cleanseth us from *all* sin" (1 John 1:7).

ERWIN LUTZER

My father was one hundred years old when Satan brought to his mind the sins of his youth. My father said to my mother, "You know, Satan is just assaulting me about my past sin," and he was going to again ask forgiveness for his sins, but my mother wisely said, "No you don't. This is not a time to ask for forgiveness for sins. This is a time to praise God that your sins have been forgiven!"

That was indeed wise counsel. The devil uses guilt, even guilt for sins that have already been forgiven. And no victory is achieved by confessing and re-confessing past sins. We must affirm the promise that "if we confess our sins, he is faithful and just to forgive us our sins and to cleanse us from all unrighteousness" (1 John 1:9). We must receive both forgiveness and cleansing; in other words, our conscience must cease to condemn us.

So, with the shield of faith we ask, "Are we going to believe God's promise or are we going to believe our feelings and circumstances?" The promise is that God has removed our sins as far as the east is from the west.

PRAYER

Father, even if I still see the consequences of my sin,
may I rejoice in Your forgiveness.

AN ANCIENT QUESTION WE ALL MUST ANSWER

But the LORD God called to the man and said to him, "Where are you?"
GENESIS 3:9

D. L. MOODY

A man once said to me "How do you know that God put that question to Adam?"

The best answer I can give is: Because He has put it to me many a time. I doubt whether there ever has been a son or a daughter of Adam who has not heard that voice ringing through the soul many a time. Who am I? What am I? Where am I going? So, let us put the question to ourselves, personally, Where am I? Not in the sight of man—that is of very little account, but where am I in the sight of God?

ERWIN LUTZER

So, "Where are you?" On a scale of 1 to 10, where are you spiritually? In your work habits, your relationships with friends, family, and coworkers, "Where are you?" Can you honestly identify where you stand? Of course, God knew exactly where Adam was, but He wanted Adam to tell him. And God knows where we are, but He also wants us to evaluate ourselves.

As for our spiritual identity, we can reply we are "in Christ." We are born in Adam, but through the new birth, we are now "in Christ" (see 1 Corinthians 15:45). We belong to a different owner, a different relationship, and have a different future. But our identity in Christ has to be lived out in practical experience.

Take time out today and answer the question, "Where are you?" And then, "Where would you like to be?" And, "How will you get there?" As we soon enter a new year, let us take inventory.

PRAYER

Father, thank You that I am Yours.
Help me to be all that I am called to be.

DO YOU LIKE LIFE?

With long life I will satisfy him and show him my salvation.
PSALM 91:16

D. L. MOODY

I get a good deal of comfort out of that promise. I don't think that means a short life down here, seventy years, eighty years, ninety years, or one hundred years. Do you think that any man living would be satisfied if they could live to be one hundred years old and then have to die? Not by a good deal. Suppose Adam had lived until today and had to die tonight, would he be satisfied? Not a bit of it! Not if he had lived a million years and then had to die.

You know we are all the time coming to the end of things here, the end of the week, the end of the month, the end of the year, the end of school days. It is end, end, end all the time. But, thank God, He is going to satisfy us with long life; no end to it, an endless life.

Life is very sweet. I never liked death; I like life. It would be a pretty dark world if death was eternal, and when our loved ones die we are to be eternally separated from them. Thank God, it is not so; we shall be reunited. It is just moving out of this house into a better one; stepping up higher, and living on and on forever.

ERWIN LUTZER

This is an excellent transition to the new year. This is an invitation to reassess our future; after all, we are coming to the end of all things. And today, we are coming to the end of the year, preparing for an unknown year to come. Whether we will have a long life here on earth or not, the Scriptures call us to focus on our eternal future. There will be no end of days.

So, can we take this time for reflection? Some who are reading this will not live until the end of the coming year. Let us live today as if we might die tomorrow.

PRAYER

I long for You Lord.
May I welcome the new year safely tucked in Your hand.

ACKNOWLEDGMENTS

This book was a joint project that required an exceptional team to bring it across the finish line. I'm especially grateful to four remarkable individuals whose dedication and skill in collating, updating, editing, and formatting these devotionals brought this project to life:

Letricia Brooks

John Lee

Micah Shumate

Corbin Wisniewski

God is not unmindful of your efforts. Your tireless commitment will bless the many readers who find inspiration and encouragement in these daily meditations.

Erwin Lutzer

Pastor Emeritus, The Moody Church

SCRIPTURE INDEX

Acts

Romans

1 Corinthians

2 Corinthians

3 John

Jude

Revelation

NOTES

1. Fanny J. Crosby, "To God Be the Glory," *The Celebration Hymnal* (Word/Integrity, 1997), 56.
2. Bertrand Russell on God and Religion, ed. Al Seckel (Prometheus Books, 1986), 11.
3. Elvina M. Hall, "Jesus Paid It All," *The Celebration Hymnal* (Word/Integrity, 1997), 305.
4. Charlotte Elliott, "Just as I Am," *The Celebration Hymnal* (Word/Integrity, 1997), 488.
5. Fanny J. Crosby, "To God Be the Glory," *The Celebration Hymnal* (Word/Integrity, 1997), 56.
6. Bernard of Clairvaux, "Jesus, the Very Thought of Thee," *The Celebration Hymnal* (Word/Integrity, 1997), 89.
7. Augustine, *The City of God*, ed. Marus Dods, Project Gutenberg, https://www.gutenberg.org/ files/45304/45304-h/45304-h.htm, Vol, 2: https://www.gutenberg.org/cache/epub/45305/pg45305-images.html.
8. John Knox was a Scottish Reformer, John Bunyan wrote *The Pilgrim's Progress*, and John Milton wrote *Paradise Lost*.
9. Shorter Catechism, Question 1, The Westminster Standard, https://thewestminsterstandard.org/westminster-shorter-catechism/.
10. William Shakespeare, *Hamlet*, Act 3 Scene 1, Folger Shakespeare Library, https://www.folger.edu/explore/shakespeares-works/hamlet/read/3/1/.
11. John T. Elson, "A Man for Others," *Life*, May 7, 1965, 116.
12. Eric Metaxas, *Bonhoeffer: Pastor, Martyr, Prophet, Spy* (Thomas Nelson, 2010), 532.
13. John Calvin, *Institutes of the Christian Religion*, 1:11.8, trans. Henry Beveridge. https://ccel.org/ccel/calvin/institutes.iii.xii.html.
14. William Cowper, "Walking with God," *Olney Hymns*, Poets.org, https://poets.org/poem/olney-hymns-i-walking-god.
15. Aleksandr Solzhenitsyn, *The Gulag Archipelago*, vol. 1 (Harper Perennial Modern Classics, 2007), 69–70.
16. Blaise Pascal, *Pensées*, Section 8, No. 586, trans. W.F. Trotter, Christian Classics Ethereal Library, https://www.ccel.org/ccel/pascal/pensees.all.html.

17. Martin Luther, "A Mighty Fortress Is Our God," *The Celebration Hymnal* (Word/Integrity, 1997), 151.

18. This is a modern paraphrase of Augustine's teaching. For further reading, see *City of God*, Book 11.

19. Dr. Andrew Bonar was a nineteenth century Scottish minister.

20. John Newton, *John Newton: An Autobiography* (Moody, 1980), 39, 43.

21. Jennie Evelyn Hussey, "Lead Me to Calvary," *The Celebration Hymnal* (Word/Integrity, 1997), 310.

22. Quoted in David B. Calhoun, "'Amazing Grace' John Newton and His Great Hymn," C. S. Lewis Institute, December 1, 2013, https://www.cslewisinstitute.org/resources/amazing-grace-john-newton-and-his-great-hymn/.

23. Augustus Toplady, "Rock of Ages," Timeless Truths, https://library.timelesstruths.org/music/Rock_of_Ages/.

24. John R. W. Stott, *God's New Society: The Message of Ephesians* (InterVarsity Press, 1979), 82.

25. Quoted in W. A. Criswell, *Criswell's Guidebook for Pastors* (Broadman Press, 1980), 66.

26. Vernon J. Charlesworth, "A Shelter in the Time of Storm," *The Celebration Hymnal* (Word/Integrity, 1997), 693.

27. Blaise Pascal, *Pensées*, Section 7, No. 425, trans. W. F. Trotter, Christian Classics Ethereal Library, https://www.ccel.org/ccel/pascal/pensees.all.html.

28. Edward Mote, "The Solid Rock," *The Celebration Hymnal* (Word/Integrity, 1997), 526.

29. Corrie Ten Boom with Elizabeth and John Sherrill, *The Hiding Place* (Chosen Books, 2006), 44.

30. Bernard of Clairvaux, "Jesu Thou Joy of Loving Hearts!," Hymnary.org, https://hymnary.org/text/jesus_thou_joy_of_loving_hearts.

31. See Martin Luther, *Luther's Letters of Spiritual Counsel*, trans. Theodore Tappert (Westminster Press, 1955), 110; or *Luther's Works* 48:12, trans. Theodore Tappert.

32. "Ogden Nash Quotes," Encyclopedia Britannica, https://www.britannica.com/quotes/Ogden-Nash.

33. William Cowper, "There Is a Fountain," *The Celebration Hymnal* (Word/Integrity, 1997), 336.

34. Martin Luther, "Letter to George Spalatin," August 21, 1544, Weimar Ausgabe (WA Briefwechsel), X, no. 4021.

35. Augustine, *The Confessions of Saint Augustine*, Book 1, trans. E. B. Pusey, Project Gutenberg, https://www.gutenberg.org/cache/epub/3296/pg3296-images.html#link2H_4_0001.

36. E. E. Hewitt (aka Lidie H. Edmunds), "My Faith Has Found a Resting Place," *The Celebration Hymnal* (Word/Integrity, 1997), 528.

37. Charles Haddon Spurgeon, *The Metropolitan Tabernacle Pulpit*, vol. 40 (Passmore, 1894), 300.

38. While S. Franklin Logsdon started his sermons in this way, we have been unable to verify if he was the author of the poem.

39. Frederick M. Lehman, "The Love of God," *The Celebration Hymnal* (Word/Integrity, 1997), 157.

40. Anne R. Cousin, "O Christ, What Burdens Bowed Thy Head," Hymnary.org, https://hymnary.org/text/o_christ_what_burdens_bowed_thy_head.